MAKING GROUPS WORK

MAKING GROUPS WORK
A Guide for Group Leaders

Rodney W. Napier / Temple University
Matti K. Gershenfeld / Temple University

Houghton Mifflin Company / Boston
Dallas / Geneva, Illinois / Hopewell, New Jersey / Palo Alto / London

Photo Credits: Chapter 1—George Bellerose, Stock/Boston; Chapter 2—© Frank Siteman 1979, The Picture Cube; Chapter 3—Ellis Herwig, Stock/Boston; Chapter 4—David Powers, Stock/Boston; Chapter 5—Terry McKoy, The Picture Cube; Chapter 6—Mark Antman, Stock/Boston; Chapter 7—© Jerry Berndt 1979, Stock/Boston

Design and Production by The Book Department, Inc.

Printed in the U.S.A.

Library of Congress Catalog Card Number: 82-82242
ISBN: 0-395-29705-2

We dedicate this book to our children . . .

Bob, Gila, Howard, Richard, and Kenneth

Amma, Laura, and Tori

. . . who suffered through our first real group experiences and with whom we learned the real meaning of making groups work

Contents

Preface

When people come together to meet and work in groups, a certain energy is produced. If focused with skill, this energy can result in productivity, good feelings, and a real sense of success and accomplishment. But if a group leader is unable to channel this energy in a constructive fashion, the results are more likely to be unresolved conflict, tension, and inefficiency.

Audience

Making Groups Work is for anyone who works with groups and who wishes to make them more effective. It is a resource book that extends beyond any single field or area of concentration. It is for teachers, trainers, managers, and consultants, as well as for therapists, case workers, counselors, supervisors, youth group leaders, community organizers, and a wide range of human services personnel. It is for everyone who seeks to understand the fascinating, frustrating, and often-confusing dynamics of people working in groups.

We hear a great deal about collaborative management, cooperative teaching, the sharing of resources, and participative problem solving. But most group leaders and facilitators have not been taught how to accomplish these desirable outcomes. Most people working with groups in a leadership capacity have received little or no training in group development, design, team building, or conducting meetings or task forces. *Making Groups Work* is intended for those individuals and especially for those who have little hope of receiving hands-on training in this vital aspect of their job role.

Making Groups Work is a textbook that can be used in a variety of programs and courses in educational institutions or other organizations dedicated to increasing skills in areas related to group processes. It is especially appropriate for courses in the following subjects: leadership training, human relations, group therapy, group counseling, family therapy, social case work, group dynamics, management development, supervisory training, and team building and athletics.

Purpose

We have made no attempt to create a book of simplistic prescriptions or activities for the facilitator to dip into mindlessly in search of the "right" solution for a problematic situation. If that is the reader's goal, several "how to" activity books for group leaders are available. Our aim is to provide a realistic way of thinking about groups and to supply the tools for developing what we call a "design mentality" and for tapping those artistic and creative energies that separate the most successful group leaders from the rest.

Coverage

Chapter 1 establishes a context and Chapter 2 a theoretical framework for the skill-based and applied chapters that follow. In Chapter 1 we take a hard look at why some groups fail and some succeed and how the concept of group leadership has changed dramatically during the last fifty years. In Chapter 2 we expand this context and focus more directly on a particular view of group leadership that has evolved historically.

Chapter 3 explores the problems that group leaders often consider to be the most prevalent and bothersome—not problems of design but rather practical difficulties and blockages that can obstruct leadership and hamper a group from developing effectively. In this chapter we address such issues as overcoming negative norms, dealing with dominating participants, neutralizing hostile subgroups, handling personal attacks, reducing the group's dependency on the leader, and a wide range of related issues. We strongly believe that leaders who are unable to cope with these ever-present problems will find it almost impossible to direct positive energy to the critical tasks of diagnosis and design that form the keystone to effective group development.

Chapters 4, 5, and 6 focus on the topic of design and form the heart of the book. For us, design is the concept and skill that most accounts for the difference between effective and ineffective group leaders. "Making groups work" suggests doing something constructive: taking action to maintain the qualities of an effective group or improving those qualities when necessary. In Chapter 4 we look at the facilitator as an interventionist in the life of a group. The nature of an intervention, its creativity, appropriateness, and consequences are all critical aspects of the design process. As part of understanding how to design effectively, we carefully lay out in Chapter 4 the ingredients we consider to be essential to the success of any design. We also explore the critical nature of "beginnings" and "endings" and their impact on the life of any group.

Having looked in depth at the concept of design, we offer in Chapters 5 and 6 nineteen designs that exemplify interventions in a wide range of problem situations. They represent our efforts during the last twenty years to apply group theory to groups in factories, prisons, offices, television stations, convents, monasteries, schools, banks, oil companies, medical and dental offices, hospitals, and therapy centers. In every case—whether in the classic designs of Chapter 5 or the conflict designs of Chapter 6—our goal is to improve an existing situation in a manner that will facilitate the life of the group and the organization. By illustrating a way of thinking about groups and by helping to strengthen your understanding of design, we believe these case studies will enable you to intervene with more effective designs in the meetings, task forces, teams, classrooms, or therapy groups in which you may find yourself. Although our designs may not be exactly appropriate for your specific groups, they should help to make you more capable of intervening with skill, creativity, artistry, and integrity in your own unique situations.

The final chapter explores the value of evaluation for groups and organizations, especially in relation to the growth and development so necessary in a vital group. We examine a variety of evaluation methods, from relatively simple ones to an eight-stage evaluation model. Whatever the complexity of the process used, evaluation can be an important asset to a group's operation and development.

The book concludes with an extensive appendices section. Appendix A provides additional information for making life easier for you as a group facilitator. It includes specific suggestions for improving observational skills, grouping techniques, and data-gathering methods and for enhancing feedback strategies. Other appendices offer additional advice that you may also find helpful.

Acknowledgments

Over the years our editors at Houghton Mifflin have not only provided us with support and professional guidance but have encouraged a style of writing that stresses informality and readability while minimizing jargon and academic arrogance. For this, we are continually grateful.

Other individuals have been tremendously giving of their time, advice, and counsel. The following reviewers offered constructive and insightful comments, which were a great help in the development of this book: Colleen Conoley, Southwest Texas State University; Nancy Evans, Indiana University; Robert Hatmaker, California State University, Fresno; and Irving Hott, Central Connecticut State College. Marvin Gershenfeld, M.D., played a role as both critic and laborer in the minutia of proofing in addition to being a most supportive husband. Paula Leder gave editing and manuscript coordination a special care that went beyond any job. And Helen Reiner saved us more than once with typing and editing that turned impossible deadlines into realities. Our appreciation and thanks to each.

Rodney W. Napier
Matti K. Gershenfeld

To the Instructor
Ideas for Increasing the Value and Utility of This Book

Making Groups Work can work best if it involves practice—the direct application of what is read to what the reader is doing. The old saying that it is a long distance between "cup and lip" also applies to the distance between intellectually consuming the content of this book and actually utilizing it in real-life situations. Thus, we would like to suggest a few approaches to help you to maximize the value of the information presented in this text.

First, Chapters 1, 2, and 3 are keyed to the leader—the facilitator who works with groups. These chapters can be framed around a number of interesting tasks, whether instruction occurs in a formal classroom setting, in a training center, or in some other organizational setting.

1. Introduce the book by using one of the classic designs presented in Chapter 4 (many are suitable, but the first design is especially appropriate). This forces the participants to establish the criteria for an effective group leader, and the group's assessment can be used as a discussion point in relation to much that is raised in the early chapters. The remainder of the design will provide a useful review of group process and establish its value from the beginning.
2. Take basic designs relating to group norms or membership or other topical issues from a book such as *Groups: Theory and Experience** and use them to impact the learning group. Have the group begin to discuss the concept of design by analyzing the purpose and value of your own designs.
3. Have the participants generate among themselves the biggest blocks or problems they see leaders facing as they attempt to work with groups. Analyze the results and have the group create alternatives; later their responses can be compared to those proposed in the book itself.

The main point to be made here is that how the material in the book is presented should be consistent with the principles of design and effective

---

*Rodney Napier and Matti Gershenfeld, *Groups: Theory and Experience*, 2nd ed. (Boston: Houghton Mifflin, 1981).

facilitator behavior discussed in the book itself. Without the modeling of such behavior by the instructor, the teaching-learning process will most certainly ring hollow.

Second, Chapter 4 provides a perfect opportunity for exercising exactly what the chapter itself represents. One suggestion is that pairs of participants be asked to find an ongoing group and conduct a diagnosis of the group and its individual members. Using information from the first four chapters as well as Chapter 7 on evaluation and Appendix A on facilitator skills, each pair may be expected to gain a new and comprehensive understanding of their chosen group and to feed their findings back to the leader and hopefully the group as well. Observational, structural, and environmental information, interviews, and questionnaires are all available for gathering the diagnostic data. By having each member of the pair independently gather data (but using similar methods and procedures), the pair can analyze the information together while learning of their own inclinations to project and misinterpret the information before them. Again, it is the task of the facilitator-teacher to provide additional information, theory, or support in order to help the investigative process reflect the diagnostic mentality that must be present in any successful design. Once this has been accomplished, each pair may then hypothesize potential design interventions based on their diagnostic analysis.

Third, while covering the chapters on design, ask the participants to select and modify one of the designs for use in the class itself. The whole group can then discuss the design's structure, process, and goals as well as how the design was presented. A variation on this theme is to have various participants create short, perhaps thirty-minute, designs, which other members can experience and then critique based on criteria drawn from Chapter 4.

Fourth, create a problem situation in a hypothetical group. Divide the participants into clusters of approximately three individuals, and ask each cluster to meet (in or outside the group) and design an appropriate intervention for remedying the problem situation. Choose one of the clusters to implement its design on the rest of the group's members who are to role play the original situation given by the facilitator. Again, the discussion and critique following can be based on the values and criteria found in Chapter 4. Other designs developed by other clusters can be discussed as alternatives to the role-played design. Also, the facilitator's behavior in the role play can be discussed using the first two chapters for criteria and comparisons.

In all of the examples to this point, the book is used as a backdrop for discussing the merits of a design and of a facilitator's behavior. If the class group itself is in need of team building, then it would be appropriate to practice with a team-building design from the book or to have one generated from the participants. Carefully focused discussion sessions with feedback for the practicing facilitators is an integral part of each example to this point.

Fifth, have each of the participants implement one of the classic or conflict designs, or an appropriate variation, on an outside group. Part of the task is to solicit feedback on the experience after it has been completed by utilizing approaches from Chapter 7. Each participant is also to seek feedback on his or her own facilitator behavior. Examples of groups for use in such an activity are a family group, friends, a classroom, a department in a business, a church group, or a social club. Obviously, the design created should be relevant to the interests and needs of the particular group.

Sixth, if it has been decided that the class or training group is to use itself for practicing the creation and execution of designs, then it would be a natural step to have some of the participants be responsible for designing an appropriate and useful evaluation of each design. Building creative critiques or evaluations requires the application of many of the principles explored throughout the book.

Clearly, there are many other methods for maximizing the material in *Making Groups Work*. By outlining a few here we hope to encourage you to create your own. Our goal in writing this text is to help in the development of tough-minded facilitators. To achieve this goal, all facilitators must have the opportunity to experience the art of design and to practice the tools of the trade. This type of training will reduce the chance that they will be uncreative "bagmen" (see Chapter 4) and will increase their ability to design spontaneously based on the reality of the existing situation. The more designs they are able to observe, critique, create, and personally experience, the greater the possibility that they will become flexible, artistic, and skilled group facilitators.

1
The Leadership Effect: Why Some Groups Fail and Some Succeed

At any given moment, every day, people come together at group meetings to communicate with each other—to share their experiences, opinions, skills, resources, and to work toward accomplishing their common goals. The process sounds simple and straightforward enough, but in reality the road to accomplishment is obstructed by meanderings, bypasses, roadblocks, and detours at almost every turn.

Groups: Why They Don't Succeed

Groups make many people uncomfortable. In a group you don't get your own way, you must defer to others at least some of the time, discussions can be confusing, individual differences can explode to produce heightened conflict. In addition, in a group there are fears—fears of appearing foolish or being regarded as low status, fears of being scapegoated or being "dumped on," fears of not fitting in and being an "outcast," and fears about outcomes. What will the outcomes be? A complete waste of time? A disaster? Sometimes things can be much worse after the meeting than before the meeting. The outcomes sometimes are not at all what was intended. Many of these problems can be evidenced in the following examples.

Examples of Unsuccessful Groups

Example 1. A suburban school district prides itself on how well the administration works with the faculty; there is participative decision making between the administration and faculty and between teachers and department heads as well. A new art coordinator for the district was trying to generate excitement and, at the same time, build a reputation. He thought a district art fair would satisfy both those aims. He called a meeting of the art faculty and in his best participative leadership style indicated that they were meeting to solve a mutual problem—how to generate community interest in art and how to increase students' enthusiasm about art. After three sessions, during which the teachers rejected an art fair as being too much work and as encouraging display art rather than learning, the coordinator got tough. He said that he had tried to be nice, but since they were lazy and unresponsive, he had no choice but to order them to prepare for an art fair. Furthermore, any lack of cooperation would result in unfavorable evaluations.

Example 2. A large foundation grant had been received by a group of ministers to teach minority community families how to be more effective as a family—to support each other and to raise their children. Ten ministers had been actively involved in the project from the beginning, eager to have their church members involved in learning family skills and to bring such a program into their churches. Each minister was delighted to be on the advisory board. They wanted the training to be evenly distributed and so agreed that each minister would recommend three couples for the training. (The grant called for thirty couples to be trained.) After taking the training, these couples would conduct it in their own churches.

The program was not to start for six months. Only four ministers sent three couples; four others sent one couple each. No minister indicated any difficulties, and despite repeated calls no other couples were recommended. Although the funding had been obtained, the project had to be shelved.

Example 3. Once a lengthy school strike at the beginning of the year had ended, the animosity between teachers who had come in to teach during the strike and those who had stayed out only increased. Strikers felt that the "scabs" had accepted the pay raise and other benefits of the new contract while sabotaging their strike efforts to gain the benefits. At the end of the year, the district decided to hire a consultant to conduct a two-day workshop to reduce the escalated divisiveness among the faculty of one of its large high schools. The consultant arrived to find that the faculty members who had gone on strike were reading newspapers and playing cards. They hooted and heckled every comment made by certain teachers and the consultant. The consultant later learned that the faculty were two days short of working the state-required 180 days. They had been offered the choice of attending the workshop and being paid, or not attending and not being paid for those two days. The "striking" teachers presented bodies to get paid but were going to prove that the faculty differences could not be overcome. The "striking" members continued to heckle the scabs even eight months later.

Example 4. A prestigious task force was to select state delegates for the White House Conference on Families. Those who attended thought criteria would be developed and then discussed. Instead they were presented with a list of delegates who were said to represent the diversity of populations in the state. Next to each name was the category (city, age, occupation, marital status) that made them representative. The group learned that its task was only to rubberstamp an already selected list.

Example 5. A group of mental health professionals and community religious leaders spent their very limited budgets to attend a weekend workshop to learn the skills of building a trusting, supportive community. The brochure claimed that the leader of the workshop had written extensively and had a reputation for being an innovator. Participants arrived eager to learn skills deemed essential for their effectiveness.

The leader began with a short lecture on definitions and understandings of trust, interdependence, and responsibility. He then led the group through a half hour of the most common nonverbal encounter exercises. That was it—the end of his direction. Prior to sitting down, he announced that it was now up to the group to work out how to become a trusting, supportive community. People stared at each other in disbelief. Some tried to goad him into taking some action; some smiled and pretended to be unperturbed, thinking the whole thing was some strategy that would soon end; some got angry. It didn't matter. The leader would not be coaxed or badgered, neither on Saturday nor all through Sunday until noon. On Monday people called and wrote demanding that their money be refunded.

Obstacles to Group Goals

All kinds of problems beset groups that meet to accomplish their goals. Sometimes groups meet and state their goals but later find out that those were not the same goals that the leader had in mind. Sometimes people say they are ready to meet and discuss a problem when in reality one segment realizes that the repercussions might be very serious if its thoughts are truly expressed. Sometimes people want only to be in a prestigious group. They tend to act as if they have resources they don't have and are involved in making decisions they know will not be carried out. Sometimes people's personal needs get in the way of the group goal and their behavior sabotages the movement toward the agreed-upon goal, no matter how legitimate the group goal may seem. Sometimes people are asked to make decisions only to find that a higher power has already decided, and they experience the frustration of being "window dressing."

After a series of frustrating or disillusioning experiences, people are less likely to look forward to a group experience; they are more likely to withhold their energies and hopes. They will exert limited control, will feel comfortable in the process, and will have little confidence in the quality of the outcome.

Some people become uncomfortable even thinking about the difficulties groups have in achieving their goals. There seems to be a sense of the inevitable—being in groups means being part of all of those difficulties; they come with the territory. Others display an apathetic response. They don't plan to get involved, and if they do, they will be involved as minimally as possible. There is the sense that some things can be changed and some cannot. If something can't be changed, accept that situation and don't put energy there.

Groups: Why They Succeed

Most people remember the failures, the disasters, and the disappointments that can occur in a group. But group experiences can be exhilarating. There is the bond of working with others and being mutually involved in searching for possible solutions rather than feeling alone and overwhelmed. There is the caring and closeness that develops among members who know each other as they never did before. There is the insight of listening to someone and suddenly understanding yourself. There is the wonder of watching people decide to change and then really change. There is the joyousness of experiencing the "click" of finding the right solution. There is the laughter, joking, and fun of teasing, kidding, and sparking each other. Finally, there is the pleasure of shared, solid accomplishments.

Let's look at some examples of successful group experiences.

Examples of Successful Groups

Example 1. A leader who had been trained in the autocratic school of conducting meetings was most reluctant to attend a team-building weekend with his staff. The experience proved to be one of the most momentous weekends of his life. He learned that once given responsibility for the meetings, his staff was not apathetic. He learned that he did not have to monitor everyone closely—that he was wrong in thinking that they would do only the minimum. He was amazed at the energy, the good ideas, the cooperativeness of his staff at the retreat—and how different that was from the usual staff meetings. He and his staff learned some methods to evaluate meetings. He learned how to observe the process and then to raise questions around what he saw. He observed a whole dimension of what was happening at his meetings that he had never seen before. The entire staff felt that a major change had taken place as a result of that weekend—a change for the better.

Example 2. A new staff development member, a couple of hours into a three-day principals' workshop, confided to the group that she felt like the "Wizard of Oz." She had been confidently acting as if she knew all the answers, but increasingly she had been feeling like a big fake. She admitted that she feared impending disaster, of being found out. Knowing she was new and with limited experience, the principals had been testing her. Her disarming appeal, however, was just what was needed. The principals rose to the occasion, and, instead of being divisive and difficult, they decided to make the program work. They outlined procedures, checked for agreement prior to continuing, decided to accomplish their tasks rather than harass the leader, and had one of their most productive workshops. They even joked about the workshop and created a couple of mottos: "Principals don't have experience handling easy situations, but give them a tough one, and they rise, brilliantly, to the occasion." And, "We shall overcome, magnificently."

Example 3. A "planning staff" met with a "trainer" to develop an orientation program for nontraditional college students in a new community program. In addition to a few faculty members, the planning staff consisted primarily of new middle-aged students entering the college. The students raised their questions and their fears. They asked about everything from registration to study skills, from using the library to meeting and making friends.

The orientation was designed to deal with these concerns and was a huge success. People entered alone and apprehensive and left with friends and confidence. They had met some faculty, made new friends, and generally had fun at the workshop. They felt so positive about the experience that they decided to meet every Friday afternoon to continue to keep up the friendships and give each other support and survival tips.

Example 4. The administration was increasingly concerned with the serious drug problem in its high school. The administration perceived the problem as being how to help the loner, the academically unsuccessful, and the unpopular girl or withdrawn boy to feel comfortable and befriended at school. Drugs were viewed as a symptom of the problems of relating and of the difficulties of achievement in a competitive school with very high standards. The school hired a consultant, who went through a process of bringing together diverse faculty, students from each grade, counselors, and some of the administrative staff to develop methods of solving the problems. Those six weekends resulted in vast changes in the school, and not just in areas targeted for change. Different segments of the school community came to know and work with each other. Cooperation developed and influenced the competitive norms that had existed. A realization developed that family and parents also needed to be involved where previously all elements had vetoed their inclusion. A different view of the curriculum evolved, and possible alternatives in courses, class size, and course length were suggested. Weekend programs were developed in collaboration with the adult evening school. The meetings brought about a ripple effect far beyond the expectations and outcomes that had been hoped for.

Example 5. The staff of a rehabilitation hospital felt that it had to learn to work as a team for good patient care. A patient could be seen by nine different department staff members (physician, orthopedist, psychologist, physical therapist, occupational therapist, speech pathologist, social worker, nurse, and transportation coordinator) plus relief staffs. The scheduling and treatment plan, although coordinated on a blackboard, was not working. What was occurring was the proverbial right hand not knowing what the left was doing. With a facilitator, the hospital developed a weekly series of rehabilitation staff meetings. The meetings were painful at first. The physicians, who were the team leaders, rarely attended. Certain staff members attended while others did not. The transportation coordinators (staff who transported patients to various treatment centers in the hospital) never attended. They were typically less educated and of a different race from most of the staff; they felt inferior and unable to have any input.

Each of the problems was confronted and dealt with. At the end of the year, people were experiencing the exhilaration of having seen a miracle occur. Instead of avoiding each other, staff came early (the sessions started at 7:30 A.M. before the regular workday) and brought doughnuts, juice, or cheese as they started the day together. They talked about patients and their progress. They monitored attendance and gave a mock award to the staff member with the best attendance. They also involved the transportation people and came to understand their problems with the staff. They celebrated birthdays and became friends. People even reported that work wasn't as draining, despite a hiring freeze.

Complexity of Groups

Even examples of successful groups illustrate the wide range of group situations and the enormous complexity of working with groups. Every group has its uniqueness, and it is that uniqueness that prevents cookbook prescriptions from providing methods for helping groups be successful.

Because of this complexity and the fact that there are no easy answers, some people have never experienced being part of a successful group. Even more difficult is knowing how to create one. How do you create a group experience that is productive and deeply satisfying to its members? How does it happen?

The History of Groups

Groups are everywhere. They are the fundamental building blocks of our society. Groups are our primary means of early socialization in families, in schools, in day-care centers, in play groups, on sports teams, and in clubs. They are our primary means for task accomplishment in work groups, staff meetings, budget meetings, planning committees, and boards and councils. They are our fundamental means for social support in clubs, peer groups, networks, self-help groups, and consciousness-raising groups. They are our primary means for adult learning in classes, seminars, courses, workshops, and in organization development and training. Finally, they are our basic means for personal change in personal growth groups, therapy, or special-problem groups (Alcoholics Anonymous, Smoke-Enders, and Weight Watchers).

Leadership in Groups, 1930–1960

People have always lived in groups without paying too much attention to how they functioned—they just did. People, of course, have their personal theories on what happens in groups based on personal experience and the circumstances of their times. The scientific study of groups, however, began in the late thirties and early forties and focused on two primary concerns. One was leadership. With the success of dictators in Germany, Italy, Russia and Spain, there was a real concern for the future of democracy and democratic leaders. The early studies of Lewin, Lippitt, and White were a series of classic small group experiments to ascertain scientifically the effects of an autocratic, democratic, or laissez-faire leader. Which style was the most productive? Which induced greater member satisfaction? What were the results in the short run and in the long run? These concerns with leadership and its effects on a group continue to be studied. Leadership greatly influences what happens in a group and group outcomes.

The second concern that precipitated the scientific study of groups did not occur by design but by serendipity. In the mid-forties, a training group at the National Training Laboratories (now Institute) devised a method to analyze its own behaviors. This method came to be called *experience-based learning*—that is, participants learned through analyzing, discussing, and trying to improve their own behavior in the present group situation (called here-and-now learning). These groups were led by a leader, called a trainer, who acted in a very different way from the traditional teacher. The objective of the trainer was not so much to impart content but to help members learn *how* to learn. The trainer helped establish learning norms and created a climate in which risking new behaviors was acceptable. People could express their feelings—not just nice or good feelings, but also angry or bad feelings.

A fundamental principle of laboratory training is that the leader is not "in charge" the way a teacher is in charge in a classroom; the teacher knows the curriculum, but the students do not. The trainer focuses not on content but on process, not on what is said but how it is said, not on the words but the effect of the words on others. The leader does not directly control the group. Rather, the group is responsible for its own learning. The leader might give a brief demonstration or conduct a lecture or lead an experimental exercise, but the group has power to use or not use what is taught in its training group. The group can follow the trainer's comments or ignore them. The group can initiate its own content and continue whether the trainer approves or not. Being a trainer and working with groups is very different from the traditional director of classroom or learning activities.

Laboratory training, or working with groups in experience-based learning, continued to grow. While it expanded in the fifties, by the sixties it had become a phenomenon. Viewed by some as the method for understanding interpersonal relations, laboratory training resulted in all kinds of corporations sending their executives for basic training in how to be human in an NTL Human Relations Lab. Although some people considered experience-based learning a powerful experience, others questioned its effectiveness because the results were not readily described or measurable. Some people viewed experience-based learning as a way of learning democracy, a way of teaching people how to care and to be cooperative with others. Still others promoted it with a way of creating better human beings, religious communities, and educational organizations, and as a way to elicit community responsiveness. Then there were those who saw it as a way that social scientists and behavioral scientists could contribute to improving the quality of life. For lots of people experience-based learning was simply an experience to be enjoyed like any other new experience: join a group and play the games. Groups were the theme of movies, a subject of parlor games, and a popular topic of television interviews.

Impact of Change Since 1960

Since the sixties, experience-based learning has undergone enormous changes (Miles, 1980). For example, twenty years later, experience-based learning is no longer new. It has been used to train police, U.S. ambassadors, juvenile court judges, and girl scout leaders. It has been used to improve marital communication between couples and to prepare rocket launch teams. It has been used with first graders and university faculties. It has been used to build supportiveness among religious blacks in South Africa and to reduce conflicts between Arabs and Jews in Israel.

Laboratory training has proved to be a powerful tool for creating new ways of working together and understanding differences. Of course, sometimes laboratory training can be ineffective and leave more problems unresolved than there were initially. And as time passes, the glow of the hoped-for magic answer has worn off. People are much more sophisticated about groups and laboratory training, and the games, techniques, and gimmicks of a decade ago will no longer work. Newness, like change, in itself means nothing. People who have previously experienced a game are bored, or are manipulative because they "know the answers" from a previous time and can produce the "desired" behaviors. The mood today is much less toward "let's do that because it is interesting and we can learn something from it" than toward "how does this fit with our objectives and how will we learn what we need to know directly from this learning experience?"

A second change affecting experience-based learning involves training. Because there is so much laboratory training used in almost every imaginable setting, a profession of people who are trainers has emerged. (*Trainer* is the most commonly used term for those conducting laboratory training. Other terms are *consultants, facilitators,* or *leaders.*) Master's and doctoral programs are now available to teach people the theory, skills, and practice of being a group trainer.* Thousands have already learned and thousands more are learning how to be laboratory training experts. Many people in other fields have recognized the need for skills in group training and have taken courses in designing, conducting, and evaluating training, in understanding small group leadership, or in conducting workshops. Because success or failure is not random or precarious, there is an understanding that skill and training are necessary before trainers can help the groups with whom they are working.

A third development in experience-based learning is the enormously increased interest in groups as a medium for personal growth. Since the mid-sixties, these groups have proliferated to such an extent that estimates now are that 5 million Americans have been involved in some type of personally oriented growth experience. There have been Achieving Your Potential groups, Transactional Analysis groups, gestalt groups, transition groups, women's groups, and couples' groups. In each, people come together with a trainer to learn skills or generate understanding or go beyond areas of special difficulty in a group experience.

Concurrent with the emergence of personal growth groups has been the development of groups that serve as a support to those having personal difficulties. These support groups include widows' groups that help people to recover from their spouse's death and to learn to cope with the world alone, and cystic fibrosis groups that bring young adults together to explore methods of bringing normality into their lives. There has also been an expansion of self-help

---

*Both authors are on the faculty of Temple University's Graduate Department of Psychoeducational Processes, originally Group Dynamics, which is one of the oldest and most comprehensive such programs in the country.

groups, sometimes with a professional leader and sometimes not. Self-help groups include groups that help people overcome problems of overeating, drugs, or gambling, help rape victims overcome their fears, help divorced people cope with making a new life, reeducate child abusers, and advocate support for gay people, the handicapped, and the American Indian.

More and more experience-based training is being used in organization development programs. People do not work in isolation with random groups but rather with selected participants from a department that is part of an organization. Increasingly, efforts have been devoted to working with an entire system, often over a period of years. The organization development program might be with first-line supervisors in a particular department or with all of the departments and staffs under a vice president. Although organization development programs may focus on group behavior as in a "team-building" project, they deal more frequently with issues having to do with the effectiveness of the organization and the quality of work life. They are usually concerned with improving managerial style or improving the organization through utilization of human resources.

Group Leaders: Present Focus

The present state of work with groups seems to have shifted. There is no longer the eagerness to get into a group training experience, for it is no longer the "newest" or the latest fad. People have had experience with laboratory training and may or may not have found that experience effective. Given the monetary restrictions of the present times, there is neither the money nor the time to waste on training unless it will be productive. The bandwagon days are over, and with them the grabbag of gimmicks that represented effective "training design" in an earlier era.

Increased interest in personal growth groups, with their focus on the individual, and organization development groups, with their emphasis on organizational culture, has brought about a concomitant increase in concern over how the group can be effective. Several questions emerge for the group trainer.

- How can the group trainer help the group accomplish its task?
- How can the trainer help members achieve personal learnings and skills while accomplishing the task?
- How can the trainer help members learn transferable skills of supportive, collaborative relationships in this setting?
- How can the trainer encourage a process of looking at what is happening in the group and creating a learning, experimental atmosphere?
- How can the trainer encourage members to try new behavior, to learn new problem-solving methods, to have a broadened understanding of themselves in group situations?

The group leader or trainer is not responsible for all that happens in a group. However, at least 75 percent of the effectiveness of the group can be attributed to the trainer. Tannenbaum et al. (1977, p. 129) note that "for the most part, research on processes has tended to recognize the trainer implicitly, but to ignore his explicit behavior. This has sometimes led to the erroneous impression that events occurring in a . . . group are only indirectly affected by the trainer's activities." The trainer is the major influence in determining how effective a group will be. Even deciding in a planning session that the objectives cannot be achieved in the time allotted is to influence group effectiveness.

We are writing this book because we believe groups can be effective in achieving goals individuals cannot accomplish on their own and because we believe that trainers can enhance that effectiveness. Our primary objective is to teach leaders or trainers how to help their groups achieve their goals.

Why the Difficulty with Groups?

Most of us have difficulty working with groups because we do not know how to work well with others. Although we spend much of our time in groups, much of the learning is faulty. Cultural anthropologists tell us that you can understand much about a culture by knowing its language. They point out that there are many words and synonyms for important aspects of the culture. For example, there are twenty-eight words for "snow" in the Eskimo language; thus one might surmise that snow is important. In the English language, there are forty words for war and competition. This is the land of the rugged individualist who is not constrained by anything and who constantly strives to win, beat, dominate, survive, outclass, and outlast. As a result, we tend to view others suspiciously and competitively. From that framework, how could we have learned the skills of being trusting and collaborative?

Another reason for our deficiency in group participation is that families have rarely encouraged shared participation. In early years children learn to become acculturated, which means doing what they are told by their parents. There is even the sad joke of a child wanting to understand and asking her mother, "Why, Ma?" Her mother gives the ultimate satisfactory answer, "Because I said so." Hardly a sharing norm—rather, one that says obedience to power and authority are the primary requisites of survival. And we learn little about feelings at home. A child says, "I'm scared." Dad says, "No, you're just tired. There's nothing to be scared of." A child learns early that bad feelings are not to be expressed. For example, a child coming in from school frowning might hear, "Wipe that look off your face. You want to be sad, I'll give you something to be sad about." The child learns early to mask feelings and present an acceptable image to the world while receiving a message that others can be relied on less and less.

Schools generally do not encourage shared efforts. Grades and assignments are given individually. Sharing information is frowned on—it is considered copying or not doing your own work. Teachers have been taught about statistical measurements and marking "on a curve" so that students see each other as competitive curve breakers who might reduce each other's grades. Teachers dominate the teaching time, and student opinions are rarely valued. Even chairs are often arranged to face the teacher.

Another reason working in groups is so difficult is that each of us has our own assumptions about motivations and behaviors in groups as well as what happens in the group as a unit. Many of these assumptions are wrong when compared with what is scientifically known about groups. Dr. Vytas Cernius, Temple University, gives his graduate classes in small group behavior a first assignment to ferret out these assumptions. He asks that they make a list of assumptions and then examine these assumptions and how they influence behavior in groups. Then they are asked to research whether these assumptions are valid or invalid, under what conditions, and why.

The following assumptions are listed here as a reader activity so that you can explore what holding those assumptions might mean to you.

Reader Activity

The following reader activity is an adaptation of the Cernius design. Below is a list of assumptions about behavior in groups. If people believed that assumption, how would they act? Why would they behave a certain way based on that assumption? Answer for each of the following assumptions.

1. No group member who has a serious opinion to voice wants to be laughed at or rejected.
2. Some people feel the need to lose their identity by joining a group.
3. People join groups to come into contact with ideas that are different from their own.
4. People join groups to experience a sense of belonging.
5. Members of a group may sometimes ask a question that you could not think of and that would aid you in getting an answer you desired to find.
6. Decision making about a specific topic can sometimes be accomplished easier in a group situation, particularly when consciences of the other members may be spared from having to decide individually on a matter that may not exactly win agreement from all group members.
7. A concept such as democracy makes itself known within the group.
8. At times groups tend to conform more easily and quickly than individuals.
9. Groups can be advantageous economically for each individual in light of situations that involve "group rates."
10. There is physical safety within groups in certain situations.
11. Group membership can be dangerous for the member in certain situations.

12. In certain situations groups can be a threat to others outside of the group.
13. Groups can solve problems more easily than can individuals.
14. Groups can be so intimidating that an individual is afraid to express personal ideas or feelings.

We need much reeducation. Trainers need to help their groups learn the skills of being cooperative, of being supportive, of trusting, of acknowledging behavior to improve for the next time, of learning how to achieve their objectives with other people. Trainers need to help members become effective in their work efforts or their personal learning efforts. Outcomes of group experiences must be gratifying and satisfying.

Of course, groups are not the only places where people learn. However, to think of what would happen if people could learn to become even 10 percent more effective in groups is mind boggling.

Group Leaders: For Whom This Book Is Written

This book is being aimed toward those who will be leading or facilitating groups. These persons may have a variety of titles, such as trainer, facilitator, workshop leader, consultant, counselor, social worker, adult educator, professor, or teacher. They may even have titles such as president, chairperson, foreman, supervisor, board member, or director. The essential aspect is that the person is charged with the responsibility to conduct a program.

Our goals in writing this book are to answer some of the questions that group leaders need to ask. When they don't ask, they become victims—they feel trapped and don't know what to do. The questions are as follows:

1. How can those who lead groups help their groups attain their goals?
2. How can leaders be effective — that is, what steps are necessary to help the group achieve its purposes?
3. How do leaders design programs to help the groups with which they work achieve their purposes in a manner that helps individuals as well as the group to be successful?
4. What are some of the ways in which groups fail? How do leaders help their groups avoid these pitfalls?
5. What are successful designs? Why are they successful?
6. How do leaders plan, design, conduct, and evaluate programs for effectiveness?

This book is not about groups but about how leaders who conduct groups can be responsible and effective. While we do not believe in magic answers or gimmicks, we do believe this book will make an immediate difference. We expect that group leaders will look at groups differently, think about their roles differently, and behave differently as a result of these understandings.

Certain Assumptions

We assume that prior to leading a group, the reader has had some experience in groups as a member—in a training group, in an organization development group, in a workshop, in an experiential training program, or in a human relations laboratory. There is no substitute for personal experience for understanding experiential learning, for understanding the involvement of the whole person, and for the issues of diagnosis and design.

Our second assumption is that the trainer is conversant with basic group concepts such as norms, group goals, cohesion, and group development. We will be talking about these concepts assuming the reader is familiar with them. To conceive of someone leading a group who has not done his or her preliminary homework by learning some of the basic group concepts is impossible. These concepts are essential for understanding how groups function, and from an individual perspective how individuals learn in groups. For those who need such preparation, we would like to recommend four books. Obviously, our favorite is our companion book, *Groups: Theory and Experience*, 2d ed. (1981); it is our favorite because it develops group concepts with experiential activities at both an individual and group level. Other recommended books are *Group Processes and Personal Change* (Smith, 1981), *Group Processes in the Classroom* (Schmuck and Schmuck, 1971), and *Learning to Work in Groups*, 2nd ed. (Miles, 1981).

Definitions

Despite our assumptions that trainees are conversant with basic group concepts, we do feel a few definitions are in order to explain our use of certain terms (Miles, 1981, p. 3).

Training is defined as a systematically planned approach to achieving an objective that utilizes group methods and encourages learning of better group behavior.

A *program* is a planned combination of training experiences (lectures, discussions, role plays, exercises, simulations, and training groups) taking place over a period of time.

A *group* is a number of persons (the traditional definition, two or more) working in a face-to-face setting on a task that requires their working together — for example, a curriculum committee meeting to revise the fourth grade math curriculum; or an executive director meeting with staff assistants at their weekly staff meeting; a community group meeting to make recommendations for utilizing a soon-to-be vacated school; the staff of a university department meeting to decide who will be accepted as candidates in the doctoral program.

A *group process* refers to the flow of behaviors in a group—how things are happening rather than what is happening. The group process provides the data for analysis. Process involves setting goals, exchanging ideas through communication, and developing procedures for problem solving and decision making; it is members knowing each other and expressing different forms of communication with one another; it involves its own normative system prescribing what behaviors are expected from group members; it is developing methods of support; it is resolving conflicts. The group process is going on all the time, although only on occasion is there special attention paid to that process.

A *design* is a training plan developed out of the needs of a particular group. It may be developed by the trainer or cooperatively with a planning group.

Focus on Task Orientation and Process Orientation

This book is designed to help trainers improve the work of their groups with a task — a job to be done and objectives to be achieved. It is not concerned with leadership in family groups, therapy groups, or social gatherings.

The focus is on *how* people behave in groups. There is a process orientation, which is the focus, rather than specific content. Usually, content and process are not viewed separately. In other learning situations, for example, the focus is primarily on content (a new accounting procedure, four methods of supervision, an explanation of guidelines for hiring temporary employees).

Even we sometimes forget to separate content and process. One of us received a letter from the Federal Deposit Insurance Corporation, inviting us to arrange an appointment preliminary to developing a consultant relationship. The immediate response was that the letter had been delivered to the wrong person. Dr. Gershenfeld had a cousin on the same university faculty who was a labor arbitrator; every so often mail was delivered to the other Dr. Gershenfeld. She called the director of the FDIC to indicate that the letter had probably been routed to the wrong person because, as she explained, she "knew nothing about auditing banks." The director immediately responded, "No, we sent the letter to you. We don't need experts on auditing banks: we know how to do that. It is for dealing with our interpersonal staff problems that we need a consultant." Even "experts" sometimes forget that they are not expected to be content technical experts.

In our book, the special focus is on process—how do people behave? What are the consequences of those behaviors? How do they influence other members? Skills that are learned in that process analysis can be utilized in other settings and hopefully will allow participants to become more effective in having their behavior match their intentions in other situations. That is not to say that content is never dealt with; a trainer may present a lecture, conduct exercises, or lead diagnostic periods in which methods of leadership, styles of communication, or methods of conflict resolution are examined.

Problem Focus

In laboratory training the focus is on the immediate problems people face in trying to work with others—not on imparting theory about small groups or presenting a series of lectures on organized knowledge about groups. The focus is on solving real problems of the existing group. How do we reduce the divisiveness of the faculty, which has resulted in the inability to work together after the school strike? Or how do different specialties with different professional languages and styles work together to give a patient in a rehabilitation hospital the best coordinated care? Or what can a departmental faculty do to increase enrollments in department offerings? Or how can community leaders be trained to conduct for area families a program coping with unemployment?

Summary

People are uncomfortable in groups for a number of reasons. The major reasons are that they have little experience in how to work together in a group and they do not have the same control as is possible in solving problems as an individual.

Group emphasis has changed since the beginning of scientific group study in the late 1930s. The studies of leadership and laboratory training, with their emphasis on self-analysis, were the focus in the early years. Since the 1960s, there has been an increased emphasis on groups for personal growth and in organization development. There has also been an emphasis on individual learning through a group experience as well as a macrolevel utilization of groups. Because laboratory training has been used in a wide variety of settings, people no longer see it as a panacea and are more sophisticated about what can happen in a group.

Groups can be highly successful experiences in which people feel exhilarated from having accomplished the objectives. An especially significant factor in a successful group is the group trainer. There is now a profession made up of skilled group trainers whose vocation is to help groups achieve their objectives. This book is written for group leaders to enhance their skills and increase their effectiveness.

References

Gershenfeld, M. K., and R. Napier. 1981. *Groups: Theory and Experience*, 2d ed. Boston: Houghton Mifflin.

Miles, M. 1981. *Learning to Work in Groups*, 2d ed. New York: Teachers College Press, Columbia University.

Schmuck, R. A., and P. A. Schmuck. 1971. *Group Processes in the Classroom.* Dubuque, Ia: William C. Brown.

Smith, P. B. 1981. *Group Processes and Personal Change.* London: Harper & Row.

Tannenbaum, R., I. R. Weschler, and F. Massarik. 1977. "Observations on the Trainer Role: A Case Study." *Sensitivity and the Laboratory Approach,* edited by R. R. Golembiewski and A. Blumberg. Itasca, Ill.: Peacock.

2
The Leadership Role

This chapter is for group leaders. This is not to say all of us are not leaders every day—when we help a colleague analyze a problem, when we coordinate a special project, or when we help resolve a stalemated discussion. Here, however, we define leader in a special context; we are referring to leaders who conduct groups, workshops, or training programs. These leaders may be internal or external organizational consultants. They may be professionals who work with groups and organizations to help achieve the skills, knowledge, or changes for which that group or organization has contracted. They go by the name of group leader, facilitator, trainer, psychologist, behavioral scientist, counselor, consultant, or staff specialist. They may have taken courses or perhaps are in master's or doctoral-level programs, learning and acquiring the skills of being a group leader or an organizational consultant.

Attributes of a Group Leader: Fantasized and Real

When we think of group leaders and their attributes, we subconsciously make a quantum leap into supertechnicolor fantasy. Alas, even fantasies have frames of reference and different tracks. In the T-group sensitivity track, there is the image of a handsome, sexy, six-foot, blue-eyed man with an ingratiating smile and an even more ingratiating manner. He is dressed informally, typically in jeans, and his shirt is "casually," daringly open. He wears an assortment of chains around his neck and probably a moustache or beard or both. His hair is either styled or worn longish. Moccasins, boots, or running shoes complete his attire. He has charisma and pizzazz. People listen because his nontraditional, nonauthoritarian style commands attention. He speaks with confidence but without using big words or getting overly cognitive. Simply put, he is a cross between Robert Redford and Carl Rogers.

In another frame of reference—the organization development one—the fantasy of the leader differs slightly. He is tall and is lean from running or playing tennis or racquet ball. He dresses in the ivy league tradition, impressively but conservatively. In the office he wears three-piece suits, polished loafers, and striped Repp ties. He holds a doctorate, or at least an MBA, has book-lined walls in his office, knows behavioral science theory, and is comfortable with survey data, computer printouts, and research analysis. In a training program at a retreat site, his attire is more casual—docksiders, jeans, and an "alligator" jersey. He has styled hair (that doesn't look styled), a flat stomach, a Boston accent, and an absolutely knockout manner of combining erudition, theory, and egalitarianism. He speaks sensibly but intelligently. His style induces even the most competitive, jealous males to view him as superior, and they become noncombative and grudgingly subservient. He achieves results and is comfortable giving advice to the board of trustees as well as to the foreign governments for whom he consults.

The fantasies are overwhelmingly consistent. Let's go on. A successful group leader is male, is attractive in his style, has instantaneous charisma, has a natural (inborn or highly intuitive) sense of what to do and how to do it, and leads a group effortlessly—and always successfully. If you have the magic ingredients, being a successful group leader is easy and, in fact, effortless. If you don't have the necessary ingredients, being a group leader is a struggle in which all kinds of difficulties occur—perhaps management doesn't trust you, or the proposed project is not funded, or the group is resistant and hostile, or the objectives are not carried out. But what do you expect when a mundane person is sent to do a superhuman job? Of course, you will fail.

These fantasies, with minor variations, are held, *not* by romantic teenagers or idol-seeking college students, but by all kinds of intelligent, educated, hardworking men and women. They perceive successful group leaders as having physical, visible attributes. They see an easy charm, group acclaim, a style of ready confidence in any situation and conclude the successful ones "have it"—the others are ordinary people somehow aspiring to being group leaders, but they "don't have it." It's like training a plow horse to be a race horse—you can put hours of energy and training in, but plow horses just aren't race horses. They never will win the race.

The fantasy continues. Group leaders are almost always born, although training can enhance their skills. Unsuccessful group leaders just don't have it, and training, experience, and credentials are all a waste of time. For proof, witness the myriad university professors who are failures in conducting groups or being effective as organization consultants.

Yes, the training may have failed but not because the professor and consultant didn't have the right style, but because they didn't understand their role as group leaders or how to design training or how to evaluate it. They failed because they didn't know or understand the role of a leader. Working with a group is very different from lecturing to a class.

Role and Relationships of a Group Leader

Realizing that a group leader is not an image that magically confers success and effectiveness on a program is essential. Realizing that to be an effective group leader one must fully understand the particular group or organization is also essential. What are the members' expectations of the leader? What is the leader expected to deliver? In how much time? What are the objectives for this program? What resources are available? Success comes from planning, diagnosis, implementation, and evaluation.

The leader that we are talking about in this book is not the president of the corporation, the superintendent of the schools, or the administrator of the hospital. Nor does our leader aspire to those positions. Instead, our leader is a person who would be invited to develop a program to assist those people and their organizations, to build skills in staff, to increase abilities of departments to work together, or to help the organization overcome interpersonal difficulties. The group leader of whom we speak is frequently called a trainer or a facilitator because the leadership role calls for helping the experts in the organization work together to enhance their abilities as individuals and to increase their effectiveness as an organization. Whether part of the leader's responsibility is to conduct a T-group, conduct a survey, or increase skills of supervisors, the leader's role is as a consultant or enabler.

And, of course, the group leader need not have the physical appearance and style just fantasized, nor the gender. Women are also effective group leaders. Despite the skepticism with which some organizations continue to view women's roles as group leaders, women are increasingly being hired by organizations that see beyond the traditional fantasies and stereotypes that surround the image of female group leaders. What insightful organizations are buying goes far beyond sex, color, age, or religion.

Still, fantasies are perpetuated even by those training group leaders. For example, listen to this description of a group leader from a recent book on the subject (Merritt and Walley [1977], p. 12): "A group leader is creative, nonjudgmental, democratic, excited, exciting, sharing, inspiring, strong, sensitive, perceptive, a member of a team, patient, growing, learning, open, alive, honest, exploring, feeling. You." Again, a junior deity. These authors cringe when we read that list. We have been successful group leaders for over fifteen years. We know that we can be creative, but at times we have chosen to utilize standard training designs that we and others know work well. We know that we are judgmental and autocratic in more situations than we would like to be and that groups feed back information on our biases, but we also know that on many occasions we have been exceedingly "democratic." We have been excited, but we have been bored. We have even seen others excited but then sometimes bored. We have been strong but at other times felt powerless. We have prided ourselves on being sensitive but have on occasion been shocked by our insensitivity. We have been a member of a team but have also felt isolated and alone. We have grown—if learning from mistakes is growing—and we continue to grow, sometimes joyously and sometimes painfully. In essence, we are not perfect, nor do we aspire only to perfection.

Just as teachers do not arrive in class every day, loving every child and eager to teach every subject, so too are group leaders human. They have weaknesses and blind spots along with their strengths and sensitivities. As authors, we are not in search of attributes as qualities to ensure success. We rely instead on leaders learning to understand themselves and the tasks to be accomplished.

Special Responsibilities of a Group Leader

We view a group leader as a person with special responsibilities for helping an organization achieve its contracted objectives or helping an individual or group members learn from their experiences. This chapter is directed toward the person taking on, or considering taking on, the role of a group leader. It is a difficult role.

One of the major difficulties lies in the wide range of group situations. This range underlies the complexity of groups. It is why leaders are successful in some groups and not in others. It is why a certain method of training is effective in some groups and disastrous in others. It is why some people in a group situation make major gains and others feel upset and even harmed. There is no simple answer.

There are any number of theories about effective leadership—whether it is a trait theory, a situational theory, a contingency theory, or a life-cycle theory. Here we are clarifying our own conception of leadership and group behavior. We are focusing on the person who has the responsibility for helping the individuals or the group have a learning experience compatible with their goals. There are certain assumptions:

1. *Group leadership behaviors can be learned.*
2. *The focus is on behaviors, not intelligence or traits or sex.*
3. *Leadership is shared.* The group leader does not fill all the leadership functions of the group. Other members of the group can be involved in planning, giving information, confronting, harmonizing, giving feedback, or whatever behaviors are needed by the group.
4. *Process skills are essential.* While knowledge of content in an area is important, it is not sufficient for effective group work. How it is said, when it is said, who replies, the tone of the reply—these are the important things.
5. *Diagnostic skill is basic.* The fundamental process skill is that of diagnosing group difficulties and sensing needed but missing functions. When an incident occurs (a segment of group behavior), the process goes something like this:

   Sensitivity: Can I notice that person A usually (describe behavior)?

   Diagnostic ability: Do I understand why person A usually does this?

   Action/Skill: What information do I need? How do I get it? Do I have the skill to do it? Am I willing to take the risk—now, when, under what circumstances?
6. *Just as a diagnostic mentality happens at an individual level, it also occurs at a group level.* The leader and the members take a diagnostic experimental approach to improvement of group life. Outcomes are accomplishment of the task and, in the course of accomplishment, more accurate seeing and hearing in groups and greater ability to give support, to work interdependently, and to work with a greater range of people.
7. *The leader operates habitually.* The leader operates as an ongoing process by noting missing functions in the group and supplying them. When difficulties occur, the leader pays even more attention to utilizing behavioral data to understand what is happening. The

leader is "on"—working all the time at understanding what is happening at a content level and also at a process level. The leader's skills will increase the learning experience for individuals and achieve the agreed-upon objectives of the group.

8. *Group leadership is an art more than a science.* Much of an effective leader's actions emerge from a process within the leader that is based on experience, a developed sense of what is happening, and the kind of intervention that feels appropriate and "right." Leaders, like skilled craftsmen, work by "feel." Leadership remains more a performing art than a science.

There are assumptions—not cookbook steps in how to proceed. A group leader needs to understand the steps, the processes, the methods that work. At each level there must be a reexamination of what is happening, when things are going well, when they are not, what needs to change. In short, the continuous, experimental, learning diagnostic mentality in which the content as well as the effect of the individuals and the group are considered, and the caldron in which all this takes place, is the organism of the group leader.

The Trainer Role*

We will use the term *trainer* as synonymous with the term *group leader.* Despite its earlier named difficulties, it is the term most commonly used. A reader uncomfortable with the term is welcome to substitute another term—whether it is group teacher, facilitator, enabler, or consultant.

The trainer's responsibility is to facilitate the group's accomplishment of its objectives. Like a teacher, the trainer basically guides and facilitates learning. However, being a trainer requires a different kind of behavior than is traditionally associated with being a teacher or group discussion leader. For example, the trainer involves others more in the "curriculum design" process than does a traditional teacher. The trainer also focuses more on an analysis of "here and now" behavior as differentiated from content. In addition, the trainer may spend some time in lecturing but is not the traditional discussion leader.

The emphasis is different as well. When a group is apathetic, bored, bogged down, or in the midst of an argument, the trainer's role—unlike the teacher's—is *not* to restore order so that the lesson can proceed but to help the group learn from the disrupting events. Learning as a group of individuals to work together to accomplish objectives is an essential aspect of meeting the group's objectives.

The trainer role calls for the trainer to be the initiator of the training, the planner prior to the activity, the guide during the activity, the evaluator after the program, and the planner of new or follow-up activities.

---

*Much of this section is derived from ideas in Miles, *Learning to Work in Groups*, 2d ed. (New York: Teachers' College Press, Columbia University, 1981), pp. 236–263.

The Trainer as Initiator

Often a trainer is invited by an organization to conduct a group, lead a program, or be an external consultant on a project. The trainer then begins a process of discussion and negotiation to determine who will be the participants, the objectives of the training, the extent of management's involvement, the time allocated, the duration of the project limited or ongoing over a period of months or years, the amount of remuneration, and the method of program evaluation. While those areas are being explored, the trainer is thinking about whether the problem described is the real problem, whether the organization wants "real" outcomes or is "going through the motions" for some reason, and whether enough time has been allotted to meet the described objectives. In essence, do there need to be substantial revisions?

Sometimes the trainer proposes the project. For example, the trainer may make an appointment with a school superintendent, or the station manager of a television station, or the administrator of a hospital. The trainer may then describe a program that could benefit the organization—perhaps by helping the organization be more effective in its relationships among members, or deal with women coming into management positions, or deal with the frustrations of a "freeze" in employment or promotions, or train new principals in how to function in a particular district.

In either situation—whether invited by an organization or soliciting an organization—the trainer is in an *initiating position.* The trainer needs to "sell" the program, including the method of proceeding, the analysis of the situation, the vision of the kind of training that will be most effective, the ability to meet organizational objectives, recommendations of first steps, contingency plans for revisions, and plans for evaluation. Too often training fails because the trainer is not the initiator but rather passively agrees to conduct a proposed package, only to find the "package" doesn't make sense in this situation. At that point the trainer is tempted to delete parts or change the emphasis without informing others. Sometimes trainers get hooked into promising to fulfill objectives that are unrealistic in view of the time limitations or the nature of the population. Trainers need to be excellent salespeople who can clearly convey their ideas of how the organization will benefit, how this approach is compatible with achieving the organization's objectives, how benefits can be measured, and how the organization will view the results. And most important, trainers need to see themselves as initiators actively involved from the moment of being contracted—initiators in what will happen, how it will happen, what they expect, how they will help, and how the organization will help.

The Trainer as Planner

During the planning process, the trainer's primary responsibility is to ensure development of a training design that takes into account the participants, the time, the resources available, and the training objectives. Practical, promising plans for learning need to evolve.

Such a planning process does not take place alone in the stillness of the trainer's study. Rather it is an interactive process in which the trainer works with a group of planners designated by the organization or with a group of previous participants or other trainers. Nor does the planning process involve modifying a previous program. Rarely is a program that was previously conducted with success a sure fit for another population at another time. The trainer as planner is involved in the following functions:

1. *Creating a planning group.* The trainer must get a group of people together for help in creating a training plan based on their knowledge of the participants or the organization, for feedback during training, and for help in evaluation and follow-up activities.

2. *Being a knowledgeable, technical expert.* If the planning group says, "In our organization people never talk—they wait for the boss to say how it will be done," the trainer must suggest a number of alternatives. For example, the trainer might propose an exercise to encourage group participation or suggest grouping members into five-person discussion groups (support groups) to encourage a place in the design that allows for behaviors different from the usual organizational ones. In order to display this flexibility, the trainer must be knowledgeable about group theory and methods of conducting laboratory training. A wide array of techniques, exercises, and designs must be readily available for adaptation by the trainer. The planning group will rely on the trainer for this expert information.

3. *Being aware of how the training process is going.* The trainer needs to make sure that the objectives of the planning group are clearly stated, that the group is focused on the objectives, that people in the planning group feel psychologically safe in expressing their ideas, and that the group is being educated in the norms to be established in the training—that is, having opportunities to speak and be listened to, valuing people, practicing new kinds of behavior as appropriate, learning as an individual, and feeling as a respected member of a group. As difficulties occur in the planning group, the trainer needs to help the group understand the process—what seems to be happening, what can be done to resolve the difficulties, and how the group can continue to recognize differences but move on. From time to time the planning group needs to pay attention to the process.

The Trainer as Guide: Building Group Norms

During the actual conduct of the program, the trainer's role is to carry out the training design so that there is movement in the direction of learning and meeting the objectives. But on the way to those cognitive, declared objectives, the trainer's own behavior helps to set group norms (informal standards of what is expected, appropriate, acceptable, or valued by members of a group). The trainer influences group norms from the minute the group begins. Even before the official "opening," participants watch what the trainer does and form opinions about the training. The norms that the trainer influences encourage the behaviors that will lead to successful development of the training design and the desired objectives. Some of the norms that the trainer can encourage are as follows:

Norm 1: People should be listened to and recognized. The trainer acknowledges raised hands, a quizzical look, a tentative question. The trainer encourages a divergent thought, a statement of discomfort, or a questioning of the relevance of an exercise. Expressed in the trainer's behavior is the idea that people have all kinds of opinions and that these can be examined—it's even OK for people to express their own ideas. The norm of each person's being respected and having rights of membership in the group is established.

Norm 2: It is safe to be here. The trainer reassures members that what happens in the group remains in the group. If people have something to say to the trainer or another member, it is safe to say it. The person will not be ridiculed, or shushed, or reprimanded for speaking out. A person can discuss the trainer's behavior, and the trainer will respond sincerely, viewing the comments as data to be discussed like any other data. The trainer encourages quiet members to speak more often and the talkers to speak less often. The trainer also tries to convince those fearful of expressing their feelings to consider such expression and those uncomfortable with looking below the surface to take a chance. The norm being encouraged is to try new behaviors in an environment of safety.

Norm 3: Feelings are important. The trainer encourages expressions of feelings. Feelings are data to be discussed and influence decisions. Feelings help members to measure progress—what obstacles continue to stymie the program and what satisfactions come from being part of the activity. Feelings are what determines how much change members will consider, whether they will expend little or much effort, who they will hear and who they will "tune out," whether their energy goes toward action or toward closed-down defensiveness. The norm to be established is that expression of feelings is vital if the group is to utilize its energy toward resolving problems and understanding the processes going on.

Norm 4: Feelings, behaviors, and questions of both the trainer and members can be discussed. An experimental learning process involves seeing, hearing, and feeling (internal, not touch). A person may challenge the trainer and say, "I feel we are being manipulated." The trainer's response is not, "How dare you accuse me of such a thing. It must be that you are jealous because you aren't running the show this time." (Imagine what that could lead to in the next round!) Rather, the response should be, "How do you feel you are being manipulated? What did you experience?" Expression of feelings toward the trainer is not an attack to be warded off but legitimate data for examination and discussion. The norms to be encouraged are that expression of feelings, response to behaviors, questions that may be viewed as "difficult" (nonsupportive of the trainer or the program) are not to be ridiculed, ignored, or taken "personally" but rather as "grist for the mill." Learning takes place by experiencing the freedom to express and to be taken seriously; the climate should not be one of walking on eggs and being constantly on the lookout for hurting someone's feelings or incurring the wrath of the trainer. (Do note, however, that the trainer should respond if attacked. The trainer should not get immersed in the content of group discussion but remember the primary role of focusing on the facilitation aspects of the group.)

Norm 5: Objectivity is encouraged. Discussing feelings allows members to learn which feelings or events lead to subsequent influences on the group. As a model, the trainer deals with antagonism toward him or her, and so the group learns. The group learns when the trainer asks for information or checks if others have similar feelings that feelings expressed are not dismissed from the lofty position of the trainer or smoothed over as nonexistent. The trainer remains objective in response to members' expressions and in all program activities. The trainer also encourages process observers (instruments for analyzing their data), post-meeting reaction sheets, video playbacks, tape recorders, and observation methods—all to demonstrate that we can look at what is happening and learn from it.

Norm 6: We learn from doing things and analyzing them. In creating a training design the trainer, along with the program planning group, sets up a series of experiences. Stimulated by a provocative incident, participants are involved in these simulations or surveys, or discussions—perhaps in their usual style of interacting or perhaps "off balance." These live here-and-now experiences are then analyzed. The trainer does not encourage discussions of what happened in the past, what might be in the future, what has been read, or what happens back home. Rather, the focus of analysis is on what happened just then—what those people are feeling, how others are responding to them, and how that influences what will happen next. The trainer may distribute observation instruments or give a brief lecture on a conceptual framework for help in analyzing a particular outcome. This is done to aid in the process of learning what has occurred—what was felt, how that can be dealt with differently in a similar situation, what new behavior might be attempted, what insights were gained. In the process of achieving the objectives of the seminar, workshop, or training program, the "here and now" as analyzed is the major learning method. In working toward the objectives of the program, there is a design. As participants are involved in the design situation, they can also analyze what is happening to them as individuals, in their relationships with others, and in the group as a whole. This "present" analysis is a major lesson.

Norm 7: Planning is a joint effort. The trainer is involved with others in creating a design for the program—it is not accomplished single-handedly. Others are invited to provide feedback on the effectiveness of the program, usually as part of an ongoing evaluation, including planning for the next day or the next segment. The trainer takes clues from observing the overall atmosphere—boredom, apathy, exhaustion, increasing conflict? The trainer asks questions, revises a design, or perhaps stops and has the whole group analyze what is happening. The trainer does not have sole responsibility for the success of the program.

The trainer models these norms as the group proceeds. With experience, members come to accept analyzing their own behavior. They accept process observers, expression of feelings, and being able to respond objectively to data on their behavior rather than defensively or antagonistically. This kind of experience will help the group create a climate for learning that will be the basis for the group becoming effective and successful as the program proceeds. The experience of working in a group will be transferable, even after the current program has ended.

The norms as stated are such a central aspect of working with groups that the trainer, whether an experienced leader or a neophyte, must strive to remember them, utilize them, and, in assessing his or her own effectiveness, refer back to them. Of course, all this is easier said than done. Trainers get tired, become pressed for time, or find someone who especially annoys them; they get diverted into revising what they intended to do or are scared and adhere too closely to the design when they should be processing more; and they are sometimes not sure when the time is right to bring up a difficult situation. With experience, however, the trainer learns how to reenergize when tired, how to be objective in dealing with feelings, how to express an idea briefly and to lecture less, and when to "process" knowing that part of the plan will have to be omitted. Regardless of a trainer's style, there must be a commitment to these norms, especially as displayed in the trainer's behavior. This commitment is especially important in the early sessions of the group when norms are being formed and the trainer is being scrutinized.

The Trainer as Guide: Specific Behaviors

In addition to helping create norms that will enhance the learning climate, the trainer must also perform the following functions in the training program. These functions are (1) providing diagnostic and design help, (2) guiding analysis, (3) giving support, (4) stimulating, challenging, and confronting, and (5) encouraging group growth.

The basic requisites of the trainer are to know when certain functions are needed and when they are not, when to make an intervention and when to be quiet, when to offer an alternative and when to wait for the group to suggest one, when to confront and when to support, and when to settle for a sentence and when to deliver a short lecture. The trainer makes these decisions based on diagnosis of what is happening in the group, and with the basic purpose of enhancing effective learning.

Providing Diagnostic and Design Help. The trainer is the methodological expert who knows about training designs, activities, alternatives for creating learning experiences, methods for conducting diagnostic surveys, ways to give feedback, and how to do follow-up programs. The trainer may be working with a planning group from among the participants or may be making an impromptu suggestion in the training activity. For example, typical behaviors might include interviewing various segments of the organization to obtain their diverse perspectives or suggesting a role play as a way to help groups in the training program define a problem, or using a fishbowl* to bring together representatives of work teams to discuss their alternative plans.

Beginning trainers are usually fearful of this role; they fear they don't have a big enough "bag of tricks," or methodological alternatives. Too often this fear results in trainers' buying books of exercises with the hope that after an urgent scanning they will find one that just fits. Rarely does this happen—not because they haven't purchased enough books but because the training goals and the particular group are the primary determinants of what is an appropriate activity, not the objectives stated at the top of the training exercise. After working with another leader, or often being part of a training program as a participant, coupled with experience in working with a group to design a program, the new trainer will learn to integrate the concepts of design and the steps in the process and to be creative in developing a program.

Guiding Analysis. Remember, not only does much of the group learning take place from creating the design, but also from analyzing the process of learning. In addition to encouraging process observations, the trainer will raise questions about what is happening, note any discrepancies, point out something that is happening and invite an analysis of it, ask for implications of particular outcomes, or invite participants to consider what they have learned from a given experience. The trainer may also guide analysis of the design itself and explain the rationale for certain sequences or the theory behind a given segment of the program. The trainer may analyze the group and its style of functioning, its strengths, and its obstacles. This can be done directly or by presenting a theory (for example, Gibb's, "Defensive Communication" [1961]) and asking the group to analyze its defensive behavior in light of the theory.

New trainers are often fearful that they cannot translate concepts from a book to a meaningful intervention in the "here-and-now" of the training program. There is a big difference between reading a clear concept in the book and expressing that concept in a way that participants can hear and relate to during their present experience. Timing is also a concern. For example, How often should process observations be made and what kind? Should the trainer initiate a process observation or hope a member will? When should the trainer model behavior? When should the trainer be silent so that he or she is not the

*A technique in which half the participants form a circle and speak while the others observe; after a time they reverse.

only person doing analyses of difficulties in decision making? When should the trainer limit process involvement to only a few?

There are a few general guidelines. First, when in doubt about making an intervention, don't. Wait a moment and see if a group member also feels what you feel. If you are bored, someone else may be. If you see only a few members participating, someone may be able to draw the silent ones in. The second tip is to create group methods for analysis as part of a design. Plan on a PMR (post-meeting reaction sheet) after sessions. Include a process observer as part of a simulation. In setting up interviews, create a three-person group so that one member can be an observer. Include ways so that participants also get involved in analysis, learn from it, and recognize the benefits from not only receiving feedback but also giving it. While having a responsibility to be involved in process analysis, the trainer also has a responsibility not to create dependence and to help the group be involved in analysis.

Giving Support. For many being in a group is scary. What will happen? Who will be harmed? What will be the repercussions? Members suffering from such misgivings will be silent until they get a feel for the "lay of the land"; they certainly don't want to be embarrassed or look stupid or sound obnoxious. They will wait for others to risk beginning. Obviously, if everyone is playing it safe and picking up cues rather than speaking, the norms established will be a major deterrent to the group members' trying new behaviors or experimenting with working in combinations of groups or attempting new ways to learn.

To be encouraged to speak, to try new behaviors provisionally, or to expose their behaviors to analysis, participants have to receive emotional support. The leader, being in a position of status, can have a special effect in giving support. For example, the leader can thank a hesitant questioner or reduce conflict between members by saying, "We're not deciding who's right or judging—right now we want to gather data, to hear what each of you feels." The leader can act in a warm and friendly manner, even to welcoming people as they come in and making small talk as they wait to begin or commenting favorably when someone tries a new behavior.

Initially the support comes from the leader, who is the primary norm setter in the training program. Over time, however, support will also come from members of the group since the practice of regularly affirming members in taking risks or attempting new behaviors will have already been established. Later, the group members will remember that this was a supportive, caring group.

New trainers sometimes overdo the warm and friendly style and become the ultimate of "sweetness and light." They are fearful of conflict and will do almost anything to avoid it. When conflict emerges, if smoothing it over doesn't dissolve it, they now desperately try everything and anything. They may become apathetic, feel they are hopeless (whatever made them think they could be successful trainers?), and admit they have lost it all. Or, they may try to mediate between the sparring groups. Or, they may try to "reason" with one side. None of these approaches is helpful. Soothing everything over does not allow members to understand that conflict is part of life and that its resolution is an important part of learning—not its suppression. The leader should not take on the role of a group member by mediating between sides or "reasoning" with the members who are wrong. The leader's role is to help facilitate, to help the members examine their conflicts, and to suggest strategies (in design) to work through their conflicts. The ultimate goal is to help people learn—and it is through conflict that we often learn most. The leader cannot be apathetic to the conflict, nor play ostrich (if you pretend not to see it, it will go away), nor absolve himself or herself of the responsibility (I didn't start it; it wasn't part of the plan, so it has nothing to do with me). To be apathetic (do nothing) is to let the forces that be take over. The result is all kinds of consequences, from serious harm to an individual being scapegoated to a major walkout and greater divisiveness than there was before the program started. The leader needs to deal with conflict when it occurs. And, after the conflict has been dealt with, the leader needs to be supportive of members for the new behaviors they took on and for the way the group was supportive of the difficult situation.

There is an ongoing argument, over whether groups are therapeutic or educational. If the definition of therapy is positive change, then of course, training is therapy. However, in our view we are not conducting therapy, nor is the leader a therapist. The focus of the training is not on examining personal (beyond the organization) intrapsychic or interpersonal problems. However, sometimes groups will make one person a scapegoat or dwell on one person's particular vulnerability or needle the person to explode. At these times the leader should be supportive of the targeted person with interventions such as, "What group purpose did this behavior serve?" or, "What's happening now?" (Group interventions are most appropriate in bringing the group back to its task and most effective in encouraging analysis beyond the individual.) At an individual level, the leader should ask, "How are you feeling through this?" or, "How would you like to see the situation resolved?"

At times group members want to talk to the leader about their reactions to an event in the training or perhaps their feelings about a person. The leader should be available and supportive of the person wanting the discussion. However, to the extent possible, the leader should encourage the person to bring the matter up in the group so that there can be a general discussion or change or resolution. The trainer might even help the person explore how the position could be presented or offer to be supportive in bringing the matter before the group. By encouraging private consultations, the trainer is also encouraging dependence and hindering the group from learning.

Stimulating, Challenging, and Confronting. Trainers need to be supportive, but they need to do more. They need to help people see that what they have thought "for always" needs to be reexamined. By having their experience structured in a different way, they experience themselves and others differently.

Some of the long-held false assumptions and stereotypes dissolve in the present real experience. Ideas can be challenged, and ways of doing things can be questioned. Experiences in the training program can be a challenge to what were thought to be inevitable ideas (there is only one way to run a meeting).

One of the major methods of learning, which comes experientially, involves the stimulation, challenge, and confrontation of the program. Leader behaviors would be encouraging participation, disagreeing with someone's view of what was happening in the group, noting discrepancies between what the individual said at one time and then at another, seeing a body clue and encouraging a participant to express what he or she is feeling verbally, or raising an issue group members seem to be avoiding.

One of the problems with standard exercises is that while they were once stimulating, challenging, and formed the basis for learning, they are now so common as to be boring and repetitive. They are viewed as irrelevant and a waste of time. In designing a program, the leader needs to think of being stimulating, challenging, and confronting as a significant method for participants to learn and also as a way to be helpful to the group.

One trainer who is weary of "going through the motions and having nothing happen" uses the motto, "Keep them off balance." It's his way of saying be stimulating, have the group look at things differently, confront routinization and inevitability, and encourage a fresh perspective from a new situation to risk a new behavior.

Confrontation by itself does not encourage taking risks or trying new behaviors. Only when it is imbedded in an atmosphere of support will a person explore or reexamine or rethink. The trainer must first develop support from within as well as from members. Only then will confrontation be an invitation to open a new door rather than shut down or leave.

New trainers are often afraid to confront; they are not sure when or on what issues. They are hesitant of the outcomes. They fear stimulating and challenging designs because they are not sure they can have them work as intended; they are afraid they will be considered silly or superfluous. Again, with experience and from observing others, the new trainer will learn when stimulation is needed to allay apathy and boredom, when challenges can encourage new thinking, and when confrontation enhances the possibility of trying new behaviors. The key questions for the leader to ask are, Does the group look apathetic or bored? What can I do? Is this the time to make a blunt statement about what is happening? Later? Will someone else make the comment? Can the group confront itself? How?

Encouraging Group Growth. The leader, by being involved in creating the design and suggesting activities, in helping to analyze behavior, in supporting, and in creating stimulation and challenge, is also encouraging group growth. The group comes to realize that it can have design ideas for how the program can proceed or recognize that what felt right yesterday in planning may not feel right today. As the program continues, members can feel more comfortable analyzing what is happening in the group or among themselves. They know how to do it and are more comfortable expressing what they see. They learn the rules of feedback and how to provide feedback on a person's behavior when it is asked for. They see the value of feedback and are not as reluctant to express accurately what they feel. They learn to give behavior evidence to support their comments and to include positive comments as well as negative ones.

The leader encourages group members to take on more and more trainer functions. By helping the group be effective unto themselves, the trainer ultimately works his or her way out of a job (at least on that goal with that group). So as time goes on, the leader no longer has to be the person to encourage a shy member to speak; other members of the group will take over that role, just as they will also begin to accept responsibility for confronting or analyzing behavior. The trainer is not looking for adulation or strokes for being brilliant but is committed to having the group learn and mature. To encourage this process, a leader might turn a question back to the questioner or ask the group how it would respond, point out successful decisions made by the group and how they occurred, encourage the group to design a segment of the program without the trainer present, give teams an assignment and ask them to resolve a problem, or ask the group to present a theoretical concept or design a role play. The objectives, of course, are to spread group responsibility and encourage group growth.

New leaders may be so occupied with needed functions that they may intervene too quickly and find they have encouraged a norm in which the leader functions exclusively. New leaders tend to be so desirous of being viewed as good leaders (talented and skillful) that they may be constantly demonstrating and not allowing others with skills to use them. They may forget that they are models, but not the "only" models. At other times new group leaders think they should do their job, and the group will take care of itself. They have enough to do without also encouraging the group to grow. With experience, however, leaders begin to receive recognition, realize they are good, and can focus on encouraging their groups to grow and acquire their own skills. The leadership function can be assumed by members who know what is needed, have the skills to perform those functions, and are willing to take risks. Part of the trainer's responsibility is to encourage and help the group develop all of these functions, including encouraging members to risk and try new behaviors that may have originally been defined as leader behaviors. Of course, these leader functions do not exist in discrete categories, with the focus on one to the exclusion of another. They all occur concurrently—a statement that sounds like an overwhelming task.

The Trainer as Successful Leader

The classic Lieberman, Yalom, and Miles study (1973), based on factor analysis, named four prime attributes of the most effective leaders: caring, meaning attribution, emotional stimulation, and executive function. The most effective leaders are high in caring and meaning attribution and moderate in emotional stimulation and executive function.

Lieberman et al. define *caring* as a leader style that involves offering protection, friendship, affection, and frequent invitations for members to receive feedback as well as support, praise, and encouragement. This caring dimension is often described as the Rogerian style of high empathy, high genuineness, and high "unconditional positive regard" (being nonjudgmental). Although caring behavior by the leader may help create norms for enhanced group development, by itself it is insufficient to assure a lasting positive outcome.

The second area in which effective leaders were high was in *meaning attribution*. By meaning attribution Lieberman et al. refer to providing concepts for understanding, explaining, clarifying, interpreting, and providing frameworks for how to change. Effective leaders spend a lot of time explaining why they do what they do, how they see the group members relating to each other at a given moment, and why they recommend setting up the group in a particular way. Their emphasis is not only on learning by doing but also on learning by instruction.

Another important attribute is *emotional stimulation*, and the most effective leaders were moderate in this area. By emotional stimulation Lieberman et al. refer to behaviors that emphasize revealing feelings. Challenging, confronting, and encouraging self-disclosure may encourage members to go beyond their usual facades, but too much may be frightening—members may withdraw or even leave. Too much emotional stimulation may also lead to later psychological harm if people are embarrassed by having disclosed too much too soon and are fearful of possible repercussions. Interestingly, leaders who themselves practiced moderate self-disclosure and sought feedback on their own behavior were highly rated by members—they were perceived as real people, not just a neutral trainer.

Lieberman et al.'s fourth major attribute is *executive function*, and leaders are most effective when they make moderate use of this dimension. Behaviors defined as "executive" are setting goals or direction for movement, managing time, sequencing, pacing, stopping, interceding, and setting rules and limits. Executive function also includes inviting, eliciting, questioning, suggesting procedures for the group or a person, and dealing with decision making.

Structure by the leader does enhance learning in the group. A brief training program requires that the leader takes primary responsibility (and maybe even sole responsibility) for structuring the event. With greater time available, a broader range of options are open, depending on how readily a particular set of training goals may be approached through a more structured or differentially structured format. Structure is especially useful in the early stages of a group, as it allows participants the comfort of knowing what is expected of them. The structure creates a feeling of being somewhat at ease in what otherwise feels like a totally strange situation, which would usually elicit responses of self-protection and withdrawal. Structure also allows those more comfortable in structured situations to participate. The danger of too much structure lies in having learning prove nontransferable from the training setting to the real world. The ideal approach is to begin with structure and move on to less leader-directed structure to provide an opportunity for members to take greater personal responsibility for their actions once a safe climate is established in the group.

The most effective leaders, then, are those high in caring and giving support, high in giving information, and high in explaining or clarifying what they are doing. Although confrontation is important, it is most effective when coupled with support and caring. Learning is more likely to be retained and internalized in an atmosphere in which the leaders (or other members) clarify what they or others are doing.

The Trainer as Evaluator

Just as trainers are responsible for planning and guiding their training programs, so too are they responsible for developing evaluation procedures and instruments. Increasingly, there is an emphasis on whether the goals were achieved. What were the outcomes and how effective was the training? How does one know? The answers don't fall in place in one fell swoop six months after the training. Instead, trainers are thinking of outcomes almost constantly. From the beginning of a training program or even during the planning, trainers need to be thinking of their own role and how they will accomplish their objectives. They are continuously analyzing how they are doing according to the standards. They need to evaluate activities as they take place to note trouble spots and how the design can be revised. They need to note the group climate and the extent of the participants' involvement. They need to be aware of how the training is going day by day so that changes can be made as needed—or even to realize that changes do not have to be made and to experience the satisfaction of knowing that the training is going as planned and is being well received.

At the conclusion of the training, there has to be a method for evaluating the training, a way of focusing on how the training will be used afterward, as well as a rating of the actual program. A "high" at the end of the training program is an insufficient outcome; too often the effects of training that was "fun" and "interesting" fade within a couple of days. Our emphasis is on retention and transferability of training goals. The evaluation needs to reflect these objectives.

Evaluation may include a section on how the training will be used once the members are "back home"; it may even include a more specific contract. Members may be asked to state one specific problem they will tackle or a new behavior they will try as an outcome of the training. They may then agree to practice that behavior and return for a follow-up session at some later time from two weeks to two months. During the follow-up session, the effectiveness of the training is evaluated in the light of the practical experience of members having tried the new approaches; subsequent training programs may be revised based on the experience of the first participants.

Evaluations can also take the form of gathering information on the retention of learning as a result of the training. There may be six-month, one-year, two-year, and even five-year evaluations focusing on the sustained effectiveness of the training and its impact on the individual or the organization. Some training has immediate outcomes that are sustained, while other outcomes are quickly acquired and just as quickly lost. The changes, for the most part, seem to be primarily a function of the cohesiveness of the group. Although a portion of the training may be inadequately measured at the conclusion of the training, a major understanding may have taken place or a special skill have been acquired, which with practice will become more a part of a person's or an organization's behavioral repertoire two or more years later.

The leader is responsible for creating evaluation methods, and for seeing to it that they are carried out. Planning for evaluation is a part of contracting for training. Because it is an enormous subject and one that has been insufficiently dealt with as a trainer function, an entire chapter is devoted to evaluating training.

The Trainer as Planner and Conductor of "Follow-Ups"

From one perspective follow-up activities are the next training program—that is, each training unit is viewed as an experience unto itself. In some instances, this is true. Each training experience is separate. The organization contracts for a stress workshop or a communication skills program. There is a specific limited contract that the trainer designs and conducts. There is an evaluation at the end that might include recommendations for follow-up, but whether the organization contracts for follow-up or not is a separate issue.

However, there is increasing concern about "one-shot" training in which knowledge about the effect of the training, about what was retained, and even whether the training has caused harm is limited. One of the major changes that has been advocated, especially during the last couple of years, is an emphasis on follow-up programs built into the original contract. Even in a two-day communications workshop, a two-hour follow-up two weeks later can be built into the contract. One of the several advantages is that participants will practice what they learned. Also, there is a sense of reporting back two weeks later and wanting to report being successful.

This new trend counters the assumption that new behaviors are appropriate in the training but are not to be taken seriously when applied to the real world. Further, follow-up allows any "unfinished business" to be raised and to be acknowledged as such even if not resolved. Sometimes after completing the training, people are aware of something they did that they would like to clarify; the follow-up gives them that opportunity. In addition, follow-up allows any harmful repercussions of the training to be identified. The group can then explore how those problems can be dealt with. Finally, and not to be taken lightly, is the memory of the infusion of hope, the experimental attitude and the support felt in the training program, that is recalled during follow-up. Those attending are reminded to continue pursuing the changes they sought in the training.

We believe an important function of a trainer is to initiate, design, and guide follow-up activities as part of the closure and evaluation of the training. Such activities will create a mentality of continuous learning, revision of learning, and expansion of experience.

New trainers are frequently timid about approaching follow-up. In addition to being inexperienced in designing follow-ups, they are often fearful that their follow-up efforts will be viewed as featherbedding (making work or making limited work stretch for more money). They need to understand that follow-ups are essential for evaluating the training and for retaining the training experience.

Ethical Guidelines for the Group Leader

As we describe the functions of the trainer and enumerate the norms the trainer should be encouraging and modeling, one might assume that we have listed everything. One important norm, however, is yet to be mentioned. That norm is the matter of ethics. Underneath, there needs to be an understanding of what is ethical, and what is not. There is a difference between going through the motions and sabotaging an organization, and helping an organization increase its effectiveness. There can be ulterior motives in designing the group training as well as explicit motives that are known and acknowledged. Training, like any other enterprise, including "scientific research" (even to the subject of the research) is value-laden. Unless we are aware of our own values and feel certain about what is right in our work with people and our groups, we can be working at cross-purposes. We may be saying one thing, but doing another. We may unknowingly be sabotaging our client organization or be encouraging others to do so. Most important, we may unknowingly be harming people.

Miles (1981) has developed what he calls a set of ethical "rules of thumb." This list is not meant to be all-inclusive, but at least it calls attention to ethical issues of which group leaders should be aware. Although the "right thing" to do is rarely crystal clear, and although the application of these guidelines is fraught with ambiguity depending on particular circumstances, we think that these principles help remind us of what our role as a trainer "should be." It is as if as trainers, we dressed our various styles and guises, but understood that these outer ethical understandings are our common core. We may have many outer styles, but underneath we are agreed in these areas.

Awareness of Ethical Choice

Ethical choices exist from the very moment of contact with an organization. Would you conduct a training program for the CIA, IBM, an order of Catholic nuns, or the U.S. Army? Are the values of the trainer and the organization from which the members will come compatible? If they are not, should that trainer continue or even start, knowing there is no commitment or desire to be helpful? There is no such thing as value-free training. Who the trainer is and how he or she operates determines the effectiveness of the training program and its outcomes. Much as judges disqualify themselves from certain cases, shouldn't trainers be aware that working with systems that are contrary to their belief systems can cause ethical problems?

Sometimes the ethical choices are obvious; sometimes they are not so clear. For example, how do you handle a contract with a school system in which you are asked to work within the professional system with minimal parental contact and involvement when you believe that parents should be involved in the schools since they are ultimately responsible for the quality of their children's education? Would you not take that contract? Would you inform the school administration that you believe that parents, in addition to the faculty and administration, need to be more involved? Or would you work within the parameters of helping the professional staff be more successful in coping with the school's problems?

Awareness of One's Own Power

Trainers can have tremendous power in a group. Often they are viewed as experts on everything from how to listen more effectively, to how to improve the quality of participants' marriages, to how to deal with difficult adolescents. They are viewed as having magical powers. Out of that amalgam of a doctorate (or other "fancy" degrees), a style of expertise, and the usual transference phenomena, there are those who listen to every word and take it seriously. A quip by a trainer in a moment of exasperation may be taken quite literally by the recipient and result in that person's feeling punished or "bad."

Trainers, like any member of the group and more so because of their position, need to remember that behavior has consequences—their behavior as well as the behavior of group members. For a trainer to disavow any responsibility for what happens is a denial of the real situation. The trainer cannot say, "Each of you is responsible for your own behavior." Trainers have to remember they are in a position of leadership and are responsible for designing the training program, guiding the activities, and creating group norms. In addition, trainers should be open to receiving feedback on their own behavior, based on analysis by the group. Feedback will enable trainers to become even more aware of their influence on the group. Furthermore, behavior found through feedback to be incompatible with the objectives of the training can be changed. Finally, feedback is one of the best safeguards against leader-dominating behavior turning trainers into self-styled autocrats.

Truth in Packaging

Doctors are currently paying giant premiums on malpractice insurance to protect themselves from suits in which patients claim they were insufficiently informed of the risks of the treatment or the limitations of the outcome. Doctors have operated (no pun intended) in an aura of "the doctor knows," with little responsibility for explaining or discussing alternatives with the patients. They have learned, only too late, that they have lost public confidence, and that their silence has produced rage, even to a willingness to enter into expensive, protracted court proceedings.

Trainers, too, have been guilty of exaggerating the benefits of their training. They have insufficiently informed the participants of dangers, and they have not provided a sense of how the training will work or what is expected of potential participants. Although trainers are rarely sued, the situation is similar. One of the reasons training has diminished so substantially is that organizations who once eagerly (and naively) looked to training as an effective (and magical) method for dealing with interpersonal or organizational difficulties have been "burned." Although they aren't the "suing type," they become suspicious and very "anti-training." During negotiations about a training project, the president of a large hospital was very direct:

> I need to invite a number of trainers and listen to their proposals and then decide which one will be the best for us. Or if any sound right. If you fail at this job, which represents only one of scores of organizations with which you work, you will end up with a 5 percent failure rate—excellent for you. For us, that failure rate will be 100 percent. For us the training will have failed. Not only will we have not accomplished our objectives but our people will be more wary and less trusting in future training. We will set ourselves way back, and we don't need another of those experiences.

Although the actual nature and outcomes of a training program can never be fully anticipated, there should be full, clear information on the training, how it will be conducted, what the benefits are, and what the risks are. We have found that one way to reassure participants beyond words and exaggerated expectations or fears is to conduct a mini program (usually a half-day program) with members of the organization or even with potential participants in preparation for a longer training experience. We can then answer questions and have participants understand what we mean by directly experiencing a sample of the training.

Volunteerism

Ideally, people in a training program have volunteered to come; they are there because they want to be part of the learning stated in the objectives of the program. Coercion can be psychologically dangerous; for example, people already coping with more than they can bear in their personal lives may, when confronted by a simple piece of feedback, break down or so distort the feedback that the "giver" becomes an "enemy for life." Being "forced" may invoke determined resistance in which the primary motivation is *not* to learn. The participants in their anger at being ordered into the intrusive training may join forces in resisting the norm, with the result that the company will lose. The proverb about bringing the horse to water but not being able to make him drink applies—they will present their bodies at the training, but they can't be induced to learn.

Coercion also looms in team development programs in which the training goal is to enhance the relationships among all of the members of a team. Hopefully from a meshing of personalities will come ways of learning how to be more effective and how to reduce conflicts as a work team. Yet how transferable will the training be if only 60 percent of the team participates and, as is commonly stated, the ones who are the biggest "monkey wrenches" opt not to come?

One way out of the dilemma is to ask all members of the team to come but have the training during work time. To protect the person who is reluctant to speak (giving feedback to the boss may not be considered "constructive" and may rightly be felt to have possible repercussions) any person can "pass" when it is his or her turn. A further safeguard is to give anyone who requests it the right to not participate in an activity. Trainers do not automatically know best; persons should decide for themselves when to participate in an activity and when to stay out, when to speak and when to remain silent.

Privacy and Confidentiality

Some of the major fears participants have in training relate to the issues of privacy and confidentiality. One fear is that they will be gossiped about—that any self-disclosure will become common knowledge with the embarrassment of having "everyone know." Another fear is that a revealed inadequacy will stand in the way of a future promotion or will give a competitive colleague an edge. Yet another fear is that a mistake made in trying new behavior will be reported to the boss. Many fear that the training program is not "safe" but is really a method of employee evaluation that will be sent back to the organization. Unfortunately, these fears are real; these things have happened.

Agreements need to be made at the beginning of the training about confidentiality and privacy. The trainer needs to explain that members will not be pressured to make any self-disclosures unless they want to; the real learning is the present relationships among participants in the program. Another point that needs to be clear in the beginning concerns members who want to discuss something privately. They must be reassured that the matter will not be brought before the group by the trainer without permission from the person or better yet that the person can raise the issue in the group only if he or she feels it is appropriate. If there is to be any evaluation of participants in the workshop as part of the trainer's contract with the organization, the trainer should say so at the outset. If a staff of trainers will be discussing what happened in their groups (seemingly breaking the agreement that the group will not be discussed on the outside), that too needs to be expressed to the group at the beginning.

Some trainers play favorites and become emotionally involved with one or two participants. The other group members become concerned that they are being talked about or that the favorites are privy to special information. The group is apt to treat those "favorites" differently, deferentially in some circumstances, antagonistically in others. There is also the question of whether the person with whom the trainer has this special relationship is being exploited, such as the client being sexually taken advantage of by the therapist. Most trainers wisely decide not to have outside contact with individual group members during the training.

The most important point is to make the rules clear. Privacy and confidentiality are essential for trust to emerge and for individuals not to be harmed.

Competence

By competence we do not mean perfection or being supremely confident. Rather we are talking about not believing the magical powers that the group may project on the leader. We are talking about the trainers' knowing the level of their competence. They should be operating out of knowledge and experience. They should not be involved in an activity they have not participated in or do not fully understand. The danger of "getting in" and not knowing how to "get out" is real.

It is one thing to feel new and apprehensive, to know the material but to be fearful about having the ability to work with the population. It is quite another thing to be so overwhelmed with a training assignment that prayer and the fact that you are a good person are all that sustain you. Going beyond your level of competence is dangerous. It is not taking a risk; it is inviting disaster.

Value-Behavior Congruence

Just as going beyond the trainer's level of competence is dangerous, saying one thing and doing another is phony. Trainers who encourage members to express their feelings but carefully avoid expressing their own are creating a discrepancy that will interfere with the training. Trainers who stress the need for conflict resolution but avoid dealing with conflicts among their training staff are giving messages that conflict resolution is really futile or even dangerous. As participants engage in their work while simultaneously observing the trainer, they form ideas about what is acceptable and what is not. They are more apt to be influenced by the trainer's modeling and behavior than by the trainer's words.

Avoidance of Harm

No trainers intentionally expect to harm members of their training program or any organization with whom they work. It usually doesn't happen. Sometimes, however, an intensive training program has the potential for being psychologically damaging to some of the participants. That damage may be a loss of self-esteem or self-confidence, weakened relationships with others, depression, or a fear of groups and an accompanying reluctance to participate in groups in the future. Members of a training group who come as an organizational team are not as likely to incur psychological damage but are even more prone to organizational damage. Information revealed in a training program may have repercussions for future promotional opportunities, or bring to the surface unresolved interpersonal conflicts, or create such serious antagonism with a supervisor that resignation is called for. Trainers need to be alert to such possibilities. The training needs to be designed in such a way as to allow members to withdraw from particular exercises and to understand that they can withhold information as they choose. The trainer should ask for volunteers to speak rather than naming people to respond. Of course, as people withdraw from a particular exercise or "pass" when it is their turn to speak, full team involvement becomes limited. But a more important consideration is to be aware of how each person feels and to "do no harm." The trainer must protect each person's boundary. Goading, shaming, sarcasm, and scapegoating are more likely to cause detrimental effects than enhance learning.

The previously discussed Lieberman, Yalom, and Miles study (1973) found that psychological distress was most likely to occur when trainers used highly confrontational methods, provided little support, or tacitly permitted a high level of intermember attack. Conversely, harm to participants was least likely when trainers provided support and allowed members to move at their own speed. As an additional safeguard, trainers consulted with other trainers (or members) to guard against the tendency not to notice members who were experiencing a difficult time.

There is a tendency not to think about the ethical "underwear"—a tendency to assume that because (like real underwear) it doesn't show, it may not exist. But it does exist, and is highly significant. There are real ethical dilemmas for a trainer, and no clear or certain answers; the answer will vary according to the situation and/or the population. Also, if the trainer is congruent with what she or he says, to that extent s/he will feel that the participants are being truly helped, and without loss of integrity on the part of the trainer. Therefore, trainers become better trainers by getting in touch with their own beliefs and codes of personal ethics, and making what they say and what they do as trainer consistent with that ethical framework.

Leader Training

How does a person who would like to become a group leader go about it? The best way is to have seen a group program in operation—to have watched the trainer, to have seen the varied reactions of participants, and then to think, "I would like to do that." Once having mulled the idea around, the next step is to participate in even more training programs. With the heightened awareness of maybe becoming more involved, you will find yourself listening to trainer interventions and noting training activities in terms of their sequencing and objectives. You will be especially aware of the processes in interaction in addition to the content.

The person thinking about becoming a trainer should have extensive experience—beyond putting in time or going through the motions. During the course of these experiences the potential trainer must be able to demonstrate that as a group member he or she can learn some of the skills. The person must demonstrate a willingness to give and receive feedback where appropriate, an ability to self-disclose, an awareness of personal needs as well as the needs of others, and the leadership capabilities to carry through a variety of initiating behaviors in group settings. In the course of these experiences, the potential trainer will have tried a number of new behaviors, will have attempted varying methods of relating to others, and will have attempted varying methods of relating to others, and will have developed increased awareness of behaviors that he or she is most comfortable with as well as more difficult areas. Learning to be a trainer means to try, analyze, and then try again. Like learning to be a member, learning to be a trainer is an experience-based program.

The would-be trainer should next enter a formal process for attaining conceptual knowledge—theories and empirical data that underlie training practice. A number of excellent programs include courses in group dynamics and organization development.* The training need not be confined to a formal degree-granting structure but can also take place through various trainer programs offered as workshops or training-of-trainer programs. Our only caveat is to check the credentials of those giving independent programs.

Reading books, such as this one, is another way to comprehend the leader training process and to build both understanding and skills. Our book, for example, will be most effective if discussed with colleagues or people in a course or if it is used in designing a training activity. It is not like a mass-market novel to be read once and finished with; it is a resource for regular referral and discussion. What seemed obvious, or perhaps unimportant, can become crucial at a later point.

Concurrently, there should be a number of other learning experiences. One experience is to be an apprentice to some experienced trainers. There would be excellent opportunities for discussing what happened and what was seen. Another learning experience would be to design a small workshop as part of a class or with a group of colleagues to share in the responsibility of creating and conducting such a workshop. Co-training experience (as the junior co-trainer) is another possibility. In this experience there can be an opportunity to discuss each session afterward and to build understandings and skills as a result of those discussions. The experienced trainer can be observed closely, and interpersonal relations that develop between the junior and the senior co-trainer can be a model for future co-training experiences. Working as part of a training team is

*Temple University has such a program in the Department of Psychoeducational Processes for such training at a master's as well as a doctoral level.

another way to learn to be a trainer. Observing several trainers with their different styles will help build technical skills (suitable ways of contributing to groups in which one is a leader) and design skills (so important when planning a program).

There are many other activities that will increase your skills as a trainer. They include keeping a journal of training experiences, especially if entries are made immediately after each session. The journal should not only contain notes on the content of the sessions, but also on the trainer's analysis of what was happening. The trainer's notes should include instances of uncomfortable situations as well as "just right" situations. Questions to ask a colleague or issues to be especially aware of in the next session should also be recorded. Groups can be videotaped, and the trainer can learn through instant replay. The trainer's flow, interaction, and personal style can be noted. Tape recording the sessions also allows the trainer to review the sessions and to analyze the interventions—"Why did I stop here instead of there?" "Maybe I should have waited before intervening."

Although new trainers are often too fearful, a feedback activity with members of the group after each unit is a good way to learn how the participants are feeling toward the group's progress and how they are feeling about the trainer. If a trainer indicates an interest in feedback, members are more likely to ask for it also. In the course of all these activities, the new trainer becomes increasingly self-aware, but not so much as to give personal needs priority over those of group members. For example, a female trainer had to force herself not to back down almost automatically when an older man shouted; a competitive male reported he had to curb himself from getting into conflicts with other competitive men in the group; a religiously oriented trainer had to steel himself not to flinch when "hell and damn" appeared liberally sprinkled in the conversation. The new trainer learns to recognize blind spots and any special problems that are apt to occur. Most important, the new trainer develops a style and becomes genuine.

Finally, there is the continuous practice of being a trainer and a learner. In every training program a trainer learns something new because of a different population, a different task, an unanticipated problem, a new co-trainer, a new theory, a revamped design. The list goes on so that being a trainer is a constant learning experience, exhilarating and challenging. The challenge can be tiring, but the energy that goes into planning and conducting a program can turn into exhilaration at the conclusion when the program has gone well.

When do you stop learning and when do you know your craft well? Never. There are always new programs to attend and new theories to learn. There are new trainers to watch and new clients with special needs to help. Training to be an even better trainer never ends.

Probably the primary difficulty in the path toward becoming a group leader is the enormous diversity of current applications of group work. Most leaders find some styles more congenial than others. The dilemma is that the more they focus on their favorite style, the less they leave themselves open to the expressed needs of their members. Trainers are coping with this problem either by specializing in certain areas (with business organizations, or women, or education) or by working in collaboration with other trainers whose skills supplement their own.

Although the trainer role is one that can be learned and is not dependent on appearance, sex, personality, or clothes, to be an effective trainer takes self-awareness, knowledge of groups, diagnostic and design skill, and experience.

Summary

Training does not happen by itself. Rather, it happens through the guidance of the group leader. Who that leader is and how that leader performs influence the training outcomes.

The leader or group trainer is held primarily responsible for what happens in the training programs. The leader is not expected to be a superhuman, just fully aware of and capable of performing the functions of a group trainer. The leader is a prime mover in setting group norms and has special functions in initiating, planning, guiding, and evaluating the group program. The leader must be aware of the ethical issues and be able to handle the ethical dilemmas that might arise. The person we are describing is a well-trained leader—that is, a leader who has participated extensively as a member of a group, a leader who has ample self-awareness, a leader who has the ability to diagnose and design, and, finally, a leader who has acquired technical and methodological knowledge about groups.

There is no evading or stating this last thought too strongly: The leader has to be well trained because of the major impact a trainer has on a group in creating, in designing methods by which people learn, in encouraging interpersonal relationships to become more effective, and in fostering objectives for which programs are created.

References

Gibb, Jack R. 1961. "Defensive Communication," *Journal of Communications* 11 (3): 141–48.

Lieberman, M. A., I. D. Yalom, and M. B. Miles. 1973. *Encounter Groups: First Facts*. New York: Basic Books.

Merritt, R. E., Jr., and D. D. Walley. 1977. *The Group Leader's Handbook*. Champaign, Ill.: Research Press Co.

Miles, Matthew B. 1981. *Learning to Work in Groups*. New York: Teachers College Press, Columbia University.

Smith, P. B. 1980. *Group Processes and Personal Change*. London: Harper & Row.

3
The Questions Leaders Ask

We want this book to be helpful to new leaders and to those who are more experienced leaders but find themselves "getting stuck." We want it to answer questions of "What do you do when . . . . " Of course, as experienced trainers we like to think we know both the questions and the answers, but like any trainer initiating a consultation project, we don't know. After a decade and a half of training, the questions we figure beginning leaders will ask may not be the questions they really do ask. We have to ask them, just as we would ask any client, what do they want from the training or, in this case, a book for leaders.

In the course of our research, we asked and we asked. We asked graduate students enrolled in a course entitled "The Role of the Consultant." We asked students in a class on "Training Design." Many of these people had had considerable training experience. We asked trainers in programs to which we are consultants. These people included the training staff at Pennhurst State Hospital in Spring City, Pennsylvania, the extension staff at Michigan State University, conference participants in a workshop on developing training skills, and training directors in the Philadelphia area who had signed up for a program on women in management. We asked recent doctoral graduates, and less scientifically, but with mounting curiosity, almost anyone with whom we were working.

All this asking consisted of the following four questions:

1. As a group leader, what is one question you have?
2. As a group leader, what is one problem you have?
3. What in your opinion is the biggest problem group leaders have?
4. What is the most important advice you would give a new group leader?

We wrote the response to each question on a separate piece of paper; then we grouped together "repeats," so that we had separate piles of responses that had recurred frequently, those that recurred less frequently, and finally those given by only one person. In our first draft, we took each of the piles of responses, ordered them into an outline, and created a discussion that included the answers to the most often asked questions. We were unhappy with our results. It all seemed so bland, the answers so obvious—and worse, we thought it sounded pedantic and boring. Just as in a training program, it was "back to the drawing board." We had created a design, but it didn't meet our objectives. It wasn't stimulating, it didn't have a sense of urgency, and it didn't allow people to learn directly.

We decided on another approach. We would start with the questions our own questions generated. Then, as in a clinic or training-of-trainers program, we would devise ways to understand how to answer the questions. In an actual interactive program we might create simulations or role plays so that participants could viscerally get a feel for the questions and then test some alternative responses; here we will answer the questions with ways to think about the issue involved, and present alternative ways for handling the problem. The questions are not ordered; we like the format of a question to think about and a response that encourages continued thinking and understanding. Therefore, the questions that appear in this chapter, and our replies, get at what are the especially important problems you have that you want answers to.

The Most Asked Questions

What do I do about my lack of confidence in being a leader?

There is a wonderful anecdote told about the late Arlene Francis, an actress who was known as a sparkling, spontaneous conversationalist under any and all conditions. She appeared totally at ease, with a ready quip for any occasion. The story goes that she had just redecorated her bedroom. A visiting friend saw the room and gasped. The walls, the curtains, the bedspread, the chairs, and even the ceiling were covered in the same print of giant butterflies. Arlene explained, "I always have butterflies before I 'go on.' I thought maybe if I lived with them and was surrounded with them I would get used to them and the scary feeling would go away." Who would have thought that beneath that urbane sophisticated exterior there lurked butterflies?

Even the most assured, long-time trainer experiences a lack of confidence and has butterflies when working with a new population, beginning a very different design or running a conflict resolution workshop with widely differing participant perspectives. Some situations are scary, and sometimes we enter thinking, "Who, me? They're relying on me? Good luck!" One incident remains vivid in our memory. One of us conducted a program with senior military officers who doubted the competence of a female trainer. It was not just an initial reaction of feeling like a "not too bright kid" amidst all that brass (literally): it was three days before she breathed normally.

Like Arlene Francis, the best way to overcome fear is to learn to live with the butterflies; they are part of the job and come with the territory. After that there are a number of other things you can do. First of all, be prepared. Have a training design that is well thought through. Know the activities by having practiced them. Don't go out there alone the first time. Watch another trainer or co-leader. Start with a small practice project and then build to larger projects. The ways to build confidence are to have been a participant yourself, learn as much as possible about the group you will be working with, have a design, built with the clients to initially share responsibility for a program, and stay within the limits of your competence.

What do I do if they attack me? I'm scared.

Not if—they will; you can depend on it. Sometimes a group will scapegoat a member, and it is up to the leader (if not a member previously) to stop it. When the attack is on the leader, however, the situation seems different. We are hurt, angry, and perhaps not so sure about how to respond. Basically, concern about being attacked can be handled in four ways.

1. Respond to an attack with a sharp counterattack. From a position of authority the leader can definitely put the attacker down and at the same time depend on some of the members to be supportive. There will always be members who believe the leader should not be attacked publicly and will oppose those who do.

2. Develop a style that suppresses hostility and reduces the likelihood of an attack. Act as a gentle, friendly, caring father/mother figure, always couching your words in tentativeness: "Would you consider . . . ," "Perhaps it could be . . . ," "Couldn't we possibly . . . ," "I need to think about that. . . ."

3. Be aware that any situation can be explosive, and constantly be on guard to ward off an attack. Avoid conflict situations that might lead to an attack. If attacked, apologize—at least that tends to end an attack quickly. Keep an eye on participants who look displeased or annoyed. Be especially sensitive to them and use your energy to "win them over" or, at the very least, neutralize them.

4. Once attacked, convince yourself you will survive, that the attack was even helpful. Group members are encouraged to accept and respond to a wide range of feelings. If a group member was attacked, we would encourage the recipient to ask for opinions—do the others agree with the attack, do they see the recipient's behavior differently, are there circumstances during which the attacked behavior occurs and others when it does not? We would encourage the recipient and the rest of the group to explore the feelings expressed in the attack more fully and not to be satisfied with an oversimplified view of anyone's reaction to anyone else. Group members are encouraged to ask for specific examples or descriptive information. They are encouraged to ask for feedback from others regarding the attack. The trainer should respond in that same manner. There are two reasons. The first is that the trainer sets norms and models desired behavior. The trainer's response sets the example for encouraging members to respond to an attack in like manner. Second, an attack provides data on how the trainer is being perceived. The trainer should listen to that feedback and think about how to be more effective in the future.

The capacity to tolerate attack is crucial to a trainer's effectiveness. These four responses, especially the fourth method, will not only help you to avoid being attacked but also help you to deal with and learn from a situation when you are attacked.

We know leaders are supposed to help create positive norms, but what can you do when there are negative norms? How do you stop them from spreading?

A simple strategy in dealing with two or three people in the group who are very negative and are creating an atmosphere of negativism is to diffuse the negative comments among positive comments so that the effect is not as pervasive. Rather than ask for opinions from the group, the situation being that most members will be silent and the negative ones will be vocal, change the format. Break the large group into smaller groups of four (or six or eight, depending on the number in the training). Ask the small groups to discuss the question and have one member from each small group report. At worst, even if the negative members are selected to report out, there are only two negative reports heard as data among six positive reports. Another advantage of this procedure is that it offers those fearful of speaking (out of apathy or out of concern for tangling with the negative members) encouragement to express their opinions. Further, the more positive members in the small groups might just carry or influence the negative members, so that even the two negative responses will have reduced influence within their small groups.

So much for a short-run, immediate response. The real key is in diagnosis —what clues are there about why these people are negative? Listen to what they say about their concerns in connection with the training; invite data from others.

Consider any of the following reasons why these two or three people might be so negative and then develop a design to deal with the situation.

1. They were ordered to attend the training to "shape up." (Three supervisors who had complaints filed against them by women were ordered to attend a "supervising women" workshop.)
2. They had planned to go to the training in Florida (semivacation) like the last group; instead the training was conducted in the company building.
3. They start out negative and "smart alecky" to cover up fears about the subject and a resistance to the objectives of the training. (Navy engineers were ordered to take "human relations training" to alleviate serious interpersonal difficulties.)
4. They don't believe anything will change. Long-time employees have seen scores of training programs come and go. There may be minor changes for a few weeks, but then it will be back to business as usual. Why put energy in or go through the pretense that something will happen?
5. They are too old to deal with these constant changes. They have a difficult time adjusting. They hope this "new program" will go away; maybe if they point out its shortcomings, the status quo (the system known and comfortable) will continue.
6. Their boss never lets them talk, and they have built up years of hostility. They are displacing their anger toward the trainer, who is an authority "replacement."
7. They don't like the way the training program started out with members interviewing each other and reporting what they like most about their partner. They were "nauseated" with all that "sweetness

and light" and counter with some definitely negative comments to maintain some semblance of "reality."

8. They lost the vote. There may have been a decision to be made on the type of training, the leader, or the program goals. They fought hard for another alternative, the vote was close, and they lost. They hope the present project won't succeed.
9. They like the attention—what a great opportunity to stand out in a crowd! Only after a diagnosis (gathering some information, testing hypothesis, looking for cues) can the leader understand some of what underlies the negative behavior and begin to intervene?

How can I get everyone to participate comfortably from the outset — not just to talk, but to be motivated and involved?

The leader must create norms conducive to each person's being active and involved from the very start of the training. We are convinced that the norms of the training and of the group in subsequent training are established almost immediately. While claiming they are established in the first hour might be an exaggeration, we definitely believe they are set in the first half day. It is therefore essential that the first half day be well planned, with objectives of participation and personal motivation as primary goals.

Planning begins within the planning group. One of the first endeavors is a letter to each participant. The tone of the letter, the goals described, and the description of the training and the leader are all part of creating an atmosphere of curiosity, or at least grudging compliance. The letter should contain information on hours, meals (included as part of the training, or extra), and suggested attire. This information influences the participants' initial attitudes.

A primary objective of any program is participation, and that objective should be evident to all members as they arrive. For example, there might be a coffee pot, name tags, and chairs arranged for interaction. Someone should be welcoming members as they arrive, and the group leader should be present and casually interacting with participants, introducing persons who may not know each other. The leader does not descend at the appointed moment, "Johnny Carson-fashion," to "take over" center stage with an opening monologue. That kind of an approach definitely sets up a speaker-audience relationship.

The leader may be introduced or may introduce himself or herself and begin. In either case, there should not be an introduction ticking off the leader's impressive credentials. Such an approach is too intimidating; when participants are assailed with how great an expert their leader is, the distance between the members and the leader widens quickly. Most members will likely be quiet, but the antiauthority types will play games of trying to prove the expert wrong and will look for ways to trap their leader—hardly the participation desired. Although credentials are important for legitimacy, we prefer to list the leader's educational background and experience in a letter to participants or have a vita available in the back of the room for people who would like to see it.

The leader might begin by presenting an overview of the program, the hours, lunch times, and the anticipated outcomes. A brief talk about how the learning will occur and the kinds of activities with which the group will be involved should preface a request for any questions on what has just been explained. Questions could include anything from "is smoking permitted?" to "could lunch be shifted form noon to 11:45 to avoid the crowds?" to "is this like therapy—are people expected to 'spill their guts'?" Encouraging people to ask questions is the leader's first test. The leader's response to people who ask questions will help participants decide whether to talk and be involved, or whether to "sit it out," investing little and saying less. Remember, the process, not the content, creates norms. We believe an overview is essential. Recall that Lieberman, Yalon, and Miles (1973) said that successful leaders were high in meaning attribution—that is, by explaining what they were doing and why, successful leaders set the learning in a cognitive framework.

The next step is one in which leaders who want to encourage participation and involve everyone so often make an irretrievable mistake. They will say, "Let's go around the room and have you introduce yourselves." Although such a remark sounds open enough and as if it would encourage each person to speak and be involved, it doesn't. What it does is establish information on status, position, and connections and thus create classes of participants. In a new situation, people who are asked to introduce themselves bring all of their status-building devices with them. They search to introduce themselves with their highest position, their highest degree, their greatest link to power, or their most prestigious "anything they can think of." The effect on the others is just as intended. Those with high status can now identify and talk to their equals and ignore the "lower realm" participants. Those of lower status are less likely to present their ideas or even to speak, having been made aware of their lesser "qualifications." Interestingly, "higher" and "lower" are not the same standards in every situation. In a "managing schools" workshop, when 80 percent identified themselves as union stewards in their schools, the administrators present (who had higher educational degrees and higher positions) became increasingly silent and less involved.

Some of the following norms should be established early in the session: (1) everyone is encouraged to participate; (2) everyone can contribute—is needed to contribute to help achieve our goals; (3) there can be individual as well as group learning and more effective personal behavior; (4) the experience can be fun (we hear people say all the time that they found the training exhilarating, that it was exciting to be challenged and to think and interact with others, and that they felt alive).

One method of creating these norms at the beginning is to ask participants to pair with someone they don't know. In each pair have one person be a one and the other person a two. Assign ones to interview and twos to be interviewed. Depending on the theme of the training, choose a topic (use only one). One topic might be, "Get to know each other as if you were writing an article for the feature page of the newspaper; include interests, hobbies, philosophy of life, etc.'' Another topic could be, ''When do you feel most alive? Why is that so important to you?'' Yet another could be, ''What is your greatest accomplishment in life, the one of which you are most proud?'' After seven minutes, the trainer calls time, and the pairs may go around and introduce their partners to the group.

The point of this design is that everyone is involved in speaking and listening, being aware of another person and that person's style, and making connections beyond those they knew when they arrived. It has further effects of breaking up existing cliques and having participants feel as if they are no longer alone—they now each have a friend. Quite surprisingly, the relationship between the two in each pair becomes special; when one person introduces the other to the group, the introduction is usually done very favorably, and a supportive relationship between the two of them is created. The end result is establishment of a norm of responding to participants positively for the whole group.

The question, When do you feel most alive? is an especially effective one for getting two people who don't know each other to interact. One person does the interviewing for ten minutes, and then they switch. After the interviewing, each pair may be asked to join two other pairs to become a small group of six. The members introduce their partners and relate to the group what they learned during the interview, how they felt during the interview, and how they felt toward their partners. After each introduction, the person introduced can respond.

Then the trainer asks, ''What were my objectives in starting out like this?'' Groups are given ten minutes to discuss the question, and then each group is asked to ''report out.'' The trainer amplifies some of the statements by writing them on newsprint sheets or on the blackboard. In amplifying what is reported out, the leader might make some of the following statements: ''That's right, some of my objectives were to have you build skills in speaking and listening, in expressing how you feel and doing it uniquely, and in listening to another person express what he or she feels, which might be very different from what you feel.'' Or the trainer might say, ''That's right, one of my objectives was to have you respond to a question you had never thought of before and be aware of yourself in the moment. I also wanted to help you become aware that each person perceives uniquely—there is no right or wrong answer to some questions. It is what that person perceives at that time.'' Understanding that another person may feel very different from you (someone may feel most alive having twenty people for Thanksgiving dinner, and you think, all that work, I'd rather have a weekend for skiing) is an important norm to be established early in the design.

Another method for establishing norms early in the program is to have each member pair with one or two others to discuss their hopes and their fears for the training program. They might merge with another group to create a joint list of common hopes and fears that the larger group will report out. The trainer with the participants can then explore how the hopes might be enhanced if they are realistic or appropriate, and if they are not, how they can be revised. The fears can also be listed, and each group can be encouraged to express what these fears mean. For example, the members in one group might list as one of their fears that how they do in the workshop will be reported to their supervisor at work and may reflect badly on them. What then needs to be dealt with is what kind of report, if any, is being sent to the organization on the participants.

Another fear listed is that personal information divulged will become gossip back at work, or that the information may be used punitively. Here again, the leader needs to check among participants that information about members will remain in the group. Or, if there is a likelihood that such information may be used outside the group, the leader must advise members to be careful in how much they reveal.

Still another method for establishing norms is to have random groups form (count off one, two, three, one, two, three, etc. Have all ones in one group, all twos in another, etc.) and discuss the topic, "What are three outcomes we expect from this training?" Each group's three answers are then reported out; the trainer comments or invites discussion with resultant clarification or revisions.

All of these methods invite participation, as members are each expected to speak and listen on a personal level, right from the beginning; it is part of the design. Members will be motivated to be involved if that motivation is connected to a tension system (an internal motivational energy) toward a goal (as in the classic Zeigarnik, Lewin, and Hurwitz researches). Having an internal tension system related to a goal can be generated by having participants express their expectations, or goals or fears, on an individual basis. Eventually, group outcomes develop. Even if the expectations are very different, the process of discussing them together and developing a jointly agreed-upon response within a group fosters the norms desired—of creating a shared product out of individual needs or hopes or fears.

There are other methods of fostering norms beyond those used at the beginning of a program. For example, at regular intervals, if only a few members seem to be participating, divide the group into smaller groups consisting of three to five persons. Ask each group to discuss and respond to a question you may have asked the whole group. Then ask each group to report out; the concept that everyone is to be involved and that you want their input is thus encouraged and reinforced.

Another method is to use an exercise at the close of a sequence or at the end of the day that is a simple review or a personal evaluation. Members, either in small groups or as a total group, can comment on "Where I am at the end of today," or "What I got most out of today was . . . ," or "One thing I learned about me today was . . . ," or, "It surprised me that. . . ." Ask for a volunteer to start, and have one question go around (in some order) after the first person's comment. The answers can be brief and people can "pass" if they prefer. The point is that each person is encouraged to express his or her feelings at the end of the day. By listening to these comments, the trainer can understand what is happening within individuals. Often the trainer can encourage individuals to continue to explore and understand the implications of what they have just said. Often, people are surprised by what they spontaneously said.

Not everyone may start out speaking "comfortably," but with repeated practice, in twos, in threes, in larger groups, in various combinations of participants, people learn that it is safe to speak, that their ideas will be included, and they can become "comfortable." (We have seen unbelievable changes in even a one-day workshop.)

How can I keep one or two loudmouths from dominating the discussion?

The goal here is to encourage participation, which includes the entire group. The one or two "loudmouths" often are attention seekers, the fastest thinkers, the most verbal, or even supervisors who are used to explaining the "right way" to their staffs. Obviously, the trainer wants to keep them involved and include their responses. The difficulty is that sometimes others in the group become passive knowing that one of "them" will answer before anyone else has even formulated a response. Thus involvement from the whole group drops, and of course there are limitations on the outcome when only a few people express their ideas. Finally, limited involvement means limited ownership — that is, most members will not feel that the decision made was one they fashioned, and consequently they will have little investment in its achievement.

The question then becomes, How does the leader "design" to reduce participation by the overspeakers and thereby encourage others to speak? One method involves returning to the previous question. That is, instead of having discussions with the whole group, create small groups. Have the question discussed within each small group, and have one person report out. Even this method can be broadened beyond the usual few reporting out; a structure can be created in which one of the training goals is for members to acquire the skills and have the experience of reporting for their group; over the course of the training program, a different person reports out each time so that all acquire these skills. There can even be a brief processing afterward, in which people are asked how they feel about speaking in behalf of a group and how they feel about speaking before the entire group.

Another method of controlling overspeakers is to divide the group in half (have the members count off one, two, one, two, etc. or ask that all on one side of the room become a group and all at the other side to become a second group). Ask the ones to form a circle; then the leader instructs them on what they are to discuss as a group. The twos listen for ten minutes. Then they sit where the ones were and are instructed to continue the discussion or comment on the ones and their discussion. This method encourages participation because so many people find that participating in a smaller group is easier. Knowing that observers are watching, the "loudmouths" are much more sensitive to their own behavior and are reluctant to be seen as "obnoxious" or at best, dominating the group. Having observers also motivates some of the quieter participants to speak, so they won't be viewed as nonparticipants. This method also encourages an examination of the process of discussion. When the second group has its turn in the circle, its members are likely to comment that the session was dominated by only a few speakers and that others were not heard from. Hopefully, a new awareness is created in that group, and the overtalkers are less inclined to continue that behavior. (In this method, each group speaks twice and observes twice. In the second "round," the trainer asks that they come to conclusions or recommendations on the question discussed.)

In either of these methods to encourage participation and discourage loudmouths, the trainer can make use of interventions to encourage more people to speak. For example, the trainer can broaden participation by asking leading questions, such as "How do the ideas presented sound to those of you who have not spoken yet?" or "What other phases of the problem should we explore?" or "Are there any other opinions or comments?"

Another method to increase participation is to do a simple reaction survey. For example, a four-sentence instrument that asks about "communication" can be distributed (see Figure 3.1). Instructions are: *Please answer honestly. Check where you are on each scale.* People fill in the sheets and, of course, do not sign their names. The reaction sheets are then tallied (three groups might each take one question), and the results are reported out. Then there might be a discussion to determine what could be done to increase participation by those who feel they cannot present their ideas or are not involved in the decision-making process. One variation is for each group that is analyzing a question not only to report the data but also to make recommendations for improvement in the area of its question. Participants can thus analyze the data as a group rather than report and turn the data over to the leader; the group also has to take responsibility for creating ways to change the situation. In the process, the members are learning through their experience how to analyze and cope with problems in the group.

What do I do when I have a number of subgroups in a training program; there is little unity?

Often people come into a program from various departments — for example, in a hospital training program people would come from the departments of psychology, social work, medicine, nursing, maintenance, and administration. Each department may have limited relationships with the other departments and, in fact, even considerable hostility toward some of the others. Once assembled, there is a comfort in sitting with one's own department, both for acceptance and also for recognition of one's unit. However, one of the goals of the training may be to work as a staff across professions in patient treatment. Simply to rearrange the seating will do little to foster cohesiveness and cooperation because at the first opportunity people will gravitate back to their "home group." Depending on the goals of the program, there are a number of design strategies.

One strategy would be for the leader to explain at the beginning of the session that one of the objectives of the training is for members of the staff from the varying departments to know, understand, and work with each other. To achieve this goal, the leader explains that there will be a number of exercises in which people will be grouped in a wide variety of combinations. Each person will be encouraged to work in that group and to build his or her own skills in

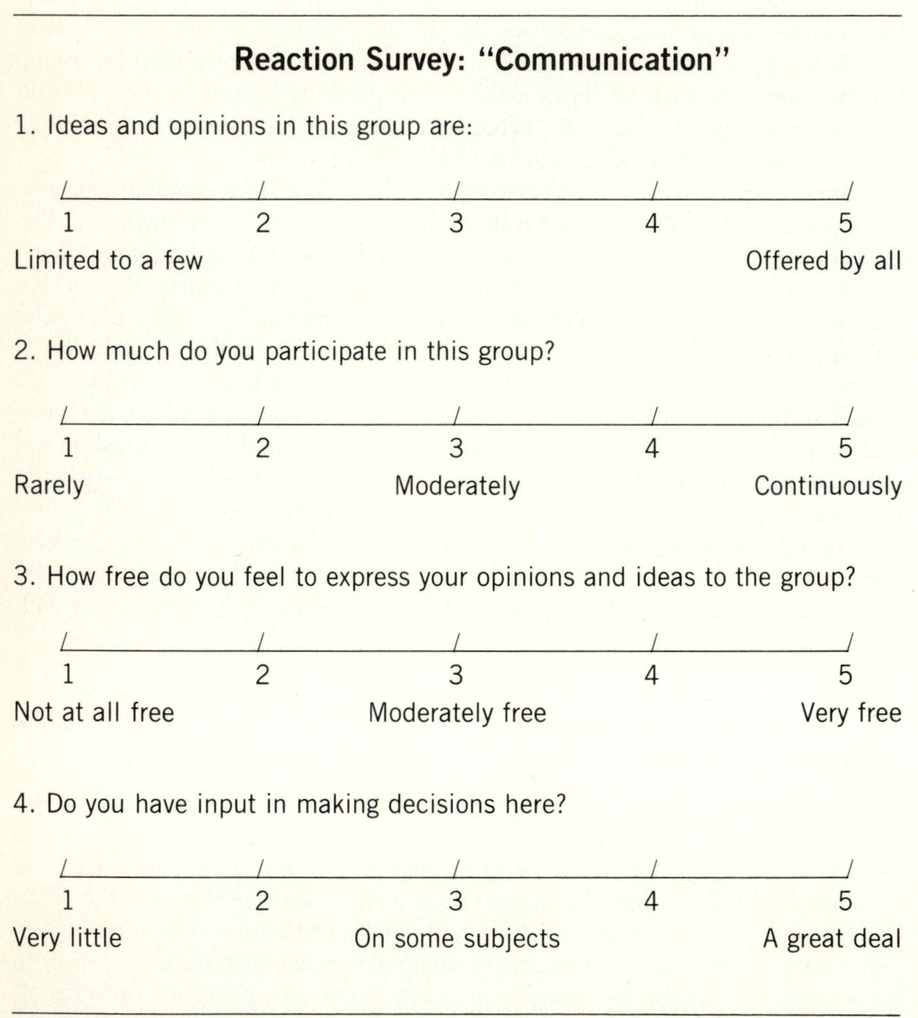

Reaction Survey: "Communication"

1. Ideas and opinions in this group are:

1	2	3	4	5
Limited to a few				Offered by all

2. How much do you participate in this group?

1	2	3	4	5
Rarely		Moderately		Continuously

3. How free do you feel to express your opinions and ideas to the group?

1	2	3	4	5
Not at all free		Moderately free		Very free

4. Do you have input in making decisions here?

1	2	3	4	5
Very little		On some subjects		A great deal

FIGURE 3.1. Example of Reaction Survey

enlarging work relationships. The leader explains all this so that participants don't think what's ahead is gimmicky, or "fun and games." No matter which of the suggested methods are used, the leader should always state the rationale of enlarging working relationships and building a staff/community working relationship.

At the outset, staff members should be asked to group with someone from another department whom they do not know. Each group should then be given a task. The idea is that people who don't know each other are immediately structured into working together. A norm of learning how to work with everyone is created. From there the dyads should be combined into larger groups of six (or eight or ten). They should work together as a group for at least half a day so that they come to know each other and are comfortable together. Having their own table and a sense of their own turf is helpful.

The next day (or at the end of that unit), members should talk about how they felt working together in this group. Each person in the group should be asked to share his or her feelings about the experience with the others in the group. This is difficult at first, but the norm is established that it feels strange and is difficult, and with time and experience we will become comfortable working with this group.

Then ask the group to become ones and twos (each group divides in half). The ones stay, and the twos move to another group as individuals occupy the seats vacated by the other twos. As they become a new group, the trainer says, "In any organization there are people staying and new people coming. Those staying know each other and have their turf; the newcomers always feel alone and wonder how they will fit in. Will you now become a group? I'll allow five minutes for you to get to know each other." Thus other groups are created, and the entire group becomes sensitive to the experiences of being an outsider in a group as a newcomer and feeling like an intruder when attending a meeting in another department.

The next day there is another grouping. The grouping can be done randomly, or by astrological signs ("Let's see if similar personalities can work well together."), by birthday months, or by number of years worked in the organization (less than six months, up to a year, up to five years, between six and ten years, over ten years, etc.). People not only accept the method of grouping as legitimate but also it becomes fun; they look forward to finding out how they will be grouped next. Each day people are asked to sit with the group they ended up with the previous night, and then there is a new grouping. There is a rush to talk to each other in the morning before they are "moved on." Along with the mock groans of "here we go again" is a sense of excitement about who will be drawn this coming time. The grouping works because it doesn't feel punitive. It doesn't feel as if medicine is being "broken up," as if blacks are being distributed throughout the group, or as if principals are being interspersed among teachers. It feels legitimate and becomes a real way of getting beyond the comfort and stereotypes of subgroups.

Another method in design can be illustrated by the example of a management/union one-day workshop in a state hospital. Both management and the union wanted to work together, even though relations had been stormy over recent years, for there was now the even larger but common problem that the state hospital might be closed and the patients moved to community homes. In addition to the trend of large state mental institutions being closed, there had been a series of damaging articles in the local newspaper citing instances of patient abuse by hospital aides. These articles chastised the administration for its irresponsibility in allowing the abuse to exist and to continue. The staff claimed the incidents were isolated and had been blown out of proportion by sensation-seeking reporters. The administration denied knowing that the abuse even existed and claimed that the staff only acted in that way when "no one was around." It was decided that the way to create a working relationship between the administration and the union was to begin with a common goal — to stop patient abuse.

In designing the workshop, the trainer kept in mind the tradition of long-time animosity and the ease with which the blame-game could erupt. After providing an overview of the day's events, the trainer asked each person to pair with someone with whom they were comfortable (without putting it into words, that meant a union person with a union person and an administrator with an administrator). The members of each pair were asked to interview each other as people—their hobbies, their family, their pleasures in vacations, their philosophies of life. Each pair was then asked to pair with another pair different from them—a union pair with a management pair. Next, each person in the groups of four was asked to introduce his or her partner (a friend introducing a friend). Then each group of four was asked to define what the term *patient abuse* meant, so that the total group could begin with common definitions.

The design worked very well. In an atmosphere in which each person felt fearful, they started by talking with a friend. As they moved into the group of four, they experienced support from knowing that the teams were even (two and two). Then, as they became involved in discussing a definition of patient abuse, they started to feel they were on common ground building common understanding. They no longer felt that there were two camps or that is was "us against them."

What do you do about too many interruptions?

Although the idea is for people to participate, sometimes the trainer worries about having created a monster—there are so many interruptions, opinions, questions, and comments that the pace is lost and the program doesn't move. Although we will be talking about ways to handle too many interruptions, we must remember never to ignore raised hands of people who want to make a comment. To not acknowledge them is to make them feel as if they are nonpersons, that they don't count. In addition to such treatment running counter to our valuing each person, we risk the possibility of causing psychological harm.

A quick method of handling an interruption is to acknowledge the questioner with a look of recognition and a gesture—a nodding of the head that you see the person or a half-raised arm to say "hold, I'll get back to you." Then do get back to the questioner when you are at a good stopping point. Another way to deal with an interruption is to answer briefly; every question does not require a long, detailed answer. Sometimes the length of the reply is what bogs down the pace.

Sometimes trainers prefer to set aside a segment of time at the end of each day or at the beginning of the next day to deal with any questions that have arisen or comments that people want to make based on their experience of that day. Such a built-in time for comments and questions often becomes a major part of the learning, as people think about and integrate their shared experiences.

One last word of advice about interruptions is to listen—what are the questions? What do they say? Are the instructions not clear? Is there a need for greater clarification? Is the concept not clear? Does material need to be presented in smaller units? Are more examples needed or perhaps a demonstration? In other words, as leader consider the "interruptions" as feedback on how to become more effective.

How do I create a diversity of activities so that the learning experience can be stimulating and exciting?

Trainers know that learning can be exciting and stimulating. They also know it can be routine and tedious. The trick is to create an exciting learning experience that is focused on helping the group achieve its goals, that is not gimmicky, that encourages extensive group participation, and from which people learn through their experience in the group. How is such an overwhelming task accomplished? Certainly not in cookbook fashion. Not in finding a book of exercises and taking one on communication, one on conflict resolution, one on team building, and one on a peak experience. Not in trying a hodgepodge of exercises because they are "different" and "interesting." Not in experimenting with activities you have never seen and only vaguely understand.

Creating a good training design comes from experience, from having seen how to create a good design, and from being a part of one. A good design is derived from noting a learning sequence and how a particular group responds—perhaps activities followed by a lecture/generalization, a lecture/presentation followed by group examples, a theory session with examples, or a building of a group experience through preliminary extensive data collection. The number of possibilities are almost infinite. With experience you learn the best way to approach a training design with a particular population.

Creating a good design depends a great deal on listening to the group with whom you will be working, whether it is a planning committee, a segment of the participants, or those hiring you. To the extent you can get input from them, you can create a design that will be stimulating to the participants. You might even try out part of the design on the planning committee or discuss sections on which you need their opinions. You might suggest alternatives and ask for their recommendations.

Reading about concepts, theories, and training designs by other experts will also contribute to creating a good design. From your reading, try to formulate how you would translate a certain theory into a training design for a population with whom you work. What are some of the materials others have used to help participants understand their theories? How can you use them, or how can you develop a similar way to express what you want to teach? As you read, latch on to what sounds like a good idea and think about how you would adapt it to a group with whom you might be working. Mull it over, play with it; you may never use it, but it gets you thinking creatively.

Being part of a multiple staff where you can discuss options and alternatives for having the group learn in a particular area or where you can design given objectives for each block of time will contribute to a good design. So will taking a course on being a trainer or on how to design. Learning the theories of design, practicing and creating designs, and conducting those designs as part of a class experience are all essential methods of building confidence and competence.

If there is one thing you will learn from this book, it is how to think in terms of design and how to use yourself as part of the training design. Not only must you learn how to "think design" but also how to create a learning experience given your clients, the time you have, and your own areas of comfort and style. Successful programs are created through that mix of the trainer, the design, the needs of the client, and the time allotted. The interplay among these factors contributes both the challenge and excitement of creating a successful program.

The first challenge is not knowing how long an activity will take. For example, in the program participants will be given a staff problem to explore. Members of each group will create a role play of their experience with that problem. After all the role plays are enacted, there will be a discussion of how the problem arises and how it escalates. How long will this design take? Some time aspects can be figured. For example, the statement of the problem and the length of time allotted to do the role play can be estimated. If there are six groups, estimates can be made of the time it will take each group to act out its play, debrief, and hold a discussion. However, what if they may need more time than allotted, to plan their role play, and the discussion might really involve participants in thinking about how these problems occur and end up lasting three times the allotted time?

Because there is no way of knowing for sure how long an activity will take, short of having conducted the design with a large number of similar groups so that from experience you can more accurately determine a time plan, the trainer must plan on which pieces of the design will be omitted if there isn't time for it all. Part of the design from the beginning is to allow for some activities to be expanded, some to be contracted, and some even to be omitted. Time must be used to achieve the most important goals first; thus, some of the goals may have to be put on the back burner for action at another time.

Another common problem with program design is planning too much for the time allotted. It is a common failing; we forget to allow time to process what is happening or we forget that something may happen that makes us want to stop and analyze. Sometimes we think an activity that will take a few minutes takes almost an hour. Sometimes a concept we thought could be learned quickly has more ramifications than we thought—we need to back up and take each aspect individually and slowly.

Time problems happen less with experience, less when planning with a clock, and less if an activity has been practiced with the staff of the planning committee on a "trial run." However, none of these methods is foolproof, and one of the most important parts of training is learning that there must always be revision given the constraints of time. Obviously, when time runs out, the last unit cannot be lopped off, for usually that last session is the integration of the concepts of the training week. It involves transferability of the learning—how what was learned will be used back home—and often the creation of an action plan for the next steps.

The last segment is essential for completion and closure of the training program. Thus, during the program there must be regular appraisal as to how the program is going given the time schedule for the training design. There can be reappraisals with a planning committee at the end of each day or even at lunch time, with revisions based on discussion of progress to date. There may be informal reappraisals by the trainer, who, from just talking to a few participants and understanding from their responses how things are going, might decide to modify the design. Having to modify a design based on time limitations is a factor in every design.

The most serious problem with regard to time revolves around the trainer's ability to find enough time to carry out the established goals. A trainer who is called in by a client or who initiates a program promises certain goals. That is, the trainer states what is to be accomplished by the end of the program and how the program will benefit the organization and make the participants more effective. The focus is not on how much time will be needed to accomplish these goals; indeed, the time constraints are often not obvious. For example, the organization absorbs not only the cost of paying for the facilitator but also the even higher costs of the combined pay of all the participants attending the training and not doing their jobs during that time. All those people cannot be gone from their work for more than the minimal number of days, and even then only certain people can go while the others attend the patients, service the clients, or keep the plant running. Therefore, the organization wants the goals accomplished in the minimum time and the trainer needs the maximum time. However, in order to get the contract or even be considered to conduct the training, the trainer often reduces the time needed. The result, of course, is that the trainer promises too much in too short a time and ends up not having enough time to accomplish the promised goals. In many cases there may be no follow-up or money available for continuing the training. The end result is frustration and failure, all around.

Some suggestions for avoiding this kind of a bind are to set very limited goals for short-term training. Communication skills, stress management, and skills on conducting a meeting can all be designed to fit a given time allotment. Set limited objectives in a limited time frame.

A diagnosis should precede more extensive training. Through the use of a questionnaire, interviews, or a random sample of the organization, compile information on the organization's problems. Feed this information back to the organization with recommendations for first steps. Build a contract or training program for action on these first recommendations and include a realistic estimate of how much time implementation of each recommendation will take. Suggest alternative ways of approaching these first recommendations, outlining advantages and disadvantages of each approach. Make clear the limited outcomes from one approach, but then contrast that approach with another approach whose outcomes may take more time, even years. Indicate that you plan a reevaluation at the end of each segment of the training for the purpose of possibly revising or renegotiating, and definitely of informing the organization about progress. Certainly this approach is not easy in the present climate of tight money in which training is often viewed as a luxury. However, as an approach it does recognize that progress is not accomplished by fiat: we have two days and the goals can be accomplished in two days. All kinds of resistances, obstacles, changes, and new problems occur when working with people, and get in the way of solving an organization's problems.

Another approach we often mention is to plan the training in consultation with a planning committee from the organization. In that way they too will know about the unforeseen obstacles. They can then be involved with the trainer in modifying the goals or setting lower ones. Because they are initially involved in the process, members of a planning committee can help a trainer be more realistic in what can be accomplished. They will intervene on behalf of the trainer when some of the promised accomplishments do not occur. An added benefit is that the planning committee will often push for additional training in cases in which the program has been successful but too short; having played a part in helping the program and the trainer achieve credibility, they will now be advocates for more training.

A training program is never enough—there is always a need for more and a next step. We strongly recommend a follow-up to any training; such a follow-up might even be longer than the training. It is a way of ensuring transferability from the program to the job, especially in regard to experiences that may still be unresolved from the training. The follow-up also is important in obtaining feedback on the use of the training. Out of it will emerge suggestions for future training or revisions of the present program so that the program will more accurately produce the outcomes desired.

What do you do about someone who is always "one-upping" the trainer?

What do you do about someone who constantly gets in the last word over the trainer's—with an "add-on," a correction, a modification, a special circumstance, or whatever? By all means respond, but do remember your special position as the group leader. Consider which of the following alternatives would be the most helpful in your situation.

1. Present your credentials in advance so that members have a chance to look at them. Sometimes the "one-upper" is questioning your legitimacy or competence. Their "one-upping" is an attempt to prove they know more than you. Sometimes seeing your credentials will put a stop to their testing. This is especially true when trainers look youthful, female, or both.
2. If the comment is helpful, reply, "That's a good point." It may be a bid for recognition of their expertise; acknowledge it and recruit an ally.
3. If the comments constantly belabor the opposite view, the trainer might say, "I wonder if we could discuss this further at the coffee break rather than here." Or, "You're right, there are many approaches, but for now I would like to concentrate on this one."
4. Handle "one-uppers" with humor: "Enough already. You may not believe it, but I can bumble through without help. Let me try." Tone and manner are everything—comments should be made gently and with mock expression.
5. Express how you feel: "I feel as if I'm being constantly tested, and I'm not very comfortable under these conditions."

There are any number of appropriate replies using facts, humor, or a diversion. The important thing is to remember to reply humanly, with initial patience. Replies are of little help in establishing a collaborative atmosphere if they are sarcastic or if they embarrass a participant.

How can I do a more effective job of processing at the end of a workshop?

Processing at the end of the workshop should not be just the trainer's responsibility; rather, the group should be involved with the trainer. Although the trainer may have initiated analysis of what is happening in the group, the members should play a role as well. They should be familiar with the concept of analyzing their group behavior. Having the group reflect on its experiences is infinitely more valuable than having the trainer do it, no matter how brilliant, how talented, or how erudite he or she is. The participants are the ones who need to process what they have accomplished and what have been their limitations. Out of their tension systems and feelings of accomplishment or understanding will come action.

The following are some suggested methods of processing at the end of a workshop:

1. Have a "go-round" at the end. Each participant expresses what was learned in the course of the program. The session can even be in

two or three parts based on responding to questions such as these: How did this workshop turn out differently from what I had expected? What is one thing I learned that I will remember? What is one thing I expect to do as a result of being here?

2. Form support groups that are made up of people who will stay in contact with one another after the program. Have them discuss what they learned from the workshop and their next steps after the program. Have one person from each support group report out for the rest of the members.
3. Distribute a feedback evaluation measure, which is a survey. Have small groups analyze the responses and report out the data to the whole group. The whole group then discusses or comments on the findings. There are questions such as the following: "How would you rate this program?"

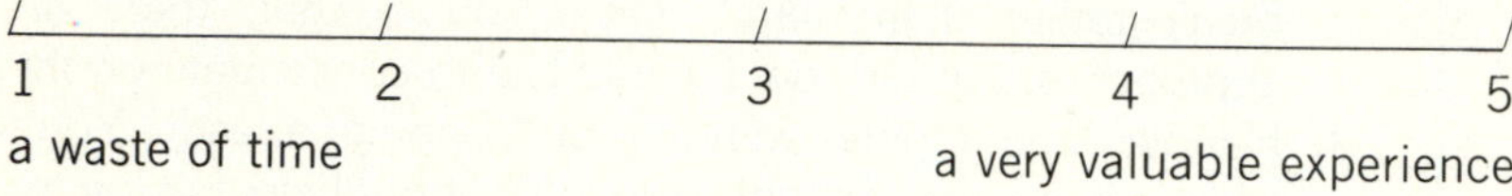

What three things did you like best?
What three things did you like least?
What would have improved the program for you; what is one recommendation?
What do you think needs to happen next as a result of this program?

There is another approach to processing. About halfway through the program ask a cross-section of the participants (six to nine) to interview a given number (let's say five) of the other participants. Have them take notes and based on these notes analyze the workshop. On the last day, the "interviewers" become a panel that processes the program. This method works best when the panel is representative of all segments of the program—younger, older; liberal, conservative; experienced, newcomer; worker, administrator—whatever the diversity in the group. Following the panelists' presentation, there can be a question and answer period, a discussion as a total group, comments by the trainer, or some combination of these ideas.

A variation of the interview technique is to randomly group participants into groups of four; the members in each group interview each other on their feelings and on what they have learned at the end of the program. Each small group discusses its agreements and then reports out to the total group.

Processing can be accomplished with less formal methods. One way is to ask groups of members to create a song about their experiences. They sing it the first time, and then with the words on the board or on newsprint, everyone joins in. The trainer may write a chorus and each group a verse. The whole group can sing the chorus, and each small group can sing its own verse. Then back to the chorus.

The idea of a song may sound overwhelming or silly. Yet actually participants respond after some initial hesitancy to creating in a different mode. They will select a familiar tune, like "I've Been Working on the Railroad" or even "Yankee Doodle," and create a chorus representing some key ideas. Then they may each do a verse. The verses may involve the simplest rhymes, but they represent ideas in a different way. Certainly, much can be said in a song that would be more difficult with words.

This kind of activity not only works well with creating a song or a stanza but also with creating a poem. Or a group slogan can be created, reflecting what has happened during the training. Each group can write its slogan and set it on the group's table, march around with it, or use it as the basis for a "campaign speech," analyzing the program as if it were a presidential candidate's platform. These suggestions generate creativity and a wonderful sense of having fun at the end. Most important, they are yet another way of working together and trying new behaviors.

The "Heavy" Questions

Some questions are "heavies"; they are difficult questions with which all trainers are confronted. The answers are neither simple nor straightforward.

What do I do so that the group is not so dependent on me, looking to me for the answer to almost everything?

The one area that frustrates trainers at both an emotional and a rational level concerns the right mix between "taking over" and being "out of it." On the one hand is the approach of guiding, telling, and being the expert who has answers but then having the group become subservient, dependent, and unable to learn from their experiences. On the other hand is the laissez-faire approach of saying what happens will happen—participants are responsible for getting themselves in and out of difficulties. This approach doesn't sound like a professional kind of leadership; leaders haven't leaned toward laissez-faire since the early days of T-groups. But how strong should leaders be? When should they give answers and when should they not? These are the difficult questions. For one thing, getting co-opted is easy. Having all those people asking your opinion is flattering. When you are having all kinds of difficulties in your own life, having participants listening to you, hanging on to your every word, and turning to you for advice is a terrific psychological boost. Sometimes you even start to believe you are all-powerful and know all the answers.

Then there is a terrible realization, the hour of reckoning. They won't do anything without checking with you; in a "discussion" they all look toward you; when there are administrative details to be taken care of, they assume it's your job; when a problem occurs or a conflict arises in the program, they do not handle it as a mature, problem-solving group, but as dependent children—maybe listening to mommy or daddy now, but not for long.

When the trainer realizes the group is too dependent, the time has come to take a serious look. Some time needs to be set aside to analyze how it happened. What did you do to set it up? You might review what happened in the workshop, focusing on what you did and could have done differently so that dependence did not continue to this point. You might review the problem with a colleague, with the idea that both of you might better determine how it occurred and some methods to prevent its continuance. In the long run you have to figure out how you allowed dependence to develop and, more important, how you will stop it.

In the meantime, the dependency must be dealt with if the program is to be salvaged and meet its objectives. Remember, you are an expert in process—you know a variety of ways to design and structure outcomes other than supplying the answers. The following strategies are all designed to turn dependency into independency.

When participants ask you a question, rather than giving the answer, name some alternatives of how an answer might be obtained. In the process the participants learn to analyze and examine and eventually to find their own answers. You are providing an interim method in which they don't feel you are abandoning them, but at the same time you are not giving them "the" answer.

Once a question has been asked, divide the participants into groups. Ask each group, "What do you see as the next step in solving this problem?" Each group discusses the problem and then reports out what it views as the next step. Then there is a group discussion of what has been suggested. The discussion continues until there is agreement on what the next step will be. The objective, of course, is for participants to feel competent in the process of decision making and to see that they can indeed find ways to cope with the question. The discussion has broadened, and each person has become involved in thinking about what could be done rather than passively waiting for the trainer's answer.

Another way to recover from a situation of dependency is to divide participants into groups and ask each group to do a role play of the present problem, ending with being stuck. The idea is for the entire group to understand *how* they get blocked. Once each role play is analyzed to see how the problem occurs in each situation, the entire group can then proceed with finding answers. Or, with an even number of groups, half the groups can be consultants to the other half, helping them analyze the situation and how it might be altered. This approach encourages creativity, analysis of a problem, seeing it in new ways, and taking on the role of the "consultant"—in other words, building skills in trainer behavior. One outcome may be that the "consultants" have an opportunity to help their clients and to take on behavior somehow regarded as only appropriate to the trainer.

Yet another way of dealing with dependency is to set the dependency up as a problem to be solved by the group. The trainer might observe that too often the participants expect answers to be handed to them. Then the trainer might go on to explain that their mutual goals are to build skills in problem solving, resolving conflicts, and becoming an interdependent group. At that point the trainer can begin a force field analysis (what are the driving forces that increase the group's dependence on me? What are the restraining forces that limit greater independence?). The members take these questions on as a group problem for analysis and proceed with solutions for overcoming the restraining forces. Force field analysis can be a way to understand how a problem emerges and how it can be solved; it is a good method for problem solving that is applicable to many situations.

The trainer can begin working with a planning committee, consisting perhaps of one person from each small group or from each department. As they evaluate and plan, committee members are assigned specific aspects of the program—reporting the previous day's feedback, the overview of the day, or even conducting parts of the program. This is done so that participants will see others in addition to the trainer taking on administrative and leadership roles; with that visibility, questions will be asked of others and not just the trainer.

Preventing dependence is a pervasive trainer problem that needs to be confronted in designing a program. The trainer must make sure that methods of group decision making and group development of answers are built into the program. There must be less "expert" lecturing. There must be an ongoing process analysis, paying special attention to the group's involvement in decision making, conflict resolution, and problem solving. The trainer needs to confront dependence whenever it arises, and if the trainer's own needs had anything to do with creating that dependence, he or she must find other ways of meeting personal ego needs. This concern with dependence leads into other ubiquitous concern—the question of trainer responsibility.

Is the trainer responsible for everything that happens in a group?

Of course, the trainer is not responsible for every sentence spoken, for who is angry and who is sad, for who is combative and who is passive. People bring into a training program a variety of problems, concerns, and attitudes. The trainer, however, is responsible for designing a program that will not intrude on people's personal lives or force them to divulge more than they want to. The trainer's responsibility is to make certain that individuals are not scapegoated, harassed, or badgered as part of a so-called "learning experience." The trainer must also create a design that helps the group achieve the agreed-upon goals or outcomes. The trainer cannot promise one program and then switch to another that goes in a different direction. For self-protection and because circumstances can be very different from those anticipated, the trainer should work with a planning committee that will convene when special problems arise.

Some people in a program may have severe personal problems. When possible, participants should be interviewed before the program begins. Those viewed as having difficulties might be referred to a different kind of experience. When interviewing is inappropriate, as when a work group comes as a team, the trainer is still responsible for what happens during the training experience. If one person's behavior seems irrational or markedly inappropriate, the trainer cannot ignore the situation. The action the trainer takes will vary, but under no circumstances will the trainer cause harm to that person.

The trainer is responsible for encouraging and modeling positive norms for the program—norms in which people are encouraged to analyze their behavior and that of the group, to try new behaviors that will give them increased self-confidence and competence, and to work supportively with others. The trainer is also responsible for designing a program that helps the group or organization achieve its objectives. One of the major safeguards that a program will be appropriate and not harmful is for a trainer to discuss the objectives with the organization and with a planning committee. The trainer is a professional who knows group methodology and has group skills and who has earned legitimacy for what he or she does. What can never be avoided is the special responsibility for the outcomes that a trainer must demonstrate on behalf of individuals and the organization.

The "Nitty-Gritty" Questions

There are the "heavy" questions, and then there are the "nitty-gritties"—those little questions that are an embarrassment; trainers are often ashamed that they need to ask these questions and even more ashamed that they feel them. They can be gathered under the heading, Questions I want answers to, but am afraid to ask. We'll deal with these briefly and realistically. Although suppressed, we have all at times asked each of these questions.

What do you do when you're nervous about getting started?

It's a little like giving a speech—you go over your notes, worry about whether you will remember all the points you have to make, and wonder if it will come out all right. Often the anticipation is the worst part. Once you start, the nervousness usually goes, and the words start to flow. The anticipation—the awareness of all your inadequacies, of all the things that could go wrong—is what scares you, even though you are set with the design and know how you are planning to begin.

The best way to relieve pre-program tension, and also the nervousness of the participants, is to come early and check that everything is set up the way you want. You will feel as if you are in control of something. Have coffee set up at the workshop; it gives you and the others a way to cope with opening anxiety. Chat and make small talk with whoever is there. You will both feel as if you have a friend, even of the most momentary and casual kind, but it helps. Ask some of the members of the planning committee to arrive early and meet before the program starts, if only for a couple of minutes so that you don't feel as alone. Review your notes on the opening part of the design and remind yourself of the reasons why you are beginning in this manner. Reassure yourself that it is a good design. Take some deep breaths. You're on.

How do you make sure everyone feels all right? How do you remove their anxiety at the beginning?

Participants are always anxious before the beginning of a new program. What is the leader like? How will they fit in? Will they be comfortable doing what they have to do? What is expected of them? Will there be protection against group pressure?

According to the Schacter (1959) research, under conditions of anxiety people are more comfortable with others than being alone. Some ways to dispel feelings of being alone are to have coffee, which creates a reason for interacting, have name tags so there is a legitimacy for engaging in conversation, have people enter and sit in groupings or at tables and have someone greet people as they arrive.

In the opening part of the design give participants information on the time structure and an overview of the program. They will be less anxious when they have some sense of order. Tell them something about yourself. If possible, do it informally. Any humor you can muster helps—not a corny joke but any comment that seems appropriate. A touch of humor will help set the norms you want.

In our training designs, we have found that in many instances beginning by pairing two people who have not previously known one another is helpful. They interact around a question appropriate to the design and immediately make a connection. They soon feel they are not alone and they stop worrying about how will they fit in or who will relate to them. The hurdle is over; a connection is made.

What if you're scared and feel you won't be able to control the group?

Don't become overwhelmed and start to go through every possible horror, imagining, "If that happened, what would I do?" Remember, you have legitimacy, you have a design, you know what your objectives are, and you know how you plan to achieve them. Hopefully, you also have a planning committee that will be there to help you if "catastrophe strikes."

Keep in mind there are any number of ways you can influence the group. You can comment of what you are seeing, and ask the group to figure out what is happening and why. You can stop the ongoing discussion and announce that you don't understand what is happening and would like to ask what others see. At various times you can set up process observers who will observe what is happening for a given segment of time and then report out what they observed. In this situation you don't have to control the group; the process observers through their report indicate what they saw. There can then be a general discussion. Sometimes just the reporting out influences participants' behavior—once they are cognizant of what was happening, they resolve not to do that again.

The groups can also be influenced by changing the design. If certain activities produce too many overgeneralized statements rather than a real focus on the problem, the design can be changed so that participants do start to focus. Remember, imagined catastrophes are for the most part very unlikely. You can control the group through a process intervention in which participants control their direction; you can redesign; you have the resources of the group to change direction.

What if something really does go badly and you fall apart or start to cry?

Once in a while during a program a trainer does become overwhelmed, can't think, feels terrible, and wishes he or she could somehow be "swallowed up." It is a very frightening experience. If there is a co-trainer or a member of the planning committee, simply say you need to be excused for a few minutes, and ask the person to take over. If there isn't someone, try to steady your voice and tell the group you need to leave for a few minutes.

Once you leave, go where no one can see you. Look at your watch; you have a maximum of ten minutes to feel competent again. A couple of minutes can be spent crying or calling yourself names for losing control or being disappointed in yourself. After that, remember that participants are depending on you and that you are a professional. Talk to yourself; list all the competent things you have ever done and decide you are returning—competent and effective. Return. You might begin by saying, "I'm OK now" (because they were wondering) and continue. Apologize if what you did previously was not what you intended. If someone attacked you, consider how you will move with that problem. If the incident is over, proceed with the design.

Of course, you will think about such an incident that night and for days to come. Do think about it, once more processing what happened and how it affected you. Also, you might want to ask a colleague or perhaps some of the group members about how they saw the critical incident. We don't always see ourselves as accurately as we would like; often it takes two to see one.

What if you pace or sway at a podium or have other nervous habits before a group?

The key question is how much? A slow pacing or occasional foot tapping or swaying at a podium will hardly be noticeable. If these habits are continuous and rapid, however, the eye movements of the participants follow the trainer's movements and an increased tension develops in the members. Asking people not to notice or to forgive you only brings the behavior to their consciousness more.

One way to break these habits is to create alternative habits. That is, if you pace, sit at a table; if you rock at a podium, don't use one. Another method is to develop a signal. Ask a member of the planning committee or a class member during a "practice" session to help you by giving you a signal, such as holding up a pencil, when you start your intrusive behavior. When you see the signal, you will stop. Finally, practice in front of a mirror. Act as if you were conducting the group or giving the instructions. Monitor yourself so that when you see the offensive behavior you stop it.

What if the participants ask how you are qualified?

We recognize that part of a trainer's legitimacy is the trainer's credentials—education or experience or both. Having qualifying credentials means that participants are likely to give you time, maybe even a whole day, when they will go along with whatever you say. This is incredibly important, for it allows you to create norms, to have participants follow your direction in role plays or a simulation with which they may be uncomfortable, and even to let participants feel comfortable processing events.

Obviously, as in a job interview, present yourself to participants at your best. If you have education but no experience, stress the education. If you have experience but no formal training, dwell on the experience. If you are doing the project as part of a doctoral class, introduce yourself as member of your professor's staff. When possible, have someone else introduce you; there will be an understanding that the person can't name everything, just the high spots. Finally, in responding to questions about your credentials, don't apologize or admit to what you don't have; emphasize the qualifications you do have.

How do you get people to participate in role plays, divide into groups, or do any of the things that you ask of them but which they consider strange or uncomfortable?

As noted earlier, effective leaders are high in meaning attribution. Before you ask people to do anything, tell them why. You need not give a laborious speech. Keep it direct and simple, such as the following: "In this program we will want you to expand your ability to work with all kinds of people, and thus we will be grouping in a variety of ways so that you can have that experience. We'll start by grouping randomly. Please count off one to five." Point to someone. "Will you begin." Like that. Simply explain what you are doing, and then begin.

In role plays, ask for volunteers. Some people are quite shy about acting in front of an "audience." In setting up a role play, explain that the characters are assigned (volunteers draw a piece of paper with their assigned role) and that people are not acting out their own personalities. After the role play be sure to debrief by asking participants how they felt in their roles. Be sure that the connection is made that people were acting out roles and that their personalities were not what came through.

The key is to create an understanding of why you are asking participants to do an activity. Expect people to respond to your requests, and if they don't, repeat the instructions or ask if there are any problems in carrying out the instructions. Our experience is that if you expect people to do it and are supportive, they will do it. If someone refuses, allow that person to observe.

What if you don't know "the answer"?

What if you know something is wrong, but you don't know what? What if you are not sure of the nature of the problem, but you can sense that there is one? What do you do and how do you do it without losing face? You don't have to know the answer. Knowing that something needs to be looked at is the essential clue. Instead of looking for a solution, begin by noting the observational data that raised questions for you. Then consider some of the following choices:

1. Create a hypothesis. What could that behavior mean? Watch and see what happens. You may be picking up first clues, the meaning of which may become evident later.
2. Report your observations to the group. Tell members you just noticed a discrepancy between what was said and what is happening. Ask them what it could mean.
3. At some time, perhaps at the end of the day when people are commenting on their experiences of the day, mention what you observed, and note that you wondered what that was all about.

Keep remembering that you value analyzing behavior and examining what it means. You do not have to have the answers; indeed, you encourage others to be involved with you in finding the answers. Others may have information about a person or about the organization that you do not have. Behavior or a situation that you question, may make sense to them. Inviting them to share in the analysis will encourage a collaborative, problem-solving process.

What if you are bored?

Assume if you are bored, so are they. Now figure out what to do. Change the pace. Have a break. Suggest a couple of minutes of relaxation exercises. Change the design and shift to another activity. Change the groupings of participants.

In a one-day workshop we once ran, participants looked apathetic and tired. We knew they had worked very hard, that the pace was unrelenting, and that too much was being crammed into a one-day workshop. However, the material had to be covered in that one day. At lunch we had talked to a participant who had once been a professional juggler and who had developed a routine on modes of therapy as patter for his juggling act. We bought four oranges and asked him if he would consider "entertaining." He was surprised, but he agreed. When the tired look came in the middle of the afternoon, we announced we had a diversion. The former juggler did his routine for ten minutes and captivated everyone. He got a standing, prolonged ovation; it had been a wonderful surprise and fun. The afternoon went on with a whole different energy level and a renewed interest.

What if you need ego reinforcement from the group?

Not all trainers are altruistic, objective, and neutral. All trainers, however, are human. We all need to feel that we are doing a good job (even better than good), that we are liked, and that we are thought of as intelligent, competent, and talented. We all need a pat on the back. Pick up clues—you will see people listen attentively while you talk; you will hear people laugh at your jokes; you will have people ask you questions and then wait for your answer; and you will hear people rate the program highly and you highly. These compliments are to be savored—they are the real rewards for having accomplished your objectives well and for having the participants become at some level friends or colleagues.

Needing praise isn't wrong; indeed, praise is part of what motivates us to work so hard. Of course, when the need for praise turns into a primary need for ego reinforcement, your needs have gotten in the way of the training objectives.

A Concluding Note

We have dealt with a number of questions that trainers ask. Another question not often asked but so often implied is, Will I be a successful trainer? How do I know if I will be good at it?

Instead of repeating what we have already said about being flexible, being aware of yourself and your own needs, and being well-trained, we would use a more intriguing way to measure how you would do. We have designed a questionnaire, and with tongue-in-cheek have given it an erudite title (Figure 3.2). There are no standardized norms; it has been used with ten colleagues to check its validity; they enjoyed doing it.

Answer each statement *yes* (usually true of me) or *no* (usually not true of me).

1. Assuming I have formal training in groups and good technical knowledge, I can create the best program working alone.

   Yes _____ **No** _____

2. I use the same basic format in all my training work.

   Yes _____ **No** _____

3. I have developed my training style, and it is consistent.

   Yes _____ **No** _____

4. Once I develop a training plan, I adhere to it; revisions tend to suggest yielding to group pressures and not completing the program.

   Yes _____ **No** _____

5. I, as a leader, am not responsible for member outcomes; members are responsible for themselves.

   Yes _____ **No** _____

6. Assuming leaders are professional and objective, there is no room for the imposition of a personal value system in conducting training.

   Yes _____ **No** _____

7. Effectiveness of a program is directly related to the leader's technical and methodological knowledge; the greater the knowledge, the more effective the program.

   Yes _____ **No** _____

8. Group leaders skilled in the art of diagnosis should tell clients or an organization what they need.

   Yes _____ **No** _____

9. A group leader should be charismatic and attractive, for as much depends on his or her appearance as on knowledge or skill.

   Yes _____ **No** _____

10. Feedback is important for members but unnecessary for the group leader because he or she is not a member of the group.

    Yes _____ **No** _____

11. As a leader, my own needs never intrude on any group with whom I am working.

    Yes _____ **No** _____

12. I immediately stop any criticism of me or my work; it reduces confidence in the leader and encourages negative elements.

    Yes _____ **No** _____

13. If you do your job to the best of your ability, evaluations will tend to be unnecessary since it will be obvious from the behavior of the group how successful you have been.

    Yes _____ **No** _____

14. Confrontation is an essential element of the trainer's behavior; it is the primary way for participants to learn.

    Yes _____ **No** _____

15. Once you know the basics and have experience, you don't have to be concerned—you will be successful with any population.

    Yes _____ **No** _____

FIGURE 3.2. Group Facilitator's Mental Health Quotient for Running Groups

If you answered yes to more than two or three of these statements, seriously consider another profession; being a group leader is not for you.

Each of the statements is dealt with in Chapter 2. You might review that chapter, especially in regard to your "yes" answers. Of course, there are extenuating circumstances and occasions where "yes" would be the right answer. Our point is that by and large a "yes" response fails to consider those factors we consider essential to being an effective group leader.

If there is one conclusion, it is this: as trainers there is a need for asking questions and searching for answers. The most essential aspect of continuing effectiveness is looking at ourselves and being sensitive to our style, progress, and fallibility. As we become more experienced, we do get better. But then our very strengths may become too strong—our very presence may become a factor in people responding to us knowing our reputations. So there are renewed questions. Even success will throw up new barriers. Successful trainers need to analyze their behavior given these circumstances and adapt. Being a trainer involves a continuous questioning, continuous analysis, continuous revision, and continuous learning. It is an ongoing challenge.

Reference

Schachter, Stanley. 1959. *The Psychology of Affiliation.* Stanford, Calif.: Stanford University Press.

4
The Fundamentals of Design

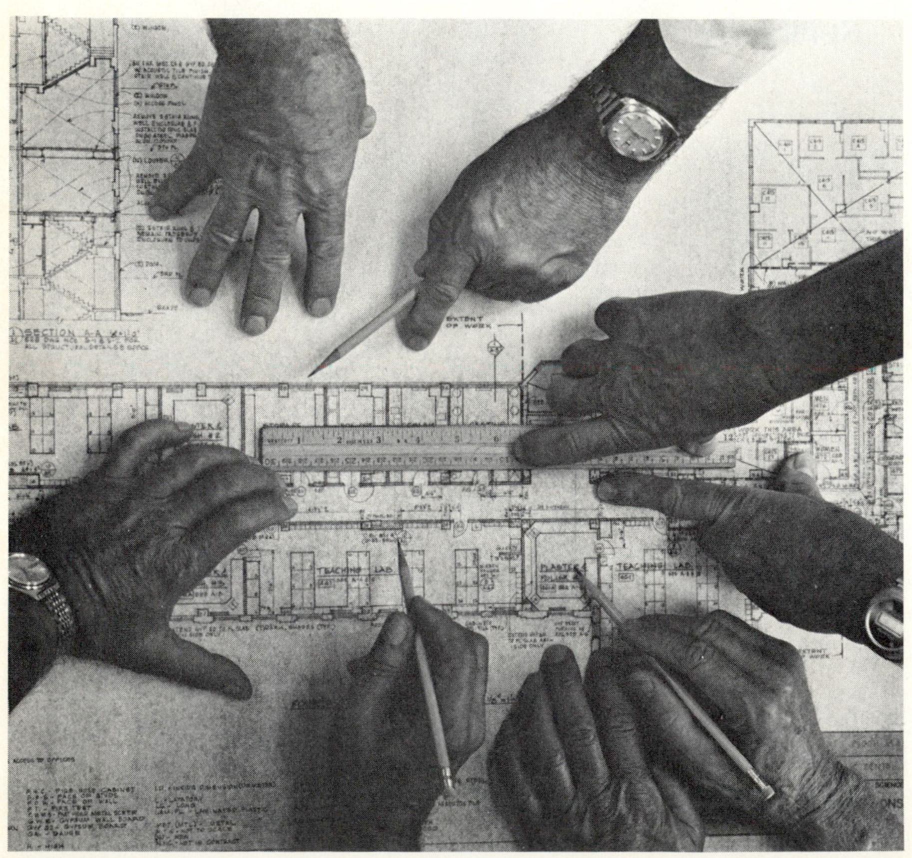

The very nature of our profession demands that a group facilitator or trainer be slightly "schizophrenic." We know, for example, that the key to successful execution of a program, workshop, or meeting rests in the degree to which we have effectively prepared ourselves and have anticipated the consequences of each step in our plan. But, at the same time, we must be "totally" flexible and spontaneous in our approach to the group or organization with which we are working. We must always be in touch with the "pulse" of the group and know when our plan no longer fits the changing needs or the climate in which we are operating. The ability to move fluently from the planning stage to spontaneous action requires a very special breed of person—one who can drop a well-prepared plan and create a new set of strategies more reflective of a group's needs and capabilities.

This chapter explores the fundamentals of "design," which for us lies at the very heart of what might be called group management. We are talking here of much more than what is traditionally referred to as "planning," which in our view is the laying out of a series of sequential steps for achieving a particular goal or set of objectives. Design, on the other hand, is the creative, artistic, or inventive part of a plan that emerges from a series of steps into a series of experiences that reflect originality, imagination, and purpose.

The Concept of Design

In translating the concept of "design" into something more meaningful for our students, we often liken it to art—at which point our students usually laugh. The fact is that most teaching and most training are not artful at all. A rather simple definition of art is "the creating of beautiful things." And designing can be just that: a blending of personalities, goals, expectations, and past experiences with realities of the environment, time restrictions, and the available resources to create an event of meaning and perhaps beauty that can stand alone. Would it not be a work of art to take a group of twenty people—cautious and perhaps apprehensive strangers—through a series of carefully designed activities and create a comfortable group that is having fun and finds itself willing to risk openness and trust amongst each other? Or is it not a work of art to take two hostile and suspicious groups of people who have developed an adversarial relationship over time and in a period of six hours through a series of carefully designed events, produce a "product" of the two groups working collaboratively, exploring and resolving their differences in a constructive and positive manner? In some ways the trainer or facilitator is the consumate artist whose canvas changes continuously as the group changes and develops. With no time to dwell on the past, the trainer must be constantly aware of changes and movement. It's like attempting to paint a landscape on a moving train: The individual must continually adapt to new stimuli and realities and draw on total resources to capture the essence of any given movement. Obviously, those with less skill will design with less creativity, with less flair, and be less responsive to what is ahead.

Avoiding the Grab-Bag Mentality

Continuing our analogy to art, the effective design involves much more than "painting by numbers." It is much more than simply reshuffling a number of pat events, games, simulations, or activities in the guise of meeting the needs of a particular group. In fact, many trainers could easily be labeled "bag people." A bag person is someone who always has at hand a group of activities or events that somehow seem to "work" on virtually any group meeting for virtually any reason. When in doubt, the bag person simply pulls from this bag of events or activities one of the tried and true designs and applies it to the group. While the event or activity is often interesting, fun, or challenging, it may have little value for the stated goals of the program. Typically, bag people do not last in the field of training because lack of creativity, dependency on their own "bag," and the resultant routine and boredom accomplish only disinterest and inefficacy.

We have carried and relied too heavily on the manuals—the training bibles, the sure things. The problem is that few situations are in fact replicable, and it is a rare design that has the staying power to be used from one situation to another. We realize that we attempt to go to "our bag" or to rely on the designs of others when we are fearful, confused, or unsure. We reach for something that "worked" previously for others or for ourselves, something that will pull us through the tough spot in the group, even though it might not be exactly what the doctor ordered. Thus, as bag people, we squeeze an event or activity into the situation because it generates interest or because the "sure fire" experience relieves our own anxieties and uncertainty and psychologically takes us off the spot of having to create and design for the needs of the group. As we mature as trainers, we find that although we will always carry the "bag," there are fewer and fewer times when we need to reach inside. We begin to see designs as unique to each situation, literally to each moment, and that the "old reliable" designs tend to have less and less appeal as we become more demanding of ourselves and the outcomes we desire for the group.

Planning for Contingencies

Most of us during our lives have at one time or another read a book or seen a film that has patiently, step by unnerving step, taken us through the excruciating tension of an escape or robbery. If we take a second look at, for example, the carefully executed bank robbery, we may gain an even clearer understanding of what must be incorporated into an effective design. The simple fact is that literally a thousand contingencies, a thousand variables or factors, must be anticipated to preclude failure. Additionally, a series of unanticipated occurrences that must instantly be dealt with cannot be predicted prior to the event itself. Since each bank is different in its physical layout, posting of guards, types of alarms, models of vaults, and possible exit and entrance routes, generalizing from one situation to the next is incredibly difficult.

For the robber, "design" means establishing creative methods for overcoming obstacles to the objective—taking the money and getting away cleanly. "Plan A" is fine if things go according to schedule, but "Plan B" is necessary in case of certain difficulties. Also required are a variety of more specific contingencies, depending on the kinds of factors that might disrupt the plan. Again, everything must be considered, no matter how inconsequential. Everything is geared to reducing risk, surprise, and error and focuses on creating a predictable and easily rehearsed situation. While one may be quite responsive to crisis situations and unpredictable events, only the fool is surprised and forced into a reactive position. Inevitably the lack of consideration of detail is what brings ruination upon a brilliant scheme.

Thus, design for a trainer or group facilitator becomes much more than simply being creative or innovative. It includes a laborious process of identifying where the crisis might lie, where the unanticipated might occur, and where the errors await, all of which demand the development of instant contingencies. Just as in any successful bank robbery, training or developing an effective group intervention demands that the facilitator first "case the joint," check all the "early warning systems," and prepare contingencies in case of failure. Concern with the design itself is not enough; its impact on the future life of the group and how it supports or undermines the activities to follow are also important. The fact is that more crooks are caught after the robbery because of their failure to consider such consequences as how to distribute the loot or how to explain their new sources of income to Internal Revenue.

Quite simply, when we talk about "design," we are talking about the core of the training and facilitating process. We are talking about the development of creative and sequentially appropriate activities or events to provide a satisfactory experience for the participant. Whether participant, artist, plumber, or therapist, the effective designer must have an ultimately holistic view of the group process. Although this chapter will continue to focus on the concept of design, subsequent chapters will look at particular designs found to be useful in a variety of situations. Having some theoretical understanding should increase the value of the application parts of this book.

Facilitator Myths That Negatively Influence Effective Design

Over the years certain misconceptions or stereotypes have emerged concerning the role of the trainer or group facilitator that influence the nature of designs utilized in meetings and workshops. It's important to explore these briefly and to suggest ways the facilitator can minimize the negative consequences of them.

The Magical Nature of the Facilitator. As a novice in the field of group process, my first experience *[RN]* as member of an organized group was with a T-group. Having advanced degrees in psychology and behavioral studies, I began with some confidence for I believed I understood human behavior and would not be lost, even within the unstructured nature of the group. Much to my chagrin during the course of the sessions, I discovered I knew virtually nothing about group behavior, very little about interpersonal communication, and even less about the dynamics of personal behaviors in a group setting. My sense of inadequacy was heightened because of the behavior of the group facilitator. By the third or fourth session I was convinced that the leader embodied the powers of a witch, a mystic, and a prophet. In addition to knowing what was happening at any moment and what unspoken forces were manipulating the group, she also seemed to be aware of what would happen in the future; she had a way of asking questions that inevitably refocused the group on something of significance and influence in the life of the group. This magical seer of a person enhanced her own qualities of mystery and power by revealing little of herself and by allowing us to endow her with as much personal influence as possible. Although some individuals would argue that her demeanor was important to the life of the T-group, still others would argue strongly that the goals of the group could have been reached with much more "normal" behavior from the facilitator.

Most groups, however, are not T-groups. And yet many facilitators seem to believe that cultivating a sense of mystery in their role is important. Because group leaders can have considerable influence over participants, such an attitude can have an important effect on the lives of members. In recent years we have reached the conclusion that such behaviors have many more costs than benefits and often result in dependency, passivity, and a sense of impotence on the part of participants, despite the fact that the group's goals probably include such things as fostering greater independence, openness, and trust.

After an opening session we try to diffuse the magical nature of a design by sharing with the participants our reasoning behind each facet of the program and our rationale for utilizing time or sequencing during a workshop. In addition, if participants have questions during a program or workshop about the nature of the design itself, and if the remainder of the activity would not be negatively influenced by providing information, we often briefly explain why we are handling a particular part of the activity in a specific way. Thus, learning can be on two levels. First, there is the goal of the activity itself, and second, there is the potential for members to learn from the nature of the design. We have found that such openness with participants greatly reduces issues of authority and helps promote an atmosphere of shared communication. Because there is a certain natural quality about the role itself that can generate a sense of mystery, trainers should attempt whenever possible to demystify the role and trust that respect and confidence in them will be created by the outcome they provide and not by mystical means.

The Myth of Nondirection. Somewhere, somehow, over the years in the areas of training and counseling, a value of "nondirectiveness" seems to have evolved, which implies that in order to draw from the participants their ideas and feelings, the facilitator should assume a role of reflection, clarification, and reinforcement. Although there is nothing necessarily negative about these types of behaviors in and of themselves, when linked to a leadership role they have in some cases resulted in the facilitator's being viewed as an individual without direction or opinion and as one who is often focused on "milking" the group while maintaining an atmosphere of pleasantry and support.

For whatever reason, what had once been an effective mode of response became for many a way of life and weakened their ability to move a group in ways that were most appropriate given the group's needs. In fact, the name "facilitator" suggests that the "best" behavior is that which effectively moves a group to meet its goals. That definition describes a person who can draw on a wide repertoire of behavior so that any given moment he or she can be direct, demanding, persuasive, humorous, outrageous, quiet, noisy, confronting, conflicting, self-disclosing, supportive, emotional, nonemotional, or angry—whatever is called for at that particular moment, whatever is right and responsive to the needs of the situation, can be drawn upon. The behavior does not have to be artificial or manipulative but can be sensitive and responsive to where the group is and where it is going. The myth of "nondirection" can cripple the facilitator by an image and a narrowly defined set of behaviors.

Going with the Flow. As group process or group dynamics has evolved during the last twenty-five years, it is becoming increasingly apparent that the most successful leaders are those who are able to recognize and adapt to the changing needs or climate of the group. Being psychologically "stuck" with a design or plan of activity that does not reflect the changing nature of a group not only can destroy the process but also result in antagonism and hostility toward the leader.

This increasing focus on the process, however, has led many individual trainers or group facilitators to swing their pendulum to the other end of the spectrum and another whole set of problems. These are the "going-with-the-flow" individuals who become so sensitized to any movement or change in the group that they inadvertently undermine any product or outcome goals of the group. There is a need to "deal" with every difference of opinion, every potential conflict, or with any individual behavior that may jar the sensibility of the group. Flexibility becomes the ultimate virtue, and preworkshop diagnosis and planning stand for rigidity and inflexibility.

Thus, only a fool would spend time designing a program when everyone knows that once the group begins everything will go up for grabs as the participants "get into it." The almost compulsive need to redesign spontaneously on the spot becomes an end in itself. But, because the leader is responding only to limited data and sometimes to personal needs and projections, such instant designing can be fraught with danger for the group since the short-term response and subsequent action by the facilitator may not be sensitive to the group's long-term needs and goals. Of course, flexibility and the ability to adjust on the spot are essential. We merely raise a flag or warning so that trainers are absolutely aware as to why they would change the flow of the design, what the consequences of such a change might be, and whose needs are being met by the change—the group's or the facilitator's. The danger is that leaders can be so busy "mucking" around with the process of making brilliantly designed interventions of the moment that they simply lose sight of the group's overall purpose and direction.

One can see that we are creating a double bind for the facilitator. On the one hand, we talk about the "grab-bag" design in which leaders force onto a group preconceived and set designs that simply don't reflect the group's needs even though they may provide the leader with an interesting and stimulating experience for the group. On the other hand, we talk about the facilitator who is simply too flexible and too responsive, who does not allow an overall design to unfold because of constant interruptions to the process. These leaders have an overriding need to "deal" with almost everything that occurs. Clearly, we are talking about the state of the art of training. We are talking about an individual who has the skill to design creatively at the front end and who recognizes the overall goals and direction of the group. Yet that same individual is constantly alert to critical changes in the personality of the group and has a repertoire of skills and the design capability for intervening effectively at any given moment. Being able to walk this fine line is at the heart of effective training. Walking this fine line, however, also heaps the fortunate few who have this ability with a great amount of unsolicited work.

Limiting Behaviors and Their Effect on Design

Effective training and facilitating within a group context weave together into one fabric the artist's intuition and skill, a certain cognitive understanding of group process in interpersonal relationships, and a heavy dose of understanding of one's own needs, strengths, and limitations. As any good therapist knows, the difference between mediocrity and excellence rarely lies in the individual's formal education as much as it does in self-understanding. Unfortunately, many of us are corrupted by not being able to see what there is to see in a group or by not being able to overcome our personal biases or needs. The therapist who is unaware of personal needs, fears, and the influence of past life experiences will be unable to respond to the subtle cues and shifting readiness of the client.

Because so many of us have been carefully conditioned to a relatively limited range of behaviors for which we have always been rewarded, we tend to respond in a situation as much in relation to our own needs and comfort as to those of our clients. And because we have been successful in the use of these behaviors, we resist change even when we reach a point in our lives when they no longer have the benefits they once did. Thus, how we have gotten ahead—whether by being "nice" or humorous, sticking to the task, avoiding conflict or generating it, dealing with authority issues or not dealing with authority issues—or how we have resisted dependency or chosen to become dependent really doesn't matter. What matters is that we have a limited range of behaviors that make us comfortable and that we tend to overuse in a variety of situations. Obviously, the problem might be unimportant for an accountant, a plumber, an artist, or anyone but a group leader. To be effective in that role often demands the utilization of behaviors for which we have not always been rewarded, and with which we certainly may not be totally comfortable.

The following example illustrates the problem of limiting behaviors. One of our friends, who is relatively successful, was raised as a child by a father who never gave him anything, who always demanded that he learn by doing, and who believed that individuals should always be pushed beyond their capacities. As one might expect, our friend became a highly independent, demanding, and successful individual who expects the same from those working with him. As a result, in a group setting he rarely gives directions or instructions and feels no discomfort when people flounder or seek the information and wisdom that he so tenaciously holds. As a result of his needs, our friend rarely utilizes the group as well as he might and rarely provides information that could move the group rapidly ahead and into new experiences. He confuses his value for struggling, floundering, and self-learning with what is good for the group. As a result, many of the individuals in his groups become angered, frustrated, and "turned off" to the experience. These are not his goal, of course, but by failing to be sensitive to these repercussions because of his own rigid set of values and past experiences, he fails in achieving his true goals.

Another individual we know was called for years the "great teddy bear" of group facilitation. His own needs for acceptance, cogeniality, and warmth created an unrealistic atmosphere of harmony in his groups. Conflict and issues of authority were seldom allowed to surface. Although members of his groups always gave him high marks and loved and approved of him, their own experiences were being shortchanged by his own inability to deal with conflict and his inability to see the dependency he was creating. After several years of therapy in which he learned to open himself to a variety of other experiences, he was eventually able to see the pattern and rigidity of his own responses. As his leadership style began to reflect these understandings, his groups were "freed" to work with a much wider range of issues.

Because we so easily become victims of our own narrow experiences and needs, it is absolutely crucial that people who plan on helping others in a group context be continually open to personal feedback so that limiting patterns of their own behavior can be identified and that they will have the opportunity to grow and develop in their own right. The issue is not that we have limitations and personal needs that are influenced by our own personal histories; rather the issue is whether or not we are willing to face these clearly and do something about them.

Again, if we believe an important part of a facilitator's success depends on the ability to organize and assimilate observational data almost instantaneously so as to make an intuitive diagnosis of the group, then the individual must be acutely aware of his or her own impact on the group at any given moment of time. Thus, the facilitator not only sees what needs to be seen but also helps to create the environment that is influenced by his or her responses and behavior, which, by the way, may well corrupt the very data being received. In other words, how you as a leader dress, what you say and how you say it, how you sit or stand, your tone of voice, your eye contact, your use of nonverbals, the way you act during breaks, the type of language you use, how you ask or answer a question, how you deal with conflict, and how you show feelings and express your concerns have an incredible impact on the group itself. You simply cannot underestimate the degree to which you are influencing the attitudes, the behaviors, and ultimately the outcome of the group.

Whether a group is ultimately successful or not often depends less on the technical sophistication and appropriateness of the design as on how the design is delivered and supported and on the indirect behaviors of the facilitator who works with the group. All we can do as writers is reiterate again and again that a great part of your success as a facilitator will depend on your awareness of your own impact through feedback from a variety of sources. Furthermore, since we are always changing (or at least recognize that change is possible), feedback should be continuous and obtained from as many perspectives as possible.

At one point in my own career *[RN]*, after several years of successful teaching, I began to feel that I was not reaching my students as I had in the past. Having become complacent, I had not been receiving enough information about my own teaching style. Thus, I solicited some direct feedback from my students (anonymous to be sure) and found much to my surprise that I was intimidating many of them through what they perceived as "well-placed" caustic and sarcastic humor. My first inclination was to deny the data and to justify myself by the fact that I had always abhorred the use of such humor. But, by using the data and asking a few people whom I could trust to be absolutely candid, the information was corroborated. I then realized that because of a crisis in my own personal life I was inadvertently taking out my frustrations and tensions on my students.

This behavior was not only influencing my effectiveness as a teacher, but also was establishing a pattern of behavior that could have had a long-range effect on my own career. The pain of recognition resulting from the initial feedback was nothing compared with the discovery of the problem I was creating. The gift of awareness that I had given myself as a facilitator allowed me a "real choice" of whether or not to continue that particular kind of behavior. Without such choices in our career we become victims of unknown forces that we ourselves create. The impact of all this can be remarkable on the success or failure of a particular design.

Most successful facilitators like to believe that their integrity as a group is unquestionable and that they do not prostitute themselves in order to be liked by the group members. A question that needs to be raised, however, is how much of ourselves do we give away by our need for future work? Since one good group can lead to another, there is constantly a subtle tug at the trainer to give the group what it wants rather than what it needs. The same is true in consulting with a client; there may be a tendency to soften the truth or be selective in the data we give back in order to avoid alienating ourselves or jeopardizing future work. As a writer it feels almost like heresy to raise the issue because I have never known trainers or facilitators to admit to giving away their own integrity for the possibility of future contracts. The fact is I strongly believe the shape of our workshops, meetings, or consultations is often influenced by such factors. I am also aware that the more experienced and skilled we become and emboldened by some personal reputation, we are increasingly direct, confrontational, and even outrageous with groups and clients. At first this behavior is usually received with some misgiving and suspicion and later with relief since the people now know they can trust us. With this trust our credibility and our value go up. For those beginning in the field of training and consultation, such directness and candor will pay off, but we certainly realize how difficult it is when other uncertainties about your own performance are causing apprehension.

Finally, it seems important to end this section with an example of how our own irrational needs—in this case values—can destroy the objectives for a group. Some years ago we were working with the thirty-five principals of a large urban school district. The program was held during the course of a year. Initially we had to overcome a tremendous amount of resistance and hostility on the part of the participants. They had not had the choice of participation and were additionally suspicious because of some previously ineffective training experiences. However, most of the obstacles and resistances were slowly reduced as the program unfolded, and we provided the participants with specific tools for increasing their effectiveness on the job.

During a two-day follow-up session nearly a year later, we brought on board a staff member who we thought could contribute significantly in the area of organizational conflict. The individual had a fine reputation although a rather unorthodox approach. Because of problems in our own scheduling, we had only a few moments to be briefed by the individual before he took charge of a day-long session on how to resolve organizational conflicts. The meeting started smoothly enough, and by eleven o'clock in the morning we felt comfortable enough to leave for an hour to do some follow-up planning. On our return we found what could best be described as bedlam and chaos. Five of the participants had already left, and many of the others were packing up in anger. The leader was standing in front of the group with a countenance of patience and satisfaction, obviously feeling that things were going very well indeed. Aghast at what was occurring, we watched a year of hard work disappearing out the doors.

Later, when we debriefed the session, we discovered that our new staff member had presented the group with an approach to conflict resolution that was totally alien to the experience and values of at least half the members. His attitude had been basically, "if you can't stand the heat, get out of the kitchen."

At one point half the group left. He believed so strongly that a personal confrontation approach to conflict resolution was the only way to proceed that he felt quite comfortable working with those who had remained and were dedicated to this viewpoint. His unwillingness to accept the readiness level of the other members or to place his design in the context of the whole training experience resulted in failure for the program but a psychological success for him.

Unquestionably, some trainers must maintain their personal integrity by holding tightly to certain values. But, if those values are not accepted by the participants because of inexperience, lack of education, or limited previous opportunity to practice them, the trainer should design a program that will educate and provide opportunity for members to become familiar with the values rather than dictating and coercing members to accept values they are unfamiliar with. The trainer we used as an example had become so committed to a narrow standard of values and behavior that he lost his ability to see the impact of his behavior on other aspects of the training process. Instead of creating alternatives, possibilities, or real choices, he created a sense of manipulation and impotence on the part of some of the members who had no choice but to leave.

The success of many training programs, workshops, or particular designs will be greatly influenced by a variety of factors and may have little to do with former trainer experience or skill development. Facilitators must know their own values, know their own needs, and known their own behavior. The influence of these factors on the observation and diagnosis of the group, the development of the design activities, and the response of the group to them can be profound. All too often these factors are the difference between true success, passing mediocrity, and in some instances true failure. The fact is that "the fabric" of any design is laced with the impact of these variables. Thus they must be considered seriously by the trainer.

The Diagnostic Mentality

The idea of diagnosis is repeated continuously throughout this book. More than a procedure, it represents a way of viewing a group at any moment in time. It incorporates the belief that the group, just as any individual, is a continually evolving organism that can best be understood by knowing it thoroughly and realizing that change and development are a natural part of its being.

Untested Assumptions

Perhaps the riskiest thing a trainer can do is to carry "untested" assumptions about the group and to use these assumptions as a foundation for building a training design. Several examples from our own experiences will show how the acceptance of untested assumptions or the unwillingness to look at them can jeopardize an entire training effort. In one situation one of us was working with a group of teachers. It was assumed that because they were teachers they were interested in learning *per se*, were open to new ideas, and were comfortable in a teacher-learner workshop format. After an elaborate design based on these assumptions was developed, it was discovered that the group was negative, hostile, not open to change, and not accepting of the very methods they supposedly used in their own classrooms. Once the first session was over and the inclination toward "suicide" was abandoned, a more thorough diagnosis of the situation revealed that the teachers (like many students) felt manipulated, powerless, and evaluated in the eyes of the administration. Furthermore, they had learned that new ideas were seldom taken seriously, and when they were, the teachers claimed they were made to feel ignorant as if their old ideas represented failure. Being unwilling to undertake a failure experience, they dug in their heels and resisted the program. Once this information was understood and the untested assumptions were discarded, appropriate designs were developed that alleviated many of the negative attitudes. However, ignoring their existence and not dealing with them initially proved most difficult.

On another occasion the failure to test our assumptions resulted in the loss of attention and support of a group of twenty-five black administrators who had participated in a five-day off-site training program. In this instance there were three facilitators—one black and two white. We knew that the administrators for the most part were being strong-armed to attend the program. A two-hour drive from the city, the retreat center was in the mountains where many of the adminstrators felt uncomfortable.

As trainers we knew how important it was to get off to a good start and to have people feeling comfortable and motivated toward the program as soon as possible. Thus we became absorbed in designing the initial activities for the program. We tossed a number of ideas back and forth but found none acceptable. Finally, our black colleague suggested that some kind of "milling" activity to some good "soul" music might loosen people up. I [*RN*] am personally against using milling activities because I find them awkward, and they seem to create more discomfort than before. I also felt something inside me warning that this particular group of middle-class black administrators would be totally embarrassed when asked to walk about and "groove" to soul music. My own experience from working with black groups suggested that the tendency was for such populations to, at least initially, discard any black stereotypes and work from a very professional basis. I questioned my black colleague's design but then, to my later regret, voted yes in his favor at the first hint of disagreement—after all, I was not black was I? I simply did not question his assumptions, nor did we explore our own experiences in similar groups.

Our first clue that we might be in trouble was when the group came to the program still dressed in suits, ties, and high heels. We had indicated that the sessions would be informal, and we were in dungarees and shorts, looking very informal indeed. The group sat stiffly around the room, and when my colleague gave the instructions to "groove with a little soul music" and move around the room getting to know one another, there was an audible gasp. Never had I experienced such contagious discomfort. Clearly we had not understood our population. They knew it and did not let us forget it for two days. By not fully testing our assumptions and by acquiescing to my black colleague "because he was black" rather than because of his knowledge in this particular situation, we jeopardized the workshop itself. In retrospect I realized that I had not worked through my own issues with my partner's blackness and our own feelings about our relationship or I could have said what I was feeling with the conviction with which I felt it.

For a final example, let's review a situation in which we did not explore our assumptions and yet were able to save ourselves and the group from a disastrous experience. In this particular instance, a group of thirty-five Latin Americans were coming together for an intensive ten-day human relations training program. The group had previously been together for a variety of indoctrination and educational programs. The participants represented seven different Latin countries and a variety of fields from agricultural specialists to educators to business people. Our assumption in designing the initial activities was that the group would be somewhat curious, but relatively optimistic and positive, about the workshop since it was they who had signed up for the program.

When we sat down with the group for the first time, however, we were surprised. There was an obvious amount of both passive and active hostility, and what we assumed might be a bit of caution translated into suspicion. On the spot, one of our facilitator's who was quick to read the attitudes of the participants asked everyone simply to write down on a piece of paper their greatest fears and their expectations of the workshop. They were instructed not to sign their papers. We collected the papers and immediately redistributed them around the room. We then asked individuals to read what was on the piece of paper they had been handed. Thus, we protected individuals from having to reveal their own suspicions and anger and yet allowed them to reveal what was on their minds. Furthermore, by having them read back the information we could respond as if the group itself was asking us the questions. Thus, we could increase our candor and credibility for the whole group.

From the questions that were asked and from our responses and the questions we asked them in turn, we discovered that during this group's previous workshop there had been a heavy-handed indoctrination by the CIA. There was, in fact, some suspicion that a member who had left the workshop had been a member of the CIA. The group had felt manipulated and was fearful that our program would be propaganda-based and not directed at the needs of the participants. Nationalistic fervor of these Latins was rightly stimulated. This simple "design" enabled us to get a handle on the concerns of the group and provided us the opportunity to respond immediately to their needs. Our directness in confronting their real fears and concerns in turn helped to establish the beginning of trust and our own credibility.

Researching the Population

Obviously, any design will only be as good as the "fit" it makes with the group's needs and readiness. Since a number of issues can influence the group's ability or willingness to respond favorably to a particular design, it behooves the facilitator to do as much as possible before developing the design itself. Although finding out everything about a group prior to the beginning of a program is next to impossible, gaining as much knowlege as possible without creating an undue burden on yourself or the group seems crucial to us. The following questions are typical of what we ask ourselves prior to working with a new group. Usually one or two key individuals within a group will be willing to share their opinions on such questions. If there is real doubt, a brief questionnaire can be distributed to a stratified sample of the participants prior to the beginning of the workshop. Otherwise, if such information is not available—for example, if the group comes from many different places—weaving a brief diagnostic piece into the introductory part of the workshop can provide a rich basis for cutting through untested assumptions and providing more data on which to design the program itself.

1. What are the stated, legitimate goals of the program as defined by the administrators?
2. What are the goals as stated by the participants?
3. What is the experience level of the members and what workshops or training programs of a similar nature have they attended?
4. What do participants "want" and "not want" to happen during the program?
5. Do informal groups, subgroups, or cliques exist in the group itself, and what benefits or hindrances do these hold for the total group?
6. Have past experiences of the group's working together resulted in what we might call "unfinished business" among various individuals or smaller groups within the whole group?
7. Are there norms that might facilitate the goal of the workshop or program, such as norms relating to open communication, candor, feedback, participation, support for each other, or willingness to experiment?

Many other questions can be asked and information gained that will help the trainer or facilitator join the design phase. For example, in addition to questions concerning norms, communication patterns, and goals, it would also be helpful to know about critical roles that members hold, the way that decisions are made within the group (assuming the group is ongoing), and the informal and formal cliques or subgroups that work for or against the larger group itself. More often than not, however, such information is not available, which is why part of the first session is used diagnostically. Simple questions such as What would keep this group from reaching its goals? or What concerns do you have about the program? along with a statement concerning an individual's own personal goals can often provide all the information that is necessary to keep the trainer from making initial mistakes.

Assumptions About the Learner

In 90 percent of the cases in which groups are brought together, the purpose is either to pass information on to the group or to initiate some kind of learning experience. Trainers and group facilitators are most often utilized as part of a teaching-learning process. New knowledge, new skills, and changing attitudes and values all fall within this arena. Once we understand the size of a group, its past experiences, its particular learning goals, and the time constraints that are available to us, we can then begin to design particular learning strategies or activities that will facilitate the learning process. In the process, however, we make some clear assumptions about how people learn, which will dramatically influence how we design these experiences. The following assumptions about "learners" can be used as bedrock, upon which a variety of designs can be built.

1. People forget far more than they ever learn. We swamp participants with the unnecessary and the unimportant. We must ask what it is that we really want our learners to take with them—the core, the essence, what they can use, and what they should remember.
2. People learn best that which they can experience and practice.
3. People need to understand clearly why they are being asked to learn what they are learning, and more important what are the benefits for them if they do learn the information.
4. People love asking questions as long as the questions don't assume ignorance on their part. Learning through creative questioning can be most stimulating.
5. Not all learning can be inductive—learners simply don't know enough. But most learners have an enormous amount of good information that can make them feel quite intelligent about what they are presently learning. This knowledge, or past experience, should be elicited whenever possible.
6. Learning is closely related to change. If people have been doing something one way for a long time, then the idea of change is threatening since it could imply past ignorance or ineffectiveness. Thus, somehow learning needs to imply the opportunity of something positive for the learner rather than something negative.
7. Usually if learning is approached as new opportunities or options, and if individuals believe they truly have a choice in selecting what is best or good for them, they will inevitably select something to their advantage. This is especially true if they are in a group situation in which at least some individuals are likely to strike out boldly for the innovative or "better" idea.

8. Learning can and should be fun. Of course few people have enjoyed past learning experiences since attendance has usually not been by choice and the sessions have lacked personal appeal or interest, they have not been creatively developed, and they have had little direct application.
9. People need the opportunity to practice new ideas or behaviors in a safe environment before they are expected to utilize them. One reason in-service days in educational systems are so discouraging is that good ideas are pumped into people who may see the benefits but simply do not feel comfortable or safe enough to take and translate them into the back-home situation. Thus they will return to the old, more comfortable ideas rather than strike out in favor of new ones in which they feel less secure.
10. Individuals are much more willing to try new ideas and to be less than perfect in them if they know that others are experiencing similar frustrations and if they know that others are supportive rather than judgmental of them.
11. It is absurd to think that all teaching must be presented creatively or collaboratively. Straight lecturing can be a most effective means of translating new knowledge. However, people do get very "high" from shared learning and from having the opportunity to help each other accomplish mutually beneficial tasks. The more positive we can make the learning experience, the greater the chance that it will be internalized and not forgotten.
12. Establishing competition as a modus operandi for learning usually draws energy away from the cognitive experience and into the emotional one, which may have little to do with the content at the core of the learning experience. Competition in a "win-win" situation in which individuals are not minimized and egos are not at stake can be stimulating since it can focus a higher degree of motivation and energy than might otherwise be developed in the learning context.
13. Individual learning curves drop rapidly after ten or fifteen minutes of cognitive information. Being able to talk about new knowledge or put it into practice in some creative manner makes ultimate sense before "shoving" additional new information at the learner.
14. People seldom learn the cycle the first time around—to experience and practice and then to reexperience and practice again. The cycle should be developed so that new ideas are learned while building on the old. In other words, allow considerable review and reinforcement along the way.
15. Whenever people can relate personally to their feelings, attitudes, or behaviors, which in turn can somehow be related to the context of learning, their personal interest will increase dramatically. There is after all nothing more interesting than ourselves.

Although this brief list is not inclusive, it does represent the kinds of statements we generate from the questions we continually ask ourselves as we attempt to create designs for groups that facilitate the learning process. Quite simply, the facilitator first needs to make learners "believers" or, as the jargon would have it, get them to "buy into" the learning situation. This can be done by helping them understand the discrepancy between the value of what they are presently experiencing and the value of what they could have experienced with a new method. Once they have experienced such dissonance intellectually, they will be much more open to a new idea and the practice of it. Here again it is essential that the individual not feel stupid or judged but rather free to experience a new approach or a new idea without having to be defensive or justify an old way. Thus, practicing in a "safe environment" is an essential part of internalizing a new behavior.

Receiving some kind of feedback or information on performance while utilizing a new process or idea and then fine tuning or adjusting it seems to make sense. Again, too often we send people back ill-prepared or not feeling comfortable enough to experiment with a new idea while they still have the need to look effective or competent in the back-home situation. Similarly, whenever possible, a design should provide for a small or experimental effort so that reward and satisfaction can be experienced and so that even if a failure should occur, the consequences are not devastating to the individual learner. If people can feel good and recognize the benefits of what they are doing, they will continue to utilize the new behavior. Thus the distance between experiencing a new idea, applying it in some real context, and experiencing some satisfaction from that application needs to be as short as possible if the learning is to take hold.

Getting Participants to Participate

The success of many designs depends on the readiness of the participants to, quite simply, participate. Although many participants enter a group situation with minimal suspicions or resistance, just as many quite naturally harbor doubts or suspicions about the impending experience, about the trainer, about the trainer's motivations for the program, and about what the experience is going to "cost" them in time, energy, and risk. Over the years we have found it advantageous to extract from the participants the hidden fears or questions that they would never (usually out of politeness) ask and then to face these issues head on at the beginning of the workshop. By asking people to write down the critical questions that no one is asking, and in reading those questions and answering them, we eliminate many problems before they even materialize. The following are some of the questions we are most often asked; they seem to play on the minds of our participants from small groups, workshops, and organizational programs. Obviously, our responses differ according to the situation, but you will get a flavor of how we think and might respond.

When I come to these kinds of workshops, I tend to feel I have been manipulated, almost like a puppet on a string, by the trainer or facilitator. Why should this be since I find it makes me quite resentful?

Quite often trainers or facilitators fail to provide three things that help to reduce this sense of manipulation in participants. First, individuals are often not given enough information about why they are there, where they are going, and how they are going to reach certain agreed-upon goals. People need this information in any learning situation, and some of it should be drawn from them so that they have a real stake in the group itself.

Second, and closely related, people want to have a sense of their own potency, their ability to influence the environment or the programs in which they find themselves. Thus, trainers should establish a mechanism for ongoing dialogue with the participants, whether it be in the form of a participant steering group or even involving participants in the planning process itself as the program progresses.

Third, we find that people are always curious and interested in the way certain activities in a program or workshop have been designed. By taking a few minutes at the end of a session to provide this kind of information, we relieve participants' fears of being manipulated; this tactic also provides individuals with an opportunity to participate more freely in the next session. It has the added benefit of providing the trainer with some new insights into working with groups and other people. (As we stated earlier, this is one means of demystifying the role of the facilitator.)

Is this going to be another one of those "touchy-feely" workshops?

Back in the 1960s and early 1970s many organizations were inundated by what was then called "sensitivity training." Many of the activities used during that period were tremendously helpful and remain so today. But like so many good things there was a certain overindulgence by many trainers and facilitators, and they imposed involuntarily on groups certain activities that assumed a level of intimacy that was inappropriate in terms of the group's readiness or the norms of the particular organization. The reaction is still being felt to this day. Most trainers like ourselves are very careful to measure what a group wants and to provide the best mechanism for learning, which usually has nothing to do with "touchy-feely" activities. In our workshops there are clear avenues for participants to let us know if they feel we are treading on their sensibilities. We want our programs to be fun, stimulating, and exciting, and we don't plan learning activities in which participants run around grabbing each other.

Look, just how does this differ from therapy?

For whatever reason—almost regardless of the nature of the program we conduct, unless it has something to do with specific skills—there are always individuals who are fearful that they are secretly being "psychologized." In our work with groups we are guided by a basic assumption that we are not there to "change" anybody but rather to provide some information and some alternatives that might be useful for some individuals in their jobs or in their personal lives. Whether individuals choose to act on these choices depends entirely on them, their personal goals, and their readiness.

The fact is that almost anything can be therapeutic. We are not therapists, but any good teaching-learning experience can be therapeutic just as going on vacation, to the hairdresser, or to a ball game can prove beneficial to persons who happen to need such an experience at that particular moment in their lives. After all, for something to be therapeutic means nothing more than it has the power to heal, and this would obviously depend on the needs of a particular individual. The goals of our workshops are not necessarily therapeutic, but it would be inconceivable for us to call a halt because people felt that what they experienced had a positive and therapeutic effect.

This workshop is all well and good, but I'm not sure it's going to be all that useful. Isn't it true that the people who really need this are sitting back home not attending? And what's going to happen to us when we go back home and don't have the support for this workshop?

These comments are perceptive. Certainly, many of the people who really need the workshop are sitting back home. And the back-home situation may very well not be one to support some of the newly learned behavior. However, our first goal is directed toward the individuals in our workshops. We want to provide them with greater awareness, a new flow of ideas and perhaps some skills that can be applied back home or in everyday life.

Clearly, there are no guarantees. As trainers we simply don't have influence outside of our workshops. Hopefully we teach the skills necessary to create the kind of support group or to utilize the strategies needed to take what is learned to the back-home situation. One thing we are not is romantics. We are here to accomplish within the context of the workshop specific goals that should be applicable outside. But we simply can't make promises in the areas in which we have no control and no direct line of accountability.

How do I develop enough trust in this group to share what I'm actually feeling or thinking without the fear of being shot down?

The only way to build trust is for experienced trainers to be supportive and not hurtful. The fact is that participants in groups are usually very protective of each other because as individuals they simply don't want to be hurt themselves. The way we as leaders foster that trust is to take the necessary time to "process" how we are working toward a goal and how effective we are being with each other at various times while we are actually working on our task. Thus, part of the success of any workshop will be based on the quality of our work with the participants as well as on the quality of our product. In this way if people aren't listening to each other, if they are cutting each other off, or if they are trying to ram through their ideas in an insensitive fashion, there will be opportunities to look at how we might minimize these behaviors and develop a greater sense of cooperation and openness without putting anybody down. Obviously, we are trying to do much more than just "survive" during our time with participants. We are attempting to create an enjoyable work experience in which people feel comfortable and productive while working together.

Our responses to these five examples of questions that tend to play on the minds of participants and influence their involvement enable us to legitimize immediately fears that many participants hold. We can make them aware of our understanding and our intention of not letting their fears materialize. Our responses also give people a sense that we know where we are going and are in touch with the sensitive issues that people so often bring into groups.

A Prescription for Effective Design

In the previous section we could have raised twenty or thirty questions, but our intent was only to provide a way of looking at a group and to present certain attitudes that prevail in our style of response. Directness, candor, and openness are traits we must model as facilitators to provide the participants with the feeling of safety they will need in order to display the same traits. In this section we wish to explore some "basic ingredients" that we believe need to be present within most designs, and which again reflect the way that we think about groups and the facilitator's role.

Establish Clear Goals

Talking about goals seems to be so mundane. Everybody talks about goals. It is difficult for us to understand why the issue of a "goal" provides almost a constant and predictable area of concern across groups and organizations with whom we work. Lack of clarity in goals, overlapping goals, and conflicts in goals are inevitably found among the top five issues of most groups and organizations. A facilitator can quite easily become entangled by problems surrounding the issue of goals. There are five questions that we as facilitators like to ask in studying a program around which we are going to design specific activities for reaching certain goals.

1. What are the advertised goals of the program?
2. What are the goals as stated by the individual who hired you and will pay your salary (whether you are part of an internal program or an external consultant)?
3. Do you as leader have any covert or hidden goals?
4. What do the participants expect will be the outcomes of the program?
5. What do the participants actually want from the program?

All of us have been participants in or leaders of programs in which the stated goals actually have very little to do with the leaders' or the participants' needs or wants. Designs often fail not so much because they are not skillfully presented, are uninteresting, or are inappropriate according to the facilitator's expectations but rather because they simply are not pointed directly at what is needed or what people expect or want. It is not uncommon after a discussion with the leaders of a program or organization to see the goals drastically redefined simply because the goals were either too general, not measurable, or not really representative of what is needed. Leaders need to find out what the participants really want to take away with them.

Preplanning discussions will often provide some indication of just how committed the leaders are to the goals and whether they really believe the stated goals make a difference or whether the program is simply another "experience" for the troops without much hope of having significant benefits for anyone. Such attitudes are "read" by those attending a workshop and can greatly influence the participants' motivation. Most "in-service" days are simply exercises in fulfilling state mandates and all too often are painful for both participants and leaders. Facilitators who work under such conditions should be fully prepared for the flat and negative attitudes that they receive.

The following items can act as a checklist when attempting to build clear goals from which to design particular program activities.

1. Are the goals specific and descriptive?
2. Are they outcome-oriented and can they be measured?
3. Can you verbalize what it is that the participants will take away with them and how the experience will be applied outside the workshop?
4. Along the process domain, what is to be "experienced" by individuals as they move toward the goals of the program?
5. What kinds of skills or information are to be learned?
6. How should people feel during and at the end of a workshop or program?
7. Are there "process issues" that need resolving?
8. Are there hidden agendas that need to surface?
9. Is there a legitimate goal to process the group (to explore with the members how it is working) as the group progresses?
10. Is having fun a legitimate goal?
11. Are you trying to do too much, giving them everything in too short a time? If so, why? Whose need is this?
12. What's in it for you, the facilitator?

As you can see, asking these goal-oriented questions provides a natural framework around which to design any individual experience. The original five questions at the beginning of this section were basically programmatic. The next and longer list of questions was much more specific and design-oriented in nature. Finally, a number of other questions that focus more specifically on what should be happening within the design itself should be asked. Yet, these questions are rarely asked until after the implementation of design. For example, at what time does the design occur during the day? How tired are the participants? What is the previous experience from which they are coming? Is the group a new or old one? How open and trusting are the members? Is there time to develop the design, or is time in fact a factor? Is the group intellectually tired? Is it emotionally tired? Is it physically tired? How active, and what kind of activity would be best?

Each designed unit should be somewhat self-contained with a beginning, body, ending, product, closure, and a process—all of which need to be reviewed in terms of the overall program. If the group needs a rest from intellectual information and material, then the goal of that unit or section of the design begins to provide a relevant learning experience that responds to other aspects of the group and relates observed experiences to emotional and physical dimensions of group life.

The issues surrounding goals are at the heart of any effective design. The more specific the goal, the more explicit can be the design, with a better chance of meeting the needs of the population. But the more specific a goal, the more accurate must be the diagnosis and the more integrated the trainer's sense of what has been happening, where the group presently is, and where it is going. By continuing to ask the kinds of "tough questions" we have raised here concerning direction, purpose, and the present condition of the group, it is possible to design creatively for the moment in a manner that will continue to move the group more easily toward its more critical goals.

Maintain Variety

In talking about goals it becomes quite evident that a trainer or facilitator must have a holistic view of a group and the individuals within it. Consideration must be given to the emotional, physical, and intellectual needs of the group at any moment and to the creative ways of maintaining participants' energy and morale as the program develops. One of the rules of thumb that we often use is "when in doubt disorient, disorient, disorient." Whenever a workshop or program becomes routinized and predictable, it lends itself to the development of a certain natural lethargy—even self-satisfaction. People tend to learn best when there is a slight stimulation, even tension, that forces them to think and respond in ways that are not always familiar to them. Thus, changing the pace and maintaining variety in the design is one way to ensure the creative tension and interest that seems so critical in a majority of situations in which trainers find themselves. Obviously, how the pace is changed and what kind of variety is integrated within the program are by no means arbitrary but are done with considerable thought since pace and variety will influence the nature of any activity. The following examples show how "changing the pace" can influence the mood, readiness, and interest of a group.

Vary the Time. Time is one of the trainer's most easily utilized "tools." We all know the problems of trying to do too much in too little time and the impact this can have on a group. But rarely do individuals consider the positive impact that the varied use of time can have. By giving a group five minutes to do a ten-minute task and then sharing its product with another group, the trainer finds an immediate ticket into intensity. Similarly, by giving a group thirty minutes for an hour-long task and by structuring the steps of the task itself, the trainer is able to increase the intensity in a similar fashion. Creating products under time constraints taps into people's needs to achieve and usually produces a willingness to work hard for short and intense periods of time. Such a strategy should be the exception and not the rule since when done once too often it can create antagonism, reduce the trainer's credibility, and generate a "passive" response instead of greater activity. Similarly, creating specific time blocks in which people can talk, followed by a specific period of time in which they are forced to listen, can create the expectation for new patterns of communication and facilitate both task and process goals. Finally, in a workshop or program situation in which time is rather limited, a thirty-minute period of time for simply reflecting and thinking can suddenly revitalize a group that has felt hurried and pressured. The point is that time should never be taken for granted and is a variable that will always have an impact. The challenge is how to make time work for you and the group.

Varying the Risk Taking. The level of risk in a group should vary with the group's need and readiness for risk. Too much and you can immobilize or demotivate the group. Too little and complacency can set in. To measure the amount needed at any given moment brings us back to the issue of design and its relationship to "art." Like everything else, creative risk taking can be related to emotional, physical, or intellectual types of activities. Thus, risk taking can vary in relation to how much we are willing to push a group in dealing with such issues as intimacy or authority, or it can be used to challenge the group to undertake a demanding intellectual task within limited time boundaries. It can be used to stimulate the group to undertake a cooperative physical activity in which trust is demanded through mutual support. The fact is that the type and amount of risk demanded can instantly change the atmosphere within a group and move it to new levels of accomplishment. It can just as certainly render a group immobile and make its members inadequate, which can also negatively influence the total program. The potentially heavy and charged consequences around risk taking are what keep trainers from "risking." Yet, for facilitators who are diagnostically sensitive, creative risk taking can push the group beyond its normal limits and provide great benefits.

Vary the Presentation. Five minutes of an organized summary can be incredibly powerful if placed at the proper time in the group. Ten minutes of well-organized theory, at the point when the group is thirsty and receptive, can be a marvelous catalyst. A fifteen-minuted "debate," when only questions are asked but no answers are allowed, can change the whole tone of the group. Five carefully planned, ten-minute mini-lectures can provide relief for a group after three hours of working in small group activities. The use of film, videotape, and tape recordings can force a group to operate on a different level, thus disorienting the routine of the participants' senses. We all tend to become routinized in our favorite form of activity, which can turn participants into victims of our narrow biases.

Varying the Type of Interaction. Have you ever tried an experience in which a hundred people in a group felt like a small, intimate community after a mere three hours? Have you ever heard two teams of sixteen people each carry on an articulate debate? Have you ever had an executive of an organization and an individual who worked on a factory line develop a task together in which neither had previous experience and both were dependent on one another for success? Have you ever had members of a group make a list of the high talkers and the low talkers and then force the high talkers to listen and the low talkers to talk and then watch the group magically change? There are endless designs for disorienting the predictable process of interaction that we often use in groups. How we talk and relate is one of the most predictable and easily changed aspects of group life if we are simply willing to think for a moment and generate one of thousands of ready alternatives. It is an area of design that literally shouts for creativity.

Vary the Physical Setting. From rows to circles to clusters, from empty space to pillows on the floor, from bright light to candlelight—the physical environment impinges on the personality of the group and sets the tone of openness or closedness, warmth or coldness, fun or seriousness, structure or freedom, boredom or stimulation. All too often we take physical space as "given" and are unwilling to look at the creative possibilities for bringing a group to life or for painting a stimulating environment.

Perhaps a central aspect of all these possibilities attempts disorientation or keeping participants off balance—or the element of surprise. It is our experience that people need surprises; they need fun, excitement, and a little outrage in their lives. The trainer can provide these experiences and at the same time give individuals permission to enjoy them. The trainer who is afraid to step out of the bounds of what is expected will be restricted to an incredibly narrow and limiting view of the world of groups and their potential.

Be Creative

One of the exciting realities about being in this business is that we have the option of extending ourselves and trying out new behaviors. We can be creative with our lives and push ourselves and those with whom we work into new modes of understanding and experience. Some of us take more advantage of this opportunity than others, but the opportunity is there for all of us. The question becomes, How open are we to experiencing the different avenues of learning that might in turn increase our capability of being effective trainers and group facilitators?

Being able to design creatively depends on having as vast a repertoire of experiences as possible. Designing an activity is certainly difficult if one has not experienced the dimensions of that activity. Thus, we find out that the effectiveness and creativity of individuals who are designing relates strongly to how creative these individuals are in their own lives and how willing they are to push themselves into new experiences. We are not suggesting that everyone should feel equally comfortable with all the modes of learning that we support but only that, as individuals in this field, we should be open to experiencing them and to exploring the ways in which even far-our ideas and experiences can be integrated into the more formalized and structured organizations in which most of us work.

We are continually amazed at how one individual we know, who works for one of the world's most conservative and restrictive organizations, is able to apply the creative experiences he has personally. They range from going on an Indian vision quest, to Outward Bound, to a workshop on "super" learning. For those who have the good fortune to work with him, he opens doors to other worlds, although he is always careful to stay within the norms of the organization in which he works. He has developed certain "idiosyncrasy" credits that allow him to involve people in experiences they love or that would not be part of any normal curriculum within the organization. But, at the same time, he is terribly "product" oriented and fills his workshops in "between the lines" with an incredible array of interesting and fascinating experiences. It is our contention that effective design is born out of just such an extensive repertoire of experiences; they can be translated into workshop programs and other activities through the following modes of learning:

1. The use of fantasy
2. Creative physical activity and exercise
3. Games
4. Simulations
5. Role Playing
6. Competition, intergroup, fun—not at the expense of others
7. Microactivities—real life (such as interviewing, counseling, problem solving, or teaching others)
8. The use of straight lecture and theory
9. Videotaping and tape-recording for feedback and critique
10. Fish bowling and structure debates

The most unique designs tend to be part of a unique amalgamation of the trainer's own personal experiences that are somehow merged with the need of the moment. Effective designs do not usually result from a trip through an anthology of training designs. Rather, they are something unique, driven out of the needs of the situation and the spark of one's own unique style and experience.

Involve the Group

One does not "play" at participation or collaboration. For us, success is correlated to a high degree to the level of participation and involvement people feel within a group. Increased involvement occurs in three basic ways: First, and most importantly, the design itself utilizes individuals as much as possible as group resources who have the opportunity to practice new ideas in some active and involving way. Second, periodically taking the "pulse" of the group and listening to participants' assessment of how the program is going allows individuals to feel they are influencing the process. The warning here is that this cannot be window dressing but must be real. You should never ask for involvement at this level if you are not ready to respond to it and reflect it on the program itself. Third, and finally, as briefly suggested earlier, involvement can be reflected in providing participant input in the actual planning process so that participant concerns and ideas find their own way directly into the planning process. This can be done through representation, a system of rotating membership, or some other means that allows a high degree of participation by a small number of individuals.

Develop a Sequence

Here is the essence of the art of design. We are talking about weaving together a series of designs that help to move a group through its various stages of development, that reflect the pace at which the group can learn, and that provide a balance of humor, intensity, challenge, risk taking, cognitive information, structure, process, and responsibility. All too often designs are planned in relative isolation, one from the other, since having a developmental attitude demands a keen awareness of where the group is at any given moment as well as where it is going. Such an approach requires a balance between the development of an integrative and comprehensive plan and the spontaneous design intervention created as a means of enhancing the overall design effort. Like a master puzzle, sequencing places each design piece in relation to the others and forces one's attention to the variety of goal questions raised previously.

Allow for Breaks

One panic that most trainers experience comes from the realization that in a one-day, two-day, or even week-long program there is simply never enough time to provide the participants with all the wisdom we have or with all the wisdom they need to do the best job they can. Triggered by the assumption that "more is better," our inclination is to compensate for this reality by filling the group's cup until it runs over with experience and information. It is also a means of proving our own worth.

Paradoxically, however, often what the group needs is less, not more—less information, fewer experiences, and fewer lectures. The one ingredient participants need more of is time—time to regenerate their own energy and interest, time to think and integrate, time for psychological and physical rest, time for a change of pace, time to be reflective about the questions, and time to let go and have fun.

So often, trainers think of "breaks" as necessary evils to take care of participant needs. However, if as trainers we could consider breaks as being valuable opportunities and needed supplements to the "diet" of the workshop, we might be more creative and generous in their use.

Designing "Beginnings"

Beginnings are of the essence, of crucial importance, and never to be taken for granted. They set the stage and lay the groundwork for the success or failure of the entire program and for the credibility and acceptance of the facilitator. Virtually everything you do at the beginning of a workshop or program will come back later to either support or haunt you. The following example will illustrate this point a bit more thoroughly.

A substitute teacher had been asked on a particular morning to take over an English class in one of the tougher inner-city junior high schools. Short in stature and only a few years out of college, he was scared, but he needed the money. On entering the school he talked with one of the assistant vice principals, who, without hesitation, warned him above all not to lose control of the group and to make sure they knew who was boss from the beginning. This advice, of course, was exactly what the substitute did not need. He found that his initial fear was beginning to "petrify."

Just before the beginning of class, the substitute told the vice principal that he didn't think he could do it, that he knew that substitutes were regularly eaten alive in that particular school. He simply didn't know how to handle the situation and had no plan or design for entering. The vice principal gave him a big slap on the back and said in a rather patronizing voice, "Look kid, I'm going to give you a lesson in beginnings that you will never forget." The two walked in class together and our meek friend was told, "Now watch this very carefully. I'm going to place that large four-foot trash container in the doorway so that everyone who enters the room will have to walk around it. Now take my word, they'll walk around it as if it's not even there and make no effort to move it at all."

Sure enough, each individual sauntered into the room and walked around the trash barrel as if it were invisible. Soon the class was filled with loud, rowdy, and undisciplined students eager to get a look at the substitute they heard was going to try to teach them. At this point the vice principal told the substitute to go to the front of the room and that he would soon follow. Slightly bewildered and trusting that the vice principal would not leave him alone with the "animals," he took his position at the head of the class.

Less than a minute later the vice principal walked in the door; instead of walking around the trash barrel, he gave it a violent kick, crashing it across the room and making several students dash for cover. At the same time he screamed, "Who the hell left this trash barrel in the middle of the doorway? Don't you have any respect for each other, let alone for our guest?" By this time he was near the trash barrel again, and he took his fist and hit it once more, spinning it helter-skelter across the room. "If I find who did this, I'll do the same to them." Stunned silence. Gaping mouths. He then walked slowly over and put his hand on the shoulder of the substitute and said, "I'm sure you won't have any trouble with this class but just let me know if you do."

The substitute silently and profusely thanked the vice principal and proceeded to have an incredibly problem-free day.

All beginnings extract a price. In this case, the price paid for attention, control, intimidation, and fear was passivity and unresponsiveness. In the short run the "entry design" gave the teacher exactly what he needed—security and some measure of confidence. But, he also knew that if he remained for many days, the testing would begin again and he would either have to reestablish his authority in some dramatic manner or develop other, more creative ways of maintaining control. The students would eventually resent being duped by the vice principal and would probably show no mercy if they found the substitute incapable of handling their acting-out behavior.

Most groups are at least a bit "testy," waiting to be shown, watchful and cautious. In fact, for good reasons, people attending groups of almost any kind will tend to be suspicious and doubtful. People have simply experienced too many failures and disappointments to get their hopes up. To make matters worse, many participants are there for the wrong reasons. Some have been told "be there." Others want visibility with subordinates or bosses. Still others are there simply out of curiosity. Thus, inevitably, we find that groups have to be "sold" at the beginning. They need to know not only what they can truly expect but also what the workshop will not be. They need to believe that "you believe" in the program. If you fail to reflect enthusiasm, confidence, and optimism about the outcomes of the program, there is little hope that their suspicions will be alleviated.

One way to begin is to give participants the opportunity to talk in a positive manner about what they would like to take away with them from the workshop. Having individuals chair these small groups and then feed back the information gives you the opportunity to reinforce the good ideas they have and at the same time allows you to use their information as a reality test against what you know will occur. Participants have the opportunity to see you as open and candid—as providing straight information about what will and will not occur in the workshop—rather than trying to sell an "everything package" to them. In a similar fashion, giving the participants the opportunity to share their apprehensions and fears allows you again to be perceived as "in their camp," as you systematically knock off their fantasies and worries through some straight talk. Thus, in a very short time you will have been able to alleviate some of their concerns by letting them meet in small groups and by legitimizing their ideas as they are being fed back to the larger group.

Always remember that groups build subconsciously on past disappointments, past expectations, and present norms. Although you do not have to be a pessimist, you should be ready to legitimize negative thinking and to push the group into a more optimistic frame of mind. By talking about expectations and concerns, you can create an instant diagnostic in which there is an opportunity to fill in missing information, share a few ideas, break down some stereotypes, and create an atmosphere that stresses hope, enjoyment, and anticipation. Such an opening allows you to discover how ready the group "is" rather than how "ready" you would like them to be.

The "Grace" Period

Most group leaders can count on thirty to sixty minutes or even longer at the beginning of a workshop or session (the longer the program, the longer the grace period) during which any overt hostility or antagonism will be submerged under a veneer of politeness, watchfulness, and reserve. It is a period when you can do most anything. Individuals are simply not sure enough to mount a major protest at this stage of the game; as a result, you can get away with some rather outrageous designs or events that might not work later without an enormous amount of credibility. Be careful not to strike out, however; make your initial intervention a good one. Participants using this initial grace period to get the lay of "your" land are in many cases just too courteous not to give you the benefit of the doubt. Thus, it is important during these early minutes to let the group get a good look at you and get to know you a bit. Give participants an opportunity to experience what it might be like in a workshop itself.

During the grace period, participants should have an opportunity to achieve an early success—something they can feel good about or even use. The following "rules of the game" can be used to help build the group's confidence and your credibility early in the opening session.

1. "Laying out credentials" works with those who are in need of dependency. They like to hear that you have done this before, have a great deal of experience, are gentle and yet tough, and have some specific goals in mind. In some groups, however, presenting credentials may kill you. Those who are suspicious and looking for trouble will knock academic credentials as "ivory towerish"; your experience will be irrelevant to them. A question session early on can provide the opportunity to share some baseline information with the doubting Thomases.
2. Appearing generally enthusiastic and glad to be doing your "thing" so that it does not appear to be "old hat" is absolutely essential. People are resistant to "burnouts" and even an ounce of patronizing behavior.
3. Displaying self-confidence makes people feel comfortable.
4. Believing in the group and being optimistic about the group's

chances of success gives members self-confidence, even though you don't know them.

5. Giving the group an indication of your knowledge in the area through some early activity lets people know that you can take the group where it needs to go. People want to feel that the leader has things under control and that the process won't get out of hand. They want to believe that the experience will be enriching.
6. Making the group believe that you are capable of preventing a disaster, that you can handle any obstreperous personality or consequence that might occur, is important. Again, an early question session allows people to see how you handle obnoxious and overdemanding personalities.
7. Showing the group that you are organized, orderly, well planned, and that you know where you are going impresses people. At the same time, they want to feel that you are not rigid, manipulative, highly controlling, or inflexible.
8. Having some sense of humor and having the ability not to take yourself too seriously are qualities appreciated by participants. They want to have fun, too.
9. Showing the group that you actually do hear them, that you are responsive to their needs and concerns, enables you to build trust. There is always some issue in which you can show your flexibility and responsiveness to them—for example, changing the time for a meal, letting people out a half hour early some evening, or "giving away" something that is traditionally within the power of the facilitator.
10. Giving the group an early gift of success provides participants with hope and optimism that greater success is ahead.

Dealing with Negative Behavior

One of the great fears that participants have is that the competition and negative, critical behavior they experience almost every day will occur in their group. Such behaviors are often magnified as individuals work out their own needs for acceptance at the expense of others. People are not stupid. They act negatively and caustically because they often believe this is a legitimate weapon for combating what is, for them, inevitable. Thus, early in the life of the group, the effective facilitator will try to "cut the legs out" from under such negative, hostile, and divisive behavior. For example, all one has to do is to break the group down into pairs and have the members in each pair list six or eight behaviors that they don't want to occur—behaviors that turn them off, are threatening to them in a group, or have been experienced in other group situations. Usually there is an enormous overlap among the pairs. People will agree that they don't like being cut off, put down, unduly evaluated, scapegoated, made fun of in any way, made to feel unsupported, and on and on.

That many people will agree on what "turns them off" is a stroke to begin with. When these ideas are initially made visible to the group, putting them to rest is possible. Indicating the degree to which these factors are present and that the group will be measured periodically during the course of the workshop or program will act as a means of containing them and limiting their use. Such a short-term strategy is not aimed at anything more than changing what is acceptable and often practiced in groups by raising the participants' level of awareness concerning them periodically. Personalities will not change, but behaviors often will.

Thus, during the "beginning" of a group's life, the trainer needs to establish a uniqueness of style, an ability to control the group, and credibility in his or her role. The participants should experience what might be a microcosm of the workshop itself and, during the early sessions, be candid, express feelings and ideas, collaborate, and have fun while gaining something beneficial for themselves and the group. The grace period is a time for building clear expectations and expanding the boundaries that often hinder participants from taking full advantage of a group experience. It is a time for individuals to become resources instead of just listeners and to believe they can produce successful experiences while still learning. It is a time to be candid without being shot down, to have fun but not at the expense of others, and to gain support without being competitive. These are the experiences that draw the group together, that create an initial sense of optimism, while destroying the negative attitudes that often accompany people into the group.

Designing "Endings"

During the "good old days" of group dynamics, perhaps twenty years ago, the tendency was for group experiences to have similar "endings." "Euphoric" endings were "in" and expected. People would leave groups hyped and feeling good about the experience and the other participants. All too often, however, such elevated endings would end "back home" in the crashing return to reality. There tended to be no follow-up, no monitoring, no support systems, and few strategies for applying what had been learned to everyday situations. Frustration, disappointment, and anger often resulted, even though the experiences within the groups had been incredibly rich and rewarding.

Since those days an effort has been made to bring more realism to endings, to reduce the hype, to make the ending consistent with other parts of the program, whether it be part of a one-day workshop or a thirty-day situation. Thus, increasing attention has been given to integrating back-home work and the workshop, to establishing support systems in the back-home environment, and to creating a means of reinforcement, such as establishing careful monitoring of plans and follow-up action steps. Group facilitators, therefore, have had to be increasingly tough-minded, organized, and insistent of the value of carefully structured follow-up practices. As a result, their reputations as softhearted refugees from sensitivity training in the days of "touchy-feely" are fast disappearing.

A Word About Meetings

The major focus of this book is on the role of the facilitator in a variety of small group workshops or programs. Such programs tend to differ from our concept of "meeting" in that they are more specifically content focused, tend not to be periodical or regular, and seldom call for using a trainer or facilitator as an expert in moderating the planned events. The fact is, however, that the primary reason meetings tend to fail and are often unfulfilling to many of those present is that rarely do leaders take the time to design effective meeting strategies for reaching the goals of the session. Many leaders see the meetings only in terms of a narrowly defined agenda that fails to relate the structure and process of the meeting to the needs and interests of the participants.

Too often a three-hour meeting with eight individuals present (equivalent to twenty-four "people hours") is "planned" by the leader in five or ten minutes. The outcome of that planning results in a hastily drawn-up agenda received by members either at the meeting or shortly before. Meetings thus become a process of "getting through the agenda." Each item, which should warrant an individual design of its own, is handled in much the same manner. Because of the usual constraints on time, participants often feel underutilized as they watch issues being pushed and squeezed through what is called a discussion; many emotions and feelings surrounding such issues are never raised. Rather than feeling positive or rewarded at the outcome of meetings, participants often are frustrated and leave with a sense that the time might have been better spent.

The point to be stressed is that meetings deserve the same kind of attention that we expect from workshops and programs: they should be carefully designed and based on diagnostic information, with an understanding of the total group as a system. Issues of membership, norms, goals, and the interpersonal relations generated in any group setting are all important and should be considered as one prepares for any organizational meeting.

The following "checklist" of faults were identified by participants in many meetings. Most would have been eliminated if only the meeting leaders had considered the kinds of tough questions and issues raised in this chapter concerning design. Thus, most meetings tend to be:

- too orderly
- too predictable
- too lacking in humor (except at the expense of others)
- too cognitive
- too planned (agenda based)
- too boring

- too lacking in risk taking
- too nonsupportive
- too uncreative
- too lacking in participation
- too dominated by a few
- too lacking in a worthwhile product or outcome.

Simply put, meetings should provide people with a taste of success and a belief that their time has been well spent. This experience happens most when individuals have the opportunity to participate, feel involved, believe that their ideas are being valued and solicited, and know that something positive and constructive will result from the time and effort expended. In most cases effective meetings will literally consist of a number of "mini-meetings" or separate designs for each unrelated agenda item. By carefully designing the effective use of time, as well as membership participation, the chance for attaining successful outcomes increases dramatically.

Most meetings are so predictable and so lacking in creativity and fun that people attend with a certain mind set or expectation that simply precludes much enjoyment. One industrial leader we know always includes in staff meetings one exciting "tidbit" of pleasure, enjoyment, or simple learning. He might use a nonsense game, a stimulating exercise, a stress-reducing relaxation activity, or an introduction to tai chi. During one meeting employees were introduced to a problem-solving part of the agenda through the use of fantasy. Without being outrageous this leader continually keeps his staff off balance and in a state of anticipation. The effects have lasted far beyond the meetings themselves and have acted as a means of giving the employees freedom to be more than routinized and predictable in their work style and their expectations of organizational life.

Working with a Co-Leader

Working alone is just plain easy. There is less aggravation, less confusion, less opportunity for mistakes, fewer hurt feelings and fewer egos to gratify. Without a co-leader, there is less possibility of jealousy, less competition, and fewer issues of equality, authority, or rewards. Still, few experiences are more gratifying than working with a co-leader when values, expectations, experience, and styles connect in such a way that we become supportive, open to new ideas, complemented by another's style, and receptive of the feedback necessary to maximize our own performance.

The problem, of course, is that working with another person can often be likened to walking in a mine field not knowing where the mines are planted or when one will be detonated. Co-facilitating usually takes time, work, and effort, and often the outcome of all that work and energy does not seem worthwhile. And yet, again, when it works, like a good marriage or any good relationship, it seems to more than make up for the moments of failure.

The failure of the co-facilitator relationship to gel can have as great an impact as any other single design factor on whether a design is or is not successful. Some of the conditions necessary to help ensure a successful co-facilitator relationship follow:

1. There should be an understanding from the start that few co-facilitator relationships are in fact "co" or equal. Even when co-leaders themselves demonstrate equality, participants will tend to pay more attention to one of the two parties. Different levels of experience, backgrounds, and style make the perception of equality almost impossible. This reality can impinge on the needs of each leader in terms of the sense of importance, responsibility, and the visibility they have in the workshop itself.

2. Other easily discernable differences in terms of experience, skill, reputation, and so forth should be examined closely during the planning phase so that both individuals can come to grips with these facts of life.

3. Individual needs from the workshop experience must be evaluated in terms of who will take a greater leadership role, who will lead a certain kind of activity, or who will be placed in a position of responsibility for certain events or activities. These needs have to be not only discussed thoroughly but also related to the goals of the workshop and the needs of the participants. Remember, the program is for the participants, not for the egos of the facilitators. Nor should the program be a training ground if that training is going to minimize the quality of the product provided by the two trainers. Such discussions are often painful and time-consuming, but without them the success of the entire workshop could be jeopardized.

4. Once having established personal goals, the co-leaders should discuss what each can offer the other during the workshop in order to help each other meet individual goals and provide the opportunity for reciprocal learning.

5. With all this initial work as background, the co-leaders should take as much time as necessary (often hours) to talk about how they view each other, what they can learn from each other, how they perceive their own strengths and limitations of style along with those of their partner, what fantasies might block their best efforts in the workshop, and how they might get in each other's way.

6. The co-leaders should allot enough time not only for initial planning and development but also for redesign of the program. Because the design phase is crucial, plenty of time should also be allotted to "process," or air, each leader's feelings and concerns during the planning period. Of course, after individuals have successfully worked together over a long period of time, reduction of both process

and design time is usually possible. After an overall plan and its accompanying designs have been worked through, various role responsibilities should be clearly defined as well as what can be expected of the other person during that same period. Issues of responsibilities and authority as well as control over the workshop at any given time must be worked through.

7. Role playing hypothetical workshop situations can be very helpful—for example, when one facilitator feels the need to interrupt the other to add information or alter the course of discussion. Such discussion will raise ultimate questions of trust between the two facilitators and could be a good indication as to how ready each is to handle the responsibilities inherent in a co-facilitator relationship.

8. A small amount of time should be set aside after every session or design for the co-leaders to touch base and make sure that nothing in the just-finished session will cause problems in future sessions. The co-leaders should also spend a few minutes for immediate feedback concerning their own behavior. In addition, time should be set aside periodically during the program to look in greater depth at how the sessions are going and how each of the co-leaders is working individually as well as of part of a team. So often, the absence of good "process time" has proven the downfall of many co-facilitators.

9. When working with a co-facilitator, one's personal time is often "eaten up" by the need of one person or the other to "work things out" or to "deal with unfinished business between them." Again, for that very reason, defining clear and specific time boundaries for this kind of work is important. Just as important is allotting time so that each co-leader may have time to recoup, refresh, and just plain be alone.

10. When a long and rather complicated session has concluded, we advise against co-leaders spending any extensive time reviewing or giving each other feedback. This simply is not the time for hearing well or thinking clearly. A better bet is to wait several days or perhaps a week; then the co-leaders should meet for several hours in a relaxed atmosphere to review the evaluations and each other's performances. They should discuss what might have been done differently or what they might keep the same if as co-leaders they were to do the program again. The time and space allows each person to gain perspective and to better consider the merits of the entire situation.

One can easily see from these ten suggestions that co-facilitating can be terribly time-consuming and taxing in any relationship, even if the relationship is sound to begin with. Although we would never discourage working with another individual because of the potential advantages, success in such a venture is by no means guaranteed and therefore requires both time and attention to many of the specifics outlined here. Otherwise, conflict and distrust will arise and may very well negatively influence the very nature of the program.

Summary and Conclusions

The ability to develop and implement an effective design is at the heart of all training and group facilitation. Clearly, the best designs are born out of the most specific goals and objectives. These goals should be comprehensive and include much more than product or outcome direction. What the participants should experience as they are moving toward these goals also must be considered and will greatly influence the kinds of design possibilities considered.

The following questions are intended as a self-test on the quality of the design you are creating. Quite obviously, not all designs require attention to all these questions. But the questions will act as a means of keeping you honest and will force you to consider exactly what it is you are after and whether your design is built to accomplish that purpose.

1. What specific goals or objectives will the particular designs facilitate either at a process or a product level?
2. Does the design fit well into a developmental and sequential set of events or activities that comprise the overall plan for the total program?
3. Will the participants be able to identify specific products or outcomes in the design experiences from which they can gain personal benefit?
4. Is time effectively considered and utilized?
5. If new learning occurs, can it be practiced in a relatively safe environment?
6. Is the design itself inherently interesting and creative so that the participants will be stimulated and energized by it?
7. Does the design feed the predictable or the expected, or does it provide some disorientation and creativity for those taking part?
8. Are you familiar with the consequences of the design, have you practiced or witnessed it, or will you be surprised by the unanticipated?
9. Are the participants active or passive during the design, and how does this reaction fit with their physical, emotional, and intellectual needs at this point in time?
10. Is there anything later on in the program that will help to reinforce or support the product of this particular design?

Finally, every facilitator should constantly be asking the question, *So what?* How would the participants benefit from this particular experience and at what level will the benefit occur? Additionally, as individuals, the facilitators should ask of themselves several other questions. These are the real tough questions: *Am I allowing enough involvement by the participants? Whose needs, mine or theirs, are most reflected in the design? Am I letting go enough? Am I modeling the kinds of behaviors that reflect my values and those of this workshop? Am I stretching myself or using comfortable and noncreative designs when others might be more beneficial to myself and to the participants? Am I really a bag man? Am I enjoying myself?*

5
Classic Designs

We have to be careful not to sound presumptuous when talking about anything referred to as *classic*. Basically we are talking about the best of the lot—those designs that we and others know will do the job. Such designs tend to have one or more of the following characteristics:

- When used in the appropriate context, their success is highly predictable.
- The designs tend to run on their own steam; they are not dependent on a charismatic leader or, in many cases, not even on a highly skilled or experienced trainer.
- The outcomes on both the product and process level are rather predictable.
- Many of the designs can be used in a variety of situations and under different conditions; the stimulating and valuable experience they inevitably provide for the participants depends on the specific focus of the trainer.
- The designs described as classic are unique, creative, and represent what group facilitators call *state of the art*.

Obviously, any skilled, experienced facilitator could add five, ten, or even more designs to the ones we have selected. Our goal, however, is not one of thoroughness, nor are we attempting to characterize designs by type. Rather, we hope to stretch the boundaries of your imagination by providing you with different ways of thinking about your role as a facilitator and the incredible opportunities with which you are often faced. As we present each design, we intend to editorialize and provide you reason and theoretical rationale for many aspects of these interventions. In a design situation virtually everything that a trainer does should have purpose and will lend to the impact of the overall design. This is not to suggest that all behaviors are artificial, contrived, or even strategic in nature; rather, everything you do can influence the outcome of the product of your efforts, and nothing can be taken for granted.

Case 1: Breaking Traditional Learning Patterns

Most facilitators eventually find themselves confronted with a highly intelligent group of participants who are convinced they know exactly how learning should occur and are resistant to any "new-fangled" educational methods. Basically they desire straight information from a lecture format and from the "just tell me how to do it" school of learning. Many of these individuals tend to have as a personal goal "looking good" in front of their peers; they have a fear of ever appearing ignorant or having to acknowledge past failures. Even if they are learning something for the first time that may be useful to them, many will act as if they have known it all along and that perhaps the "review" may be useful. Finally, personal involvement in the learning process is to be avoided at all costs. Such groups provide an unquestionable challenge for even the most skilled trainer.

As suggested previously, there is usually a brief period of instability at the beginning of a workshop when participants, regardless of their resistance, will go along with the program. During this period the trainer must not present narrow expectations to the participants; they must be able to perceive direct benefits from their early involvement in the program. Thus, an effective design during this initial period might

- Be unusual and a bit disorienting;
- Involve the participants quickly;
- Provide a model of the style of learning to be utilized during the remainder of the program;
- Create usable learning from the beginning;
- Stimulate interest and be fun or enjoyable.

To make this kind of a design work with a resisting group is again why we call effective designing an art.

Background

Twenty-four middle managers are attending the first of three, two-and-a-half-day, off-site workshops in subjects relating to management development. Although participation is theoretically voluntary, many of the managers feel they had little choice but to attend. The two facilitators are viewed as being on the side of top management. For whatever reason, an adversarial attitude among some of the participants is evident from the beginning.

The Design

After a brief introduction, which includes sharing expectations and concerns, the group is divided randomly into two subgroups of twelve members each. One group is directed to sit in a rather tight circle of chairs while the other group is told to sit directly behind each of the individuals in the inner circle. The two trainers are quite frank with the participants; they tell them that they will experience a different kind of learning and that they will be provided a rationale for each aspect if they will just be patient and wait until the activity is completed before questioning the motives or the process. At this point one of the trainers clearly presents the method of the design in the following manner:

Each group is to have the same two tasks. Also, each group will have five periods of six minutes each—or a total of thirty minutes—to complete the two tasks. You are allowed to work on the two tasks only when you are in the inner circle. When you are in the outside group, you will act as observers and potential consultants to the inside group. You will observe how the inside group is working—what they are doing either to block or to facilitate the completion of the two tasks. Thus, members of the first group will have six minutes to work before time is called; then they will have six minutes to observe while the second group sits inside the circle. While the two groups can borrow ideas from each other's activity, the goal is for each group to develop independent results.

The first of the two tasks to be attacked is to become an "effective" working group during the thirty minutes of your time together. The second task is to define as specifically as possible in behavioral terms the criteria of effective management as it relates to you in this organization and to arrange these criteria in some order of importance. Such a behavioral list might be used as a means of evaluating your own performance as managers. In fact, we plan to use a combined list from the two groups as one measure of management effectiveness later in this program.

Questions of clarification are addressed, and the task begins. As the two groups work at their tasks, one facilitator notes how each of the groups is developing and how its development is influenced by such variables as patterns of communication, norms, roles, goals, membership patterns, problem-solving strategies, and planning and leadership initiatives. The other facilitator is busy collecting data that indicate for each group which members are speaking, how often and to whom, as well as which members are spoken to and how often. Such "who to whom data" will contribute to understanding the communication patterns that develop during the life of the two groups.

It should be noted here that despite the resistance that is present in a group, individuals find it very difficult not to accept the challenge of a task when they are in a new group. Groups, particularly the types represented here, will perform characteristically because individuals typically have a high need to appear competent and to establish themselves in leadership or follower roles within the group. Even if the task seems absurd, the initial need to perform for each other will usually prevail.

At the end of the third six-minute session in each group, the facilitator asks the members of the inside group to turn their chairs around and face the person behind them. They then divide into groups of four: two from the inside circle join with the two they now face in the outside circle. (It is important that there be an even number of participants if possible. When that doesn't work out, one group becomes a group of five or six.) The observers are asked to discuss briefly what they saw occurring and to give some rather prescriptive advice to the groups that they have been observing. The idea is for those observed to listen carefully and to take back to their groups any advice they believe will help them perform their two tasks more effectively during their last two, six-minute sessions. Thus, members of both groups have the opportunity both to give and to receive advice for a few minutes. During this "feedback" session, the noise level and involvement in the room is exceptionally high as individuals, aware of some of the problems hindering the groups' performance, share their viewpoints as candidly as possible. At the end of perhaps five to eight minutes the cycle of inner- and outer-circle activity continues until all groups have had an opportunity to complete five, six-minute sessions. At that time the groups are asked to submit their lists of criteria but to remain seated.

It is important *not* to take a break at this time and lose momentum because enough data have been generated in the two groups to provide a six-month course in group process. Thus, the participants are again told that the results will be utilized later in the week. They are also told that during the next period of time they are going to explore in some depth each group's development and ability to accomplish the tasks that have been provided. The following instructions are given:

The inner group and outer groups should count off by fours, and individuals should form in groups representing their number. Each of the new groups will have two or three members who are from the inner group and two or three members from the outer group. Our task during the next thirty minutes is to become experts in the process domain of group life.

What you have just experienced in a relatively short amount of time are the same behaviors—both blocking and facilitative—that are found in other meetings and groups that you attend all the time. The problem is we are not trained either to observe what is happening or to act on what we observe makes the groups or meetings more productive. Thus, at this time we are going to look at five aspects of group process that have a major impact on the life of any developing group, committee, and meeting. Without a keen sense of what is happening within the framework of each of these concepts, the group leader will literally be crippled in his or her ability to influence the life of the group. The two of us [facilitators] have been busy gathering data relating to "patterns of communication" that have existed in the two groups as you have worked through your tasks. Our job will be to provide you with the means of exploring with us the data we have discovered and the implications of such information for the kinds of groups you deal with all the time.

Group 1's tasks (all the individuals who have gathered with the other one's) is to explore the concept of "goals" as they have influenced the life of the two developing groups. You should look at goals from the perspective of those that were "imposed" on the group by the facilitator, those that evolved as the real group goals, which may or may not have anything to do with those established by the leader, and those that in themselves influenced the life of the group. As a group you are to develop specific examples from the two groups of how individual and group goals influenced the life of the group and helped determine the success of the group itself.

Group 2's task is to look carefully at the "membership" criteria that prevailed in the two groups. Membership in this case is equivalent to what behaviors were acceptable or not acceptable in terms of gaining entry to the group. During those thirty minutes together some individuals gained greater membership than others because of how they behaved. The group must understand not only what these criteria were but also how they influenced the feelings, motivation, and morale of the group itself. Again, please give examples of each of the criteria that you develop and examples of how they influenced the life of one or both of the groups.

Group 3 is to take an in-depth look at the behavioral norms that influenced the life of each group. Norms are nothing more than the implicit or explicit "rules of the game" that guide and determine what behaviors are acceptable within each group—how a group handles conflict and stress, makes decisions, listens, generates ideas, allows certain language to prevail, or in other ways shapes the life of the group. These norms should be understood and identified. Again, be sure that with every norm you identify you note specific examples and make comparisons between the two groups in cases in which it is obvious that some of the norms differed radically.

Finally, Group 4 is to explore the kinds of leadership that developed in the groups—who had it, who took it, to whom it was given, and who if anyone was able to establish and maintain a real presence of leadership. Of importance is exploring how decisions were made, who made them, and to what degree specific behaviors influenced the group. Equally important is what created resistance to leadership and what kind of behaviors made the group willing to accept the leadership of certain individuals. The names of individuals are not important. Specific behaviors are because we can then begin to understand how the life of each group was influenced.

You will all have thirty minutes to develop an understanding of your particular concept and to provide specific examples of what occurred in relationship to your concept within your two groups.

At the end of approximately thirty mintues the meeting reconvenes. One of the facilitators stands in front of a large blackboard with five, two-foot columns, each headed by one of the concepts distributed to the four groups. There is a fifth column on communication taken by the facilitators. The whole group is warmed up to the task ahead by simply asking, What patterns of communication developed in the two groups which either helped or hindered the accomplishment of the tasks as well as people's interest and involvement in the process itself? While ideas are being thrown out by members of the four different groups, one facilitator "editorializes" and supports examples with his or her own examples. Five minutes into this discussion the other facilitator presents the data that the two facilitators earlier had collected on the two groups. The facilitator places two large sheets of newsprint before the participants and explains that they contain the results of the "who to whom" tally chart tabulated by the facilitators throughout the time when the two groups were working. The facilitator tells the participants how to read the two charts and then asks them to be "detectives" and to discover as much as they can about the two groups. They are to decide which chart represents which group, what patterns of communication exist, and what they can tell about the "personality" of the two groups—that is, the influences on them and how individuals affected the lives of each group. Such data inevitably create broad-ranging hypotheses about the two groups and the kinds of influences that resulted during the two, thirty-minute sessions.

About ten minutes is allowed for this discussion; the purpose is to increase the participants' awareness of this simple method for observing and understanding group behavior and how it lends a certain objectivity to what is often a subjective process. Gaining awareness, not total understanding, is the purpose of the activity. Thus, the activity can end without everyone accepting or understanding everything in relation to communication patterns. One concept at a time is explored with the particular group summarizing its findings and with the facilitator drawing other ideas from the larger group or from his or her own observations. The participants are astounded by how much is observed about each group and each member.

At this point the group leaves for a lunch break (the total design takes two and a half to three hours to do it justice). The managers leave on a real "high" based on a stimulating series of experiences and their participation in the learning process—whether they liked it or not—and as a result of the kinds of humor drawn from the real-life learning that took place.

After lunch, and as a means of bridging the morning activity into what is going to occur in the afternoon, the leaders review the nature of the "design" itself and the various goals. The purpose of this workshop, of course, is to train the managers in creative ways of thinking about meetings and encouraging participation at such meetings. They are also to look at and understand group process. The discussion of the design usually falls under a number of distinct topics. Examples of these topics follow.

The Two Tasks. In theory almost all problem-solving groups are caught between the pressures of doing a specific task in a limited amount of time and also taking care of the group membership so that people feel comfortable and are able to work effectively on the task itself. Thus one job in this situation is "maintenance" of the group. Said another way, the product (task) and process (maintenance) dimensions of group life are always present, and unless both are taken care of, the group will pay a price in either the quality of the product or the feelings of the members at the end of the task itself. Balancing task and maintenance needs is one of the critical roles of the group leader. The problem is that when push comes to shove, the demands of the task nearly always are allowed to take precedence over the needs for group maintenance. If a group is only to meet on one occasion, the hard feelings or residual effects of not taking care of maintenance within the group can be written off as the price you pay for getting the job done. But, whenever a group needs to meet for a second occasion (as is the case in this particular task), the disruptive effect of neglecting group maintenance becomes quite evident.

In this activity, it is almost predictable that the group will follow previous patterns and give almost no attention at all to the task of establishing an effective working group and instead spend almost all its energies in putting together a list of criteria for effective management. Thus, what people intellectually talk about as effective management incorporates many "maintenance" functions. The hypocrisy of the list versus the actual group behaviors becomes quite evident in the debriefing session.

Two Groups. We rarely take the time to observe what is happening around us. We are too busy "doing." Forcing participants to "switch hats" and to be both participants and observers gives them a sense of the "process" that may have escaped them previously. They also begin to learn from the mistakes of the other group; there is a "leap-frog effect," with one group bypassing the mistakes of another and moving ahead rapidly through its own development as a result of what has been observed.

We also legitimize the concept of the *process observer* (someone who will be observing what is happening, by assignment, and then will be reporting the observations back to the group). This topic is essential when discussing effective meetings or commitees; so often people stray from the task at hand when they are not legitimately monitored by someone who takes the process observer role and through that "monitoring" keeps the groups on target.

Five, Six-Minute Rounds. Most meetings are colossal failures in the effective utilization of time and individual resources. Thirty minutes is quite honestly ample time to accomplish the task at hand. In fact, a considerable amount of work can be accomplished in a six-minute block. Most members in a task such as the one provided here tend to "leap to solutions" without considering an overall plan for utilizing the five, six-minute periods, and they pay a heavy price for this haste during the last several sessions of the group. Breaking the time into small blocks exaggerates our failure to use time effectively, to utilize the resources of the group in the best possible manner. Limiting discussion to a specific time block has a further advantage of allowing a group to assess its own behavior between rounds and to unblock itself from unproductive strategies. In this particular activity, each of the five-minute blocks of time should be organized with a specific end in mind so that what needs to be accomplished can be. The same is true of a two-hour planning session in a business or educational setting, which often ends with an unsatisfactory product and a frustrated group.

The Consulting Period. Again, our purpose is to sensitize the observers to the "process" of the group and to begin to legitimize an often neglected aspect of group life. It is not uncommon for the consulting period to result in a suggestion or two that dramatically increases the effectiveness of one of the groups involved. Of course, suggestions are also ignored, and the pressure of the task can dominate the group activity. However, inevitably suggestions raised in the consulting period tend to come out during the post–task discussion and relate directly to such critical issues as membership, goals, or leadership style.

The Mixed "Process" Groups. By having created four mixed groups to help us process the entire activity, we are able to understand how the two groups were similar in many ways because of the realities of time and the structure of the event itself. But, we are also able to see how each group had a life of its own based on the idiosyncrasies of its own members; this becomes a critical lesson for individuals to take back with them. The group concepts are reinforced by the facilitator whose grasp of theory and principles of group dynamics can help to summarize and integrate the information generated from the group itself. Because of the total amount of learning and the various levels on which learning takes place in this activity, the participants rarely leave the meeting without being impressed with themselves and with the learning process. Thus, the goals of early involvement, of creating a disorienting and new approach to learning, and of modeling an approach that can be used throughout the workshop are all accomplished. In addition, a tremendous amount of human interaction occurs in a short amount of time, which allows the beginning of real "team building" (if this happens to be a goal) and provides the basis for a tremendous amount of humor that will follow the group through its entire program together. Although the design appears to be complex, it is relatively simple to manage if taken one step at a time as we have done here.

Case 2: Children as Teachers for Parents

Sad as it is to admit, people need permission to listen and a climate that is conducive for listening. Being defensive and resistant usually is a natural and expected response when we fear we are going to be criticized, or come under attack or when we fear that our present level of comfort may be disturbed. Often we fear that if we listen too carefully to others, we may lose a certain amount of our own influence or control in the situation. Obviously, for people to feel open, to explore new ideas, and to generate alternatives to their present way of acting or thinking, they need to be as free as possible from these fears and concerns. Thus, a "design" that is directed toward introducing people to new ideas should among other things

- Reduce our need for self-justification;
- Legitimize past failures;
- Place high value on self-insight and the ideas of others;
- Focus on the "developmental" nature of individuals in groups;
- Allow us to experience the benefits of new ways in a climate characterized by personal involvement and the opportunity to practice new lessons in safety.

Finally, although many of us are too busy "reacting" to think in terms of "design," design is a natural process that can flow spontaneously from a situation. Designing is as much a way of thinking about learning and sharing than anything else. One of the most effective designs we ever saw came from two young girls who had never "designed" before. The product of their efforts turned a potentially tense and defense-producing situation into one of openness and pleasure that had an important lesson for everyone.

Background

Two families decide to take a week's vacation together at a "primitive" campsite to relax and play and to spend some time exploring what they can learn from each other to improve the relationships within each family. There is an agreed-upon assumption that during the course of the week several periods will be set aside in a relatively organized fashion for developing some creative methods of communication and problem solving that will enhance the lives of each family. One couple's children include two adolescent daughters fifteen and thirteen from the father's previous marriage, and two young children ages seven and four of their own. The other couple has three daughters aged sixteen, thirteen, and eleven.

The "family improvement" program begins on the third morning. The families divide themselves into four working pairs. The two oldest daughters, the two thirteen-year olds, and a husband and wife from each of the families form the pairs. The younger children are asked to observe and to participate with whatever pair they feel most comfortable. The following design is the result of the efforts of the oldest daughters from each family. The two girls are having difficulties adjusting to their home environments. They are both perceived as spending considerable time disrupting the harmony of their respective families. In this situation the four pairs are instructed to "design" an event that will take approximately one hour and that will leave everyone with something important to think about and something important that can be experienced or practiced even after returning home.

The Design

Each of the planning pairs has approximately forty minutes in which to develop its "design" and bring it back to a meeting of the two families. The two oldest daughters, the first pair, ask if they can go first and questioned whether or not they can do anything they wish during the hour. They are assured that given some sense of propriety the time is theirs and they can do what they wish as long as they are serious in trying to fulfill the established goals.

Somewhat short of an hour later the two girls return, obviously beside themselves with the pleasure of what their planning has wrought. First, they had found an old, slightly soiled, seven-foot length of butcher paper and using charcoal had outlined eight major points around the topic "What is an adolescent female?" Each of the girls alternates taking a point and describing in some detail the significance of each, the behaviors that are manifested, and the resulting implications for family life. Each could quite easily have been the basis for a chapter in an adolescent development or psychology textbook. The examples are real, sensitive, and without blame. The girls are obviously trying their best to be objective without being defensive and are trying very hard to "teach" rather than to "sell."

After each example the others are given the opportunity to ask questions for clarification but not for discussion. The girls feel that these are points they believe in as "experts" in their lives and are exactly what they want the others to hear. For example, one of the statements is, "Adolescent girls are self-conscious of their bodies and their complexions regardless of how adequate they may appear." They detail how this makes them feel, what it makes them do in terms of their sense of inadequacy, how they try to overcompensate, and how it affects their relationship with their parents and with the other children in the family.

After they are sure that everyone has heard what they are saying (this takes a total of about twenty-five minutes), they proceed with the second part of their design. They have carefully developed five "typical" situations that occur with regularity in each of their houses and that tend predictably to create conflict and stress.

Given what they have learned in the presentation, different individuals are asked to take various roles in each of the situations. One situation, for example, has one of the daughters coming home from a party, acting very brassy and flip because she is trying to cover her own sense of guilt and defensiveness. Each situation is first acted out as it normally would occur. The roles are obviously easy to act out—years of finely tuned observation and rehearsal had gone into them. No attempt is made to hide what the girls intend everyone to see. The others, seeing themselves portrayed so perfectly, react with gales of laughter.

At the end of each situation or skit, however, those who played out the particular situation are asked to replay their roles in light of what is learned in the presentation. Then the group is asked to reveal how each situation might have been handled in a more constructive and positive manner. In each case, a parent plays the child, and in one an older daughter plays the parent. Instead of gales of laughter, the replays are met with a somewhat embarrassed silence. Everyone quickly perceives how much more effectively each situation could have been handled if the parties involved could have been more sensitive to where each individual was coming from. How to reduce the reactionary quality of most of those interchanges soon becomes evident. A brief discussion summarizes the lessons from each replay, even though the point is made clearly in itself.

What we have here is, in fact, a design within a design. Two typically "reactive" adolescents were given an opportunity to be adults, to be creative, to be proactive rather than reactive, and to be mature teachers rather than hostile actors. The girls responded to this invitation with personal wisdom and sincerity. They developed a sound framework within which the others could relate their experiences and see their "theory" occur through the situational skits. In brief, they reduced the tendency of their parents to be defensive and self-justifying and allowed them to create their own self-insights from the information they presented. They enabled their parents to view them from an overall perspective and not just from reactions to a particular moment or event. And, most important, they gave their parents the opportunity of actually experiencing a more effective way of handling a stressful situation. In short, they succeeded, where so many teachers and trainers fail, by providing theory, experience, and practice and by allowing their families to remember to this day the impact of their design.

Case 3: The Medical Emergency Task: The Use of Consensus in Decision Making*

Increasingly, we find ourselves moving away from the use of simulations and game-type activities in workshops and training programs. The reason is not that they don't work, but that over the years a certain natural resistance toward them has developed. The simple truth is that many had been misused and overused by trainers during the late sixties and early seventies. Often they were utilized as quick "turn on's," almost indiscriminately. We find that people still enjoy them, but unless the relevance of such activities to their work can be clearly shown, along with an immediate payoff, the resistance to such activities can be high indeed.

When used at the right time, the following design virtually never fails; it can carry itself without the supervision of a highly trained or experienced facilitator. The person employing the design, however, should be totally familiar with it, having practiced it several times until comfortable with all aspects.

Most trainers are familiar with J. Hall's now famous NASA Moonshot simulation or with others that involve a similar tactic based on discrepancy analysis. We are presenting the Medical Emergency Task as an alternative to these excellent designs and with the intent of exploring fully all aspects of its rationale. We include it here because it fulfills so many of the criteria of a successful intervention, especially in the area of high participant involvement. In addition to being interesting, it creates a certain disorientation in regard to any preconceived expectations participants might have. It is data-based so that resulting feedback feels as though it has some sense of objectivity to it. It is fun and yet theoretically sound and easily replicable with other groups. Thus, it enables easy group comparisons.

In a short amount of time (perhaps forty minutes) the Medical Emergency Task provides a comprehensive and integrated experience that can be tapped into by the trainer at any number of levels. For example, it can be used as an introduction into group process with the exploration of such issues as communication, membership, norms, individual and group goals, or leadership behavior. In addition, it can focus more directly and specifically on problems surrounding decision making and problem solving in a group context, particularly when a consensus is used. For a more mature group it can provide an excellent entry into the observation of individual behavior and a basis for a variety of types of feedback. For individuals who have developed an adversarial relationship, it can provide a less threatening environment in which a high degree of collaboration is present and in which the factors leading to the adversarial relationship can be explored because the task does not create the

---

* This design was created by Oliver Bjorksten, M.D., and his colleagues as an alternative to J. Hall's popular NASA simulation, which has proved to be a prototype in the area of simulation designs involving the use of consensus in group problem solving. Used by permission.

same vested interests as in back-home situations. Thus, it is critical that the trainer be aware of the "potential" of the design and to decide at what level the group should focus and how best to utilize it.

Background

The Medical Emergency Task has provided small group theorists interested in research and application with a unique simulation activity that (1) allows a group to explore with some objectivity how well it uses appropriate resource people in a particular task; (2) provides an ideal situation for observing styles of leadership, roles, norms, and communication patterns in a relatively short period of time; and (3) uses data generated from the participants in a manner that is difficult to question, thus minimizing potential resistances because of the nonevaluative nature of the feedback.

For those playing, the game itself is relatively simple to understand but very difficult to accomplish. The idea is to provide individuals with an interesting task that requires a certain amount of expertise but that is foreign enough so that most of those participating will have to depend on others if they hope to accomplish the task successfully. The key is to discover who holds the critical information. By using a medical emergency format, these various conditions are met. The group must discover which individuals actually have the most expert knowledge on the subject and then use that knowledge in the most constructive manner to solve the problem. In one group the expert turned out to be a little old lady who relaxed many long winter evenings by exploring medical books. In another group the expert turned out to be an eleven-year old science whiz from a ghetto school who tried to convince everyone that she knew nothing.

A group's success depends on its willingness to seek out such resource people and to utilize them effectively in the problem-solving experience. More often than not credentials other than knowledge—for example, confidence, loudness of voice, certainty, or charisma—become influential in determining who will be heard when solving the problem. As a result, groups seldom do as well as they might. Even the effort of the best individual in the group will not ensure the best possible response. Ideally, even though the discussion process can produce tension and arguments as the group members attempt to establish their own influence, the process itself should lead to more effective decision making if individuals are utilized effectively.

Groups often play with the ideas of consensus, but few groups have the self-discipline, patience, and interest to manage the process successfully. This exercise puts the idea of consensus to the test and reveals just what a difficult but potentially valuable process it is.

The Design

To maximize the value of this design, groups should be somewhat familiar with the study of small groups at work and acquainted with various group concepts. While this exercise can be an interesting experience for groups at various levels of experience, it takes some maturity and intellectual sophistication to be able to draw from it all the lessons that are possible. Groups with six to eight participants are ideal. If there are more than ten, providing the observation and the resulting feedback in a very efficient manner becomes difficult. In a group of six to eight, withdrawal or noninvolvement of individuals cannot be blamed on size.

One facilitator can handle as many as six groups at one session (from two to three hours). However, for every two groups there should be an individual to help with the collection and analysis of the data, and each group should have at least one observer. The exercise itself is relatively self-explanatory. The difficult part for the facilitator is organizing the enormous amount of data in a fashion that can be readily understood by the participants. Some group facilitators like to have the groups compile and analyze their own data. The authors find that such an approach tends to reduce the impact and minimize the variety of experiences that are possible. Although most people will not remember all the information placed before them, some of it will usually hit home and be absorbed.

Whenever possible, having at least two or three groups undertake the task at the same time is helpful. The element of competition provides an incentive factor, and the opportunity to compare the predictably different experiences of the groups adds several dimensions to the feedback process that cannot occur when only one group is involved. However, as the following text indicates, a single group can generate enough information for a week of discussions.

Once participants are seated in their groups, they are handed the individual decision form (see Figure 5.1) and asked to read it to themselves. The facilitator may wish to read this form aloud and embellish it in ways that might stimulate interest and motivation. The participants are then requested to complete the form by themselves, without sharing their responses with anyone else. As individuals complete this task, they are asked by the observer in the group to read off their responses quickly. The observer records this information in one of the columns on the group summary sheet (see Figure 5.2) under the individual's name. This step usually takes no more than four or five minutes; the other members are asked not to talk about their ideas until all the individual responses have been recorded.

At this point the groups are told that they will have forty-five minutes (thirty minutes is about minimal) to decide as a group the rank order of the medical process. The facilitator establishes the rules of the game by suggesting how consensus actually works, perhaps by making reference to the following points.

1. Consensus is a participative decision-making process that depends on the acceptance of an idea by all members. All members do not have to totally agree, but it is essential that they feel committed to go along with the group on a particular idea.
2. Consensus does not use such tension-reducing devices as voting to reach hasty decisions.

Group ______________________

Name ______________________

You are a second-year medical student who has had a course in emergency medicine. You are on rounds in the hospital when a nurse runs up to you and screams that a patient has stopped breathing and has no pulse. You dash into the room of a fifty-five-year-old male patient and realize you must save this person yourself because help is about ten minutes away. You know all the procedures for initial care from your lectures, but you cannot remember the order in which to apply them. Your job now is to decide in what order to apply the following list of procedures. Remember, speed is vital since a person cannot live very long without breathing. Place number 1 by the first step that should be taken, number 2 by the second step, and so on through step 12.

		Item
6*	Place patient on a solid surface (floor, bedboard) and apply external cardiac compression at sixty to eighty times per minute (the heel of the hand should be placed on the lower end of the sternum just above the xiphisterum).	A
7	Observe for return of spontaneous cardiac action.	B
1	Decide whether patient is suitable for resuscitation.	C
12	Give continuous vasopressors to sustain blood pressure if necessary.	D
2	Make the diagnosis that cardiac arrest has occurred (based on apnea, no pulse, dilated pupils, cyanosis, etc.).	E
5	Give three or four rapid mouth-to-mouth artificial respirations. Continue at twelve per minute if possible and if help is available.	F
4	Summon help and begin resuscitation.	G
9	Alert anesthesiologists; perform tracheal intubation and institute bag breathing.	H
3	Make note of the time on your watch.	I
8	Inject 1-2 ml. Isuprel into the heart if no spontaneous activity after several minutes.	J
11	Apply external defibrillator if indicated by presence of ventricular fibrillation.	K
10	Obtain ECG to determine type of cardiac arrest (asystole or ventricular fibrillation).	L

*Correct scores.

FIGURE 5.1. Medical Emergency Task

Group Summary Sheet Individual Predictions

	Bob	Geo.	Dick	Al	Will	Ben	Mary	Ann	Best Poss. Score	Final Group Score	Correct Score for the Item
Item A	6_0	7_1	2_4	10_4	6_0	7_1	5_1	5_1	0	5_1	6
Item B	9_2	5_2	4_3	9_2	7_0	8_1	6_1	8_1	0	7_0	7
Item C	1_0	2_1	5_4	4_3	2_1	1_0	1_0	3_2	0	2_1	1
Item D	11_1	8_4	7_5	11_1	9_3	10_2	10_2	6_6	1	8_4	12
Item E	3_1	4_2	1_1	3_1	4_2	3_1	4_2	7_5	1	4_2	2
Item F	2_3	6_1	10_5	2_3	5_0	2_3	3_2	2_3	0	3_2	5
Item G	4_0	3_1	2_2	1_3	3_1	7_3	2_2	1_3	0	5_1	4
Item H	12_3	11_2	12_3	12_3	10_1	11_2	12_3	11_2	2	12_3	9
Item I	5_2	1_2	6_3	5_2	1_2	5_2	7_4	4_1	1	1_2	3
Item J	7_1	10_2	9_1	6_2	11_3	6_2	9_1	12_4	1	10_2	8
Item K	8_3	12_1	11_0	8_3	12_1	9_2	11_0	10_1	0	9_2	11
Item L	10_0	9_1	8_2	7_3	8_2	12_2	8_2	9_1	0	11_1	10
Sum of the discrepancies for each individual	16	20	33	30	16	21	20	30	6	21	

$$\text{Group Average: } \frac{\text{Total discrepancy scores of all the participants}}{\text{Divided by the total number of participants}} = \frac{186}{8} = 23$$

FIGURE 5.2. Medical Emergency Task-Protocol

3. Participants are urged to share their views fully and to stick by them.
4. Because consensus is based on group acceptance, there should be less inclination to "prove one's point," and more desire to meet the needs of the group.

As mentioned previously, true consensus is difficult to reach, especially in this case (and this point should be stressed) since success depends on the efficient use of time as well as on the quality of the group's responses.

Group Observer

The observer should undertake a who-to-whom observation chart (see: Appendix A). Beyond this, what is observed depends on the stage of the group's development. With a group that often works together, the observer probably will record data that are different from those that might be recorded for a group that had not been together previously. Basically, the job of the observer is to develop behavioral data to supplement the information gained by means of the objective measures. This may be nothing more than noting behaviors that inhibit open communication or cause individuals to withdraw from active participation. In one group, leadership may be the most relevant area around which to develop observations, while in another it may be membership. The exercise is adaptable to a wide range of training needs.

Immediately after a group has successfully completed the assigned task, members are given a copy of the Participant Questionnaire (Figure 5.3), which they are to complete and return to the facilitator or one of the observers. At this time the group must not be allowed to break away from the task situation. After an hour of intensive work together, developing a lively discussion is easy. Individual members can share some of their responses to the questionnaire or the observers can share some of their data. The main point here is that the groups are brimming with feelings and concerns, many of which would be lost if the natural inclination for a break were allowed. The ensuing discussion can easily last thirty minutes or more. At some natural stopping point, a ten- or fifteen-minute break should be planned before the objective data are shared with all the groups in a general session.

Group ______________________

Name ______________________

Please answer the following questions as they relate to the activity in which you have just participated.

1. To what extent were your opinions and thoughts solicited and valued by the group?

   9 Completely
   8 Quite a lot
   7 A little more than moderately
   6 Moderately
   5 Neither very much nor very little
   4 Less than moderately
   3 Only a little
   2 Very little
   1 Not at all

2. Having worked with this group for an hour, suggest three words that best describe your feelings about the group (or its members) at this point.

3. How committed do you feel toward the final product developed by your group?

9 Completely committed
8 Quite committed
7 Moderately committed
6 A little more committed than not
5 Neither very committed nor uncommitted
4 A little more uncommitted
3 Moderately uncommitted
2 Quite uncommitted
1 Not at all committed

4. How much frustration or tension did you feel as a result of other people's behaviors during the work on the decision?

9 Completely lacking in tension
8 Approving, not bothered
7 Only slightly bothered by tension
6 Aware of tension but not hindered
5 Neither tense nor not tense
4 A little more tense than not tense
3 Moderately tense and frustrated
2 Quite frustrated
1 Completely tense and frustrated

5. How good was the eventual decision of the group?

9 The best possible
8 Quite good
7 Moderately good
6 A little more good than bad
5 Neither good nor bad
4 A little more bad than good
3 Moderately bad
2 Quite bad
1 The worst possible

6. Who were the two most influential members in your group's decision-making process during this particular task?

7. Who were the two most knowledgeable members of your group on this particular task?

FIGURE 5.3. Medical Emergency Task-Participant Questionnaire

Gathering and Analyzing the Data

The key to the entire exercise is the tabulation, integration, and presentation of the data taken from the groups. There are several phases to this process.

Phase 1. The facilitator and, if necessary, a helper or two gather the group summary sheets on which the responses of each participant in each group have been recorded (the participants are allowed to keep the decision forms). While the groups are discussing the problem and trying to reach a consensus, the facilitator calculates a deviation score for each participant. For example, an individual may rank item C as 5 when the correct score as judged by medical experts is a ranking of 1. Or an individual may rank item D as 8 when the experts believe it should be ranked as 10. Thus, the facilitator can determine for each item and for each individual the *deviation* between the participant's score and the score the medical experts believe is correct. Obviously, if the participant ranks an item the same as the experts, there will be no deviation for that item. By adding the total number of deviation points a participant has for all twelve items, the facilitator can determine not only how much each individual knew about the task when compared to the medical experts, but also how the individual compares with other members of the group. Note that in the protocol presented in Figure 5.2 Bob had a deviation score of 16 points while Dick had a score nearly twice as high, or 33 points from the perfect score of 0.

By adding the total deviation scores of all eight participants (as done in Figure 5.2) and dividing by the number of participants, a group average deviation can be calculated. In Figure 5.2 that score is 23. This average deviation would have been the group response had the group not bothered to spend all the time in discussion and had merely taken an average of its scores (roughly similar to a simple voting procedure). Even at this early point in the discussion, forty minutes of trying to reach a consensus netted the group a score of 21 (see Final Group Score in Figure 5.2) or only two points better than if a quick vote had been taken and an average score presented. This suggests that the group for some reason was unable to pool its potential resources to the best advantage. The purpose of the simulation is, of course, to help the various groups explore some of the reasons why such things occur and why some groups tend to operate most successfully while others fail rather miserably.

Phase 2. The best possible score that the group could have had on any one item—if the members had used the best resource in their group—can be determined. By looking at Figure 5.2, we see that Will had the correct response for item F—that is, he ranked the item the same as the medical experts and thus had a deviation score of 0. Theoretically, if the group members had explored the question thoroughly, they would have found among themselves a resource person or persons who knew the correct answer. Thus, the group would have responded correctly to that item had it used the best resource. In this particular instance, after discussing the item, the group agreed on the ranking of 3, which was 2 points away from the ideal score of the experts. By adding all of the group's best possible responses for each item, theoretically the group would have been unable to score less than 6 points since it apparently did not have the resources necessary to do a perfect job in ranking the items. Had the group used all its resources, however, it would have scored considerably better than the final score of 21 deviation points. For what reasons were people apparently not heard and the group not more efficient in solving its problem?

Phase 3. From the participant questionnaires provided immediately after the simulation (Figure 5.3), a number of important pieces of information can be presented to the entire group. For example, the information from items 6 and 7 concerning the most influential and knowledgeable members can be presented. Information gained from observers (who-to-whom), as well as data from the questionnaire, is gathered for each group and presented (usually on large newsprint) to the entire group. The facilitator, of course, is tempted to overwhelm the group with too much important information.

Some of this information should have already been presented to the individual groups by the observer who had been "observing" during the group discussions. The observer would have fed back tallied information and notes on process to help the participants focus on the many factors that facilitated or hindered the group in its efforts to solve the problem at hand. Emphasis on both the task and maintenance levels of group operation is essential. While personalizing the kinds of data generated is not necessary, groups usually find the activity so stimulating that they do not mind personalizing their own experiences and feelings. While the simulation may be used to develop a rather intense session of personal feedback, most groups use the experience as a means of helping them see the group as a group and the factors that influence the decision-making process.

Analysis of the Data for the Group

After the simulation itself (about forty minutes) and the following discussion (about thirty minutes, although it could go on for much longer), the participants usually need a ten- or fifteen-minute break. During this time the final data from the post-simulation questionnaire are tabulated and included with the other information now available to all the groups (see Figure 5.4). Once the groups

---

1. Group score (after forty minutes of discussion): 21
2. Group average (average deviation score of all the participants in group 1): 23
3. Best possible score of group 1: 6
4. High score (worst): 33; low score (best): 16
5. The four individuals with the best scores:

   Bob: 16 George: 20
   Will: 16 Mary: 20
6. The three individuals who talked the most (taken from who-to-whom data of observer): Dick, Ann, George
7. The three individuals who were talked to the most (also who-to-whom data): George, Ann, Ben

8. Those in the group perceived as knowing the most (taken from questionnaire): Ben, George, Dick
9. Those in the group perceived as having the most influence: George, Ann, Dick
10. Extent to which members felt opinions were solicited and valued (Figure 5.3, item 1); average score: 4.5 (three of the people scored 3 or below)
11. Extent to which members felt committed to final decision; average score: 5.2 (two people scored 1 and another 2)
12. The degree of frustration felt in group; average score: 4.5 (Interestingly, the group split between the two extremes.)
13. How good the group decision was; average score: 6.5 (all scored over 5)
14. Words used to describe the group or feelings:

cut off	involved
put down	participating
not listened to	sharing
withdrawn	open
uninvolved	fun
frustrated	learning
angry	thinking

15. Other words used which did not tend to fall at the extremes included:

worked	time
pressure	unusual
debate	consensus

FIGURE 5.4. Final Data from the Post-Simulation Questionnaire

reassemble into a large group, having a discussion of the actual correct answers is helpful. The answers should not be defended by the facilitator, however. If the participants are not satisfied, the facilitator should suggest (with humor) that they contact their local doctor, the AMA, or an expert on cardiac arrest. Understanding the method of scoring is important and as much time as necessary should be spent on explaining the nature of the deviation scores. Without such understanding, the group data will mean nothing, and the value of the entire experience will be dramatically reduced.

The Protocol and Related Data

The facilitator's role is not to play magician and make brilliant interpretations from the data. The key is to place the data before the participants in a self-explanatory manner. The following information is the kind that can be shared before the entire group. With the presentation of each set of data, more relationships can be drawn between the various groups as certain patterns tend to emerge.

Data from Group 1

As noted previously, the group was able to improve its final score by only two points over what it might have scored taking a superficial vote among its members. Also noted is that fully half of the people in the group scored better individually than the group scored as a whole. Theoretically, by combining the insights of eight people, the group should have scored better than any one of its members (except in exceptional circumstances). Of course, discovering who actually are the individuals with the most information is essential.

It is important to note that of the three people who talked the most only one (George) scored among the better half in the group. In fact, two of the individuals with the poorest scores (these poor scores do not have to be reported to the group—the absence of the talkers among the high scores is enough to make the point) dominated the talk time. Similarly, for some reason, Mary, Bob, and Will, who had the best scores, talked very little and were virtually not spoken to at all. As might be expected, those who talked the most tended to be spoken to the most. This was not the case with Dick, who might have been providing an important maintenance role that did not require being talked back to. It may well be, however, that Dick simply spoke a great deal but had little influence with the group. One person, Ben, was spoken to considerably more than he talked; it may be that he was recognized as a special resource, but, for some reason, he failed to provide the group with the kind of information it was seeking.

Often groups place blame on those individuals who tend to dominate but, as discovered later, fail to have the information or background to warrant their degree of participation. The group should have taken more responsibility for its own destiny and ensured that other members had the opportunity to invest their ideas into the discussion. Some of the blame in this situation must be placed on the quieter members who failed to share information that could be beneficial or who failed to see themselves as important resources. For whatever reasons, it is essential to break a pattern of limited participation if a group is to be successful in using consensus as a tool for decision making.

Clearly the group discovered an important resource person in George, but the attention given to Ann and Dick very likely reduced the group's productivity. Both Dick and Ann were thought to have had considerably more knowledge (Figure 5.4, item 8) than half of the group, and each was perceived as highly influential.

A pattern emerges in which it appears that a few vociferous individuals dominated the group while others stood back and observed. This pattern is particularly evident in the types of words used to describe the group or the experience (Figure 5.4, item 14). Half of the group (the talkers and those actively involved) used generally positive words while many of the others reflected the attitudes of most people who do not feel well regarded or potent. This is further evidenced in the responses to other questions. For example, three or four members of the group felt their opinions were solicited and valued in the final decision; thus they felt little frustration in the task. Three or four others, however, placed themselves at the opposite end of the continuum.

Finally, it may be said with some certainty that although the group did not do badly in its actual level of performance, the potential for solving future problems is not high. Many unresolved conflicts are beginning to emerge, along with a disconcerting pattern of nonlistening and signs of competition among the more active members. In a one-hour task many of these issues can easily be swept under the rug, but in real life these same issues all too often result in destructive behaviors among the participants as they continue to meet together with no legitimate means of viewing their process with an aim toward improvement.

Again, we cannot stress too much that as much as possible the various groups should be encouraged to draw their own implications from the data and to generalize them to other groups. This process is what makes the simulation important in the eyes of the participants.

Data Reported Back During Theory Session with All Groups

The data in Figure 5.4 gathered on group 1 will be systematically reported back to the participants. Much of the learning will depend on the skill of the reporter in making the various groups understand their own data as well as the possible variables that influenced differences among the various groups.

Simulation activities are a marvelous way of dealing with very real behaviors because personal interests are not high. They allow a much better opportunity for self-examination, less defensiveness, and the opportunity to laugh at oneself and with us. Too often, however, simulations are used as an entertainment vehicle first and a learning vehicle second. In such cases, they are used out of context and for the wrong purposes. With this particular simulation the problem is to avoid overwhelming the learner with too much data or information and instead to focus clearly on a relatively narrow range of lessons that are appropriate to the particular goals of the group.

Case 4: Discovering the Real Problems Blocking a Group's Productivity or Influencing Its Morale

Background

The management of an organization wishes to involve a representative group of fifty individuals in an inquiry process that will be the beginning of some formal organizational problem solving. The organization is service oriented and carries out such activities as marketing, sales, public relations, planning, and staff support services, as well as customer services. Participants are selected from each of these areas and their related subdivisions by other individuals from those same areas, thus ensuring a representative population.

The Design

In advance of the five-hour diagnostic session, all members of the entire organization are given a brief questionnaire in which they are asked what questions they believe need to be asked in order to discover, How do we do what we do better? The purpose of the questionnaire is to bring to the surface the problems that have been reducing productivity and morale within the organization. Two executives and two subordinates are requested to take the five hundred responses and compile a list of ten concerns that most reflect the concerns of the employees. Here is the list (presented as requests for information):

1. Please identify several factors that are presently reducing employee morale and that could be positively affected by corporative problem solving.
2. What are the greatest sources of tension or conflict in the organization?
3. What factors block effective communication in the organization?
4. If you were the president of the organization, what is the very first thing you would do to increase organizational efficiency without replacement of personnel, or great capital outlay?
5. Please suggest any innovations in other organizations that might be used to benefit this one.
6. Please talk about your feelings in relation to this organization's "happiness."
7. Please talk about the word "frustration" in relation to this organization.
8. Name at least three things about the organization and its method of operation that you would *not* change because of the benefits to the organization.
9. What three innovative suggestions would you make to improve the quality of the services offered by this organization?
10. Explain two things that the organization could do that would not cost a lot of money but that would positively influence the attitude of those working within it.

The list of ten concerns is next divided into five pairs, with the two concerns in each pair being quite different. Each of the pairs is then printed on ten, three-by-five-inch cards. A Roman numeral from I to V is placed on each of the ten cards. For example, questions 1 and 5 are selected as a pair and are copied together on ten, three-by-five-inch cards with the Roman numeral I on them. Question 2 and question 6 are paired and copied down on ten separate three-by-five-inch cards with the Roman numeral II on them. This pattern is continued until each of the questions is paired with another and placed ten times on a three-by-five-inch card. Once finished, there are five stacks of ten cards each.

At the beginning of the five-hour diagnostic workshop, the fifty participants are each handed one of the cards. Next to the Roman numeral on each card is a small letter designating the particular row where they will sit. Figure 5.5 shows how the room will be arranged. In this design, each individual sits in a designated row with a card that has two questions on it.

```
     Rotate                 Rotate                  Rotate
   I  V  IV  II  III     III  I  IV  V  II       V  IV  III  I  II
A  O  O  O   O   O    C  O    O  O   O  O    E   O  O   O    O  O
B  X  X  X   X   X    D  X    X  X   X  X    F   X  X   X    X  X
   II I  IV  V   III     I    II V   IV III      IV II  I    III V
   Remain seated         Remain seated           Remain seated

          Rotate                        Rotate
        III  V  IV  II  I            IV  III  V  I  II
    G   O    O  O   O   O        I   O   O    O  O  O
    H   X    X  X   X   X        J   X   X    X  X  X
        I    II III IV  V            III V    IV II I
        Remain seated                Remain seated
```

FIGURE 5.5. Workshop Seating Plan

As Figure 5.5 shows, there are ten rows altogether; each row is paired with another. Thus rows A and B face each other, rows C and D face each other, rows E and F face each other, and so forth. Each participant has to find the row with the same letter that appears on the card. Once having found the row, the participants can sit anywhere in the row.

The design works so that each row contains a Roman numeral I, II, III, IV, and V. The participants in rows A, C, E, G, and I are told they will have exactly five minutes to ask the individual sitting directly across from them each of the questions on their card. Their job is to obtain in five minutes as much information as they can concerning the two questions. They are encouraged to take notes with the pads and pencils that have been provided. Their job is not to question the answers but simply to obtain as much objective and accurate information as possible. At the end of five minutes time is called, and the people who have been answering the questions now ask the person across from them the two questions they have on their own card. Thus, the individuals in rows B, D, F, H, and J will have five minutes to ask their two questions. They are also encouraged to take accurate notes. At the end of this five minutes time is again called. Then, as Figure 5.5 shows, all of the individuals in rows A, C, E, G, and I move to their left one seat, with the last person in the row moving all the way around and taking the now open seat at the end. At this point, round number two begins, and each individual is faced with a different partner with a new set of two questions.

This activity includes a total of five rounds, so that each person is interviewed five times and each person interviews five people. Also, everyone has the opportunity to answer his or her own two questions. All of this will occur in less than an hour. Although the activity may sound a bit confusing, it is actually very orderly and simple to follow when the directions are given clearly and the proper materials provided. Generally, people are tremendously attentive; they will try their best to be objective and to discover what the interviewee is really asking. In most situations of this kind, the people being interviewed tend to be more candid than we often expect.

Every participant will have responses from five people for each of the two questions at the end of the hour. The participants are now given twenty or twenty-five minutes, including a break, to sit by themselves and analyze their data. Their goal is to determine if certain patterns exist among the five responses. They are also to make up a series of statements for each of the questions, which in themselves stand out as "truths" among most of the respondents. There should be no interest in "extreme" responses; rather, attention should be directed toward the areas in which the majority of interviewees have some clear agreement. Thus for question 3 concerning patterns of communication an interviewer might record the following statements of "truth."

1. People are always told and never asked.
2. There are so many memos that any single one tends to lose importance.
3. Openness seems to be encouraged but not appreciated.

At the end of twenty or thirty minutes all individuals with the Roman numeral I and letters A, C, E, G, and I on their cards meet in a group. Those with Roman numeral I and letters B, D, F, H, and J meet in another group.

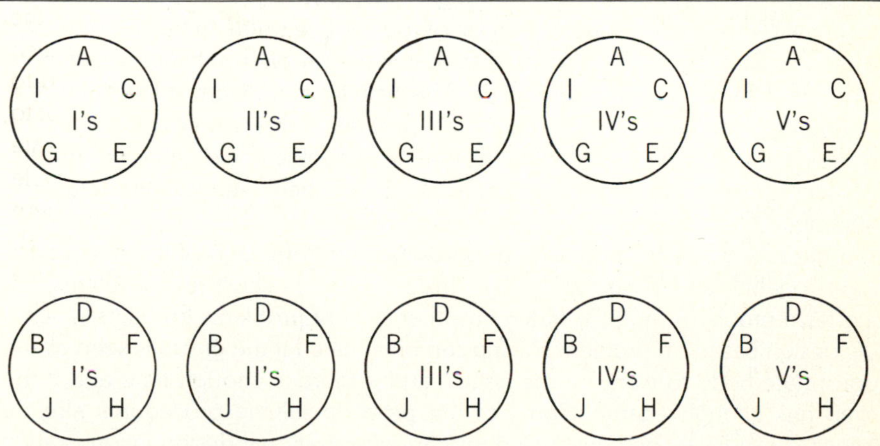

FIGURE 5.6. Workshop Seating Plan

Similarly, all those having cards with Roman numeral II and letters A, C, E, G and I meet in a group, and so forth, until ten groups are formed.

The purpose of these ten small group meetings is to share statements of "truth." The individuals within each group are not to suppose their "statements of truth," but rather are to determine which statements among the group seem to represent the real attitudes and feelings of the organization. Each group of five has approximately thirty minutes to agree on the statements it believes should be presented to the whole group and to clarify them. At the end of thirty minutes the two Group I's merge, the two Group II's merge, and so forth, until five groups of ten people are left. Individuals again compare their statements. By now there should be a substantial amount of agreement between each of the merged groups. In cases in which statements have not been agreed upon, the merged group should confer as to whether or not the statements seem fair and accurate. They then have the opportunity to add or delete items they feel are inappropriate.

At the end of thirty minutes each of the five groups is asked to write its statements of truth in large letters on a piece of newsprint and to prepare a brief presentation (perhaps five minutes) that lends some interpretation to the statements. These statements should represent the consensus of each of the groups. After a lunch break, the total group of fifty individuals reconvenes; a representative from each group makes the presentation. Although most individuals are not surprised by the truths that are uncovered, an enormous amount of enthusiasm and energy is generated because of the degree of agreement behind each statement.

Approximately four hours have now transpired, and most of the truths the group has identified represent statements of problem conditions that need to be altered. Unless the group has time to enter into the actual problem phase, it must now decide on the next steps so that the identified problems existing with the truths are not lost and action can begin. One way to proceed is to randomly form new groups of five, distribute a list of four or five truths to each group, and let each group identify the next steps so that either problem solving, research, or some other form of action can occur. This activity is a diagnostic activity. It is premature to become too specific in the problem solving unless some of the questions in themselves offer solutions that most people could agree on. In such instances the groups can explore how some of these suggestions might be implemented.

One relatively easy step is for a representative from each of the five groups to get together and divide all of the "truths" into (1) short-run problems, (2) long-term problems, and (3) statements that are not problems but facts. Then a new design based on problem solving can be initiated if the group is seen as the appropriate body to work on the issues, and if there is enough time and if the group has enough energy. Some of the problem-solving procedures already discussed can easily be constructed into an organizational design incorporating the fifty participants. Or, the meeting can end with the various truths being turned over to a steering group that would deliver perceived problems into the hands of those who should be solving them and develop a structure and support system to make sure that some action is taken.

What makes this particular diagnostic design so successful is that people feel highly involved, and a natural process of consensus develops. Any statement of truth that survives small group discussions is an issue that needs to be dealt with. People like to be listened to and are relatively nondefensive in the process; when individuals do not have to worry about solutions, they tend to be very free and honest in the diagnostic process.

Case 5: Marathon—Personal Growth for Group Leaders

One of the most difficult designs for a facilitator involves training other professional "trainers"—individuals sophisticated in the ways of groups, in role plays, simulations, and other traditional group activities, including T-groups. Furthermore, many trainers or facilitators attending such a program will delude themselves into believing they are more skilled than they actually are merely because they have experienced a variety of group courses or programs. Worse yet is the reality that many trainers know very little about their own behavior because they are so busy observing the behavior of others. Thus, some years ago we instituted a small group facilitator's program to better meet the needs of this special population of individuals.

Background

The program for the facilitators consists of the following basic parts.

- *Phase I:* A forty-hour marathon experience focusing on training, critiquing of training methods, and personal growth.
- *Phase II:* The integration of personal understandings in relation to Indian lore and self-awareness.
- *Phase III:* The design of an external workshop with a small group of fellow interns.
- *Phase IV:* The implementation and critiquing of the external workshop design.
- *Phase V:* A two-day follow-up retreat eight-weeks later that focuses on learning of design, strategies of planned change, and personal growth.

The first phase begins early on a Monday morning with all the members having previously attended a two-hour orientation aimed at clarifying the goals and methods of the program and acting as a self-screening process. By clarifying the goals and methods of this only vaguely understood program, there is an opportunity for those reluctant to be in such activities to withdraw. People know what works for them or what they expect; such clarification reduces the potential for disappointment and may also allay potential psychological problems. The program is restricted to individuals with previous training experience in the field and a range of academic course work. Thus, the population is considered to be not only sophisticated in the use of new methods but also experienced in conducting a variety of groups.

The task for the trainer is to stimulate and challenge such a group, to minimize the usually wide variation in skill and experience levels, and to provide for the participants new and interesting experiences that represent the state of the art in "design" and in conducting such a group. For our purposes, we are going to explore two of the five phases and their designs.

The Design: Phase I, the Training Marathon

For a relatively short period of years during the late 1960s and early 1970s marathons (working in a group continuously for eighteen, twenty, or more hours) were in relative vogue in certain personal growth and therapeutic programs. They are still used but much more sparingly, particularly in some of the more intensive programs involving addiction therapy. The major problem with them is not in their lack of value to the educational process but in the heavy toll they extract from the group leader and in the major commitment they require on the part of the participants. Additionally, the impact of time is a stress factor, for people become increasingly tired and vulnerable and are apt to create incredibly volatile and unpredictable situations that may require great facilitator skill. Marathons are clearly not to be played with or taken lightly, but they do offer one avenue for learning that can be appropriate under certain circumstances. Given the nature of the "trainer population" of this particular intern program, the marathon has proved a most important vehicle for learning.

The goal of the program is to provide each of the participants (who number fourteen) with the opportunity to "design" in a focused but relatively unplanned training situation in which events change in a manner that reflects the changing needs of the group. Our belief is that the essence of effective training is in the ability to develop an effective series of events that will lead participants to a predetermined goal. However, what separates the truly effective trainers or facilitators from those who are less skilled is the ability of the individual to "redesign" on the spot, based on new information uncovered as the group develops. Turning the "opportunity of the moment" into an instantaneous learning vehicle can change an average learning experience into an extraordinary one. The trainer's task is to be constantly aware of the changing needs and rhythm of the group and to be able to create an appropriate "design intervention" that reflects these needs and allows the group to continue on its way toward its goals while still savoring the richness of the moment. The marathon provides an outstanding vehicle for facilitators in training to test such skills!

The group of fourteen interns, most of whom know very little about each other, creates a "new group" situation for the would-be trainer. Over the course of a forty-hour marathon—stopping only for meals—the group progresses through an incredible number of phases and developmental cycles. Our "design" calls for the fourteen participants to place their names in a hat just prior to the marathon. Two people's names are drawn from the hat. They actually act as co-facilitators who are responsible for the group for a period of two and a half hours. The goals of the group on a personal and professional level are itemized during the orientation session so that each potential facilitator will start out with the same base line of information.

The two individuals whose names are drawn for the initial session have fifteen minutes in which to design their two and a half hours. As the group progresses and other needs become apparent, the trainers are encouraged to introduce at appropriate times new activities that might meet the needs of the group. At the end of the two-and-a-half-hour session, the total group assesses the first two individuals' design and their leadership style based on their own feelings and observations as members. How the two leaders responded to pressure, how they adapted to necessary changes, how they influenced the group members, and how they satisfactorily met the momentary goals as well as the long-range goals of the group are explored in depth. This feedback session also provides useful information for the next two facilitators who will be drawn from the hat. Thus, by the end of three hours, two more names are drawn, and they are given ten to fifteen minutes to establish an overall design for the next two and a half hours. Again, the understanding is that flexibility is the rule and that the needs of the group are likely to change at some point during that period.

The design also opens another door of awareness for the novice trainers. That is, because they are also "participants" in an intensive personal growth experience, they become sensitized to the fears, concerns, and inhibitions often experienced by participants and sometimes insensitively ignored by trainers. In this situation the participants rarely allow themselves to be ignored.

At some point duirng the forty hours every conceivable issue that one can imagine will raise its head. Issues of authority, leadership style, intimacy, goals, roles, a fear of self-disclosure, boredom, fatigue, cliques, sexism, conflict over race or religion, confidentiality, and many others grab the group by the tail. How the group leaders sensitively diagnose these issues and allow the group to deal with them effectively becomes the essence of the training task. Also, as individuals cope with the stress and tension of the moment, the degree of freedom with which they capitalize on a particular situation often determines their degree of success or failure. Feedback relating both to personal and professional style takes on much greater significance in this setting than it would in many others. Thus, while we might never again face a group that is dealing heavily with sexism at an explicit level in the thirty-sixth hour of the marathon, the individuals will tend to act characteristically in their facilitator style, which may involve flirting with female participants or discounting what women say. This behavior is rarely lost to the group in its eventual critique. Finally, the marathon acts as a sort of "initiation rite," which eventually builds an incredibly supportive group with opportunity to risk both failure and success. The shared experience allows individuals to become increasingly less isolated and more a part of a real support system.

The Design: Phase II, the Integration of Learning Through Indian Folklore

Consultants in the field of training and organizational development who over the years have been able to tolerate the unpredictability of clients and the vagaries of economic reality, as well as the changing state of the art, are usually blessed with an ability to look at their world beyond the confines of the typical nine-to-five job. Several years ago I [*RN*] was bemused to discover that the American Plains Indians had integrated within their social life and philosophical beliefs a view of personal growth and development that makes many of our approaches seem "primitive" indeed. At the time I was searching for a "design" to help training interns integrate and eventually internalize some of the wide-ranging feedback they received during and after the marathon described in the previous case. The major questions we must ask during any sincere effort toward personal growth are how much experience can we actually handle at any one time and how can we focus the information we receive from that experience into some meaningful process of change? Often what is required is a new way of looking at ourselves and the issues that pervade our lives and keep us from being as effective as we might be. My own experience with Indian folklore, including the Indian medicine wheel, the sweat lodge, vision quests, the long dance, and the shield, had provided me with a new perspective on old thoughts, concerns, and patterns.

My original fear that my graduate students—many of them in their thirties and forties—would feel this approach to be too "hokey" was laid to rest the first time I had a group of them create their own shields.* The experience allowed the child, the dreamer, and the free person in all of them to be expressed in a symbolically visual manner that became incredibly meaningful to all of the participants.

As it has evolved, the design has two central themes. First is what might be called a "mini" vision quest; while not the full vision quest of the Indian, we use a modified version serving the same purpose. The second is the opportunity for individuals to build their own shields. Here we have a perfect example of how ideas that are a way of life for one people can be adapted to help others achieve personal insight in ways that might never be anticipated and might even be scoffed at by traditionalists. By drawing on the "Indian way" in some limited degree, I did not wish to cheapen or minimize its larger significance in the lives

---

*Creating a shield for an Indian was merely one of many cultural experiences designed to help individuals explore who they were, to identify their areas of limitation and strengths, and to look toward areas that needed development.

of the Indians themselves. Thus, having personally experienced a ninety-hour vision quest in the wilderness, deprived of water and food and open to the elements, I asked myself what possible benefit a three-hour experience would have for my students on full stomachs? Wrong again; just as the shields had an impact beyond my wildest dreams, the vision quest was also an unbelievably powerful experience.

The marathon described in the previous case ended sometime after midnight on Wednesday morning. Participants were told to go to bed and when they awoke, not to speak to anyone during breakfast or afterwards. This period was to be one of reflection and movement back to some state of harmony after the intensity of the marathon experience. After their late morning brunch, the group was told about the purpose of a vision quest for Indians and the value that it played in their lives. Some Indians believe that one must "work," even suffer, for a vision; it is through personal deprivation, prayer, and isolation from the distractions of the everyday world that the spirits might present them with a vision or a series of visions that may help them gain clarity in their lives and a better understanding of themselves. Nonreligious spiritualists will tell you that visions indeed occur and that they are usually in response to one's own need and readiness to draw from our own inner sources of personal experience or understanding. Intensity of need and circumstance may simply help the process along. Whatever the truth is, we sent our fourteen interns across field and wood to find themselves an isolated spot where nature was their only companion and where for three hours they could remain silently within themselves. For whatever reason, the twenty-degree weather proved to be no deterrent, and the individuals seemed to relish being by themselves.

On their return, they silently entered the large meeting room and sat quietly. They listened to an explanation of the meaning of the medicine wheel and the value the Plains Indians placed on the creation of a symbolic shield, which revealed for them their hopes and fears, their needed areas of growth as well as strengths, and of the significant parts of life to the individual. For the interns, the shield provided an opportunity to capture visually and emotionally the impact of the marathon and the vision quest, as well as the other issues (of power, friends, intimacy) critical to their lives. The shield enabled participants to organize these thoughts and feelings through the use of Indian symbols and those they created themselves. For many the shield offered a vehicle for permission to explore openly areas of personal challenge, fear, or concern in a manner that seemed rooted in the soul, in the mystical, while still being based on the bedrock of personal emotions. Like so much in training, the design simply provided the structure that allowed the means to the search (for each to be personally, deeply involved in very central core questions of their lives) and to eventually "own" what it was they wished to see (in answers that came to them or even new questions in a different configuration) and possibly work on.

Although we do not anticipate that many of our readers will be conducting a "marathon experience" or utilizing the concept of the shield or the vision quest in their design activities, our intent is to reveal how a creative perspective—one in which the trainers thoroughly believe in what they are doing and in its significance—can create a powerful and meaningful experience for the participants when on paper the "design" might appear outrageous or even absurd. The interns—that sophisticated, experienced assemblage of group leaders—made the following comments about the mini-vision quest and the shield-building activities:

> It was the first time in my life I had ever taken even ten minutes to look inside and organize my feelings and dreams.
>
> I had never experienced the living presence of nature or heard it speak to me.
>
> The shield and its symbolism forced me to express thoughts I had hidden for years.
>
> I spoke to the tree and it answered.
>
> The marathon, the vision quest, and the shield all blended together and out dropped this picture of a person whom I had hardly ever seen, but whom I really wanted to know better. I am no longer afraid to look.
>
> There were parts of me revealed today that I have never known before and that I need to know much better.

Again, the purpose of this design is to provide a focus and direction and, if desired, the impetus for change. The problem solving that the individuals just described was based on these unusual events and was guided from the heart as well as from the intellect. As a result this design stood a much better chance of being successful. Other aspects of the program, which we will not go into here, gave the participants—over the next three days—the opportunity to build solutions to problems they had identified and to create support for change they desired in an attempt to further explore their role as trainer and trainee.

Each of us has unique experiences from which we can draw the essence of creative and meaningful designs. We stop ourselves often by being unwilling to look beyond the tried and true. In some ways our own enthusiasm—the fun and excitement that we bring to a design—is what makes it work. As a result, training rarely becomes dull or boring. It will always remain challenging and interesting for both you and your participants.

Case 6: Permission to Be Open (Taking the Starch from the Starch)

Two hundred headmasters of prominent preparatory schools are sitting in rows waiting to be lectured to about the profundity of leadership, even though in their hearts most of them believe they are already effective leaders. The participants, representing schools from across the country, have gathered for the national convention of independent schools. This particular program is a five-hour one aimed at exploring leadership behavior and skills. Cautious, watchful, and conservative might characterize the participants as a group. How to invigorate, stimulate, and open the group to new experiences is the challenge for the workshop leader. So many times the success or failure of such a program depends on the initial intervention and the energy and interest generated in the first thirty minutes. What is required is a tightly designed series of high-involvement activities that will kindle the group and start it on its ways toward self-exploration. The group needs to be rewarded early and believe almost from the outset that what follows will warrant their valuable time. The leader needs to help the participants "put on hold" their pessimism and their attitude that very little will be gained from the experience. Actually, most participants bring a spark of hope that perhaps "this workshop will be different" and just possibly they will take something back from it that they can really use. It is this cry for application that needs immediate attention.

Background

One of the most difficult situations for a trainer occurs when the workshop population consists of a wide variety of individuals with differing backgrounds and experiences in education, not to mention expectations of the program itself. In fact, many of the individuals entering this particular workshop had come to the convention for "fun" and to reacquaint themselves with colleagues and friends. Others had come in search of new employment opportunities. Of those remaining, perhaps a few had actually come with the goal of increasing their understanding of leadership and taking home some new skills.

As the facilitator of this five-hour program, I [*RN*] developed a list of assumptions about the participants that seemed to hold true regardless of age and experience. The initial design and the subsequent activities of the workshop were based on these assumptions. Thus, from past experience and from working extensively with similar populations, I could make the following observation with relatively little doubt:

Heads of schools and department chairpersons quite often find themselves isolated from sources of reliable "feedback" concerning their own leadership behaviors and their personal impact on those they wish to influence. Few of these individuals have had the opportunity for formal training in management or leadership. Many are incredibly busy with a variety of responsibilities and have little or no time to undertake any systematic "reeducation." They often find themselves in a "crises-reactive" mode of behavior that helps to dictate the kinds of leadership strategies available to them. The kinds of skills that made them effective teachers are not necessarily the ones that will make them effective administrators within the school environment.

Because most of these assumptions have been validated by me over time, I was also able to assume that many of the individuals who would be participating in the program would be "thirsty" for information about their own leadership effectiveness and how they "in fact" affect those reporting to them. Furthermore, although the group appeared to be rather stiff and a bit "starchy," I suspected that many were eager to push away conventions and stereotypes; given the slightest permission they would participate with zest in slightly unorthodox and even risky activities. Many were bored by the traditional lecture format followed for years at this particular convention. While they expected to be "talked to," they were hoping for a different level of involvement.

The Design

After a few lighthearted, introductory comments, the participants are warned not to expect a conventional workshop. They are told that leadership can only be studied by looking at one's leadership style. The workshop begins with a brief structured perception activity. A variety of designs would be appropriate here with the object being to help participants "see" that their vision and their interpretation of reality can be distorted by an enormous number of variables, ranging from emotional, structural, and physical variables, and based on their education or experience. While most of these individuals will have covered this territory previously in some other workshop or program, this twenty- to thirty-minute introductory perception activity has never failed but to generate a slight bit of "humility" as people see the degree to which they actually don't see. (See R. Napier and M. Gershenfeld, *Groups: Theory and Experience* [Boston, Mass.: Houghton Mifflin, 1981].) It also acts as a platform on which the following activity can be built.

The participants are told that what they are going to experience has over the years proved to be the most valuable and interesting of all aspects of the workshop. As a facilitator I have been able to establish my credibility through past successes and set a positive and supportive climate of expectation and anticipation. The participants are then asked to group themselves into clusters of three in which they have never met or talked with one another. They are requested to move quickly into these triads and not to talk among themselves. After a few moments of chaos, the groups form and can be given the following directions:

While we would all like to believe what many of us say—that we hold judgments about other people until we get to know them—the fact is that people are incredibly quick to judge others based on the most limited information and personal observations. Levels of trust, suspicion, and interest can be created as a result of a glance, a few words or a particular behavior, or by a person's dress, affectations, or posture. What most of us don't realize is exactly how much of ourselves we "give away" without ever saying a word. People absorb an incredible amount of information based on the "readout" of their initial observation of us and proceed to make judgments that can affect our relationship with them. The only problem is that rarely, if ever, are we told what this initial impact is and what people are actually seeing as we present ourselves for the first time. Most leaders almost continually find themselves in situations in which they are standing before "new groups" of individuals whom they need to impress, educate, or solicit support from. Unless they make a good impression and are aware of what it is about them that "turns people on" or "turns people off," they will be at a tremendous disadvantage in meeting their desired goals. Obviously, new acquaintances rarely have the opportunity, interest, or courage to be open with you about the impact you are having on them. But, that they have strong reactions is not to be doubted. Today, we are going to have an opportunity to test our impact and to explore how the immediate presentation of ourselves can influence the thoughts and reactions of others.

At this point a large sheet of newsprint that has a series of categories listed in bold print is unfolded (Figure 5.7).

Type of education
Type of student (high achiever, underachiever, bored, challenged, competitive)
Your dominant or most influential parent
The number of brothers or sisters and your position among them
Your religion and the degree to which it influenced your life
The type of music you most enjoy
The extracurricular activities in which you find greatest pleasure
The kind of house in which you were raised
The kind of home in which you currently live
Were you raised in the country, city, or suburbs?
Are you a person of many friends or a few close ones?
Are you an outdoor person?
Do you enjoy sports?—if so, what kind?
What type of leader are you?
Are you organized or not?
How do you handle conflict?
How do you handle anger?
What is your best quality as a leader?
What keeps you from being as effective a leader as you might?

FIGURE 5.7. Critical Areas for Understanding a Person

The following instructions are given:

The categories listed on the newsprint represent facts about each of us to which we all can relate. As I read down the list you will see that each item is something that we have experienced or do experience in our lives in a way that is peculiar to us. The object of this design is for each of the people in your group of three to answer the statements or to make bold guesses as to how you and the other individuals in your cluster relate to each of the categories. Thus, without talking or even introducing yourselves, I am going to ask you to look at each of the other two people in your group and to respond to each of the categories for each of them. For example, if I'm in your group, I may look at you and imagine that based on dress, posture, jewelry, and any other information I can gain from observing you that you are the oldest of four sisters and brothers (three brothers and a sister) and had a dominant father, that you were raised in the country and had a public school education, and that you enjoy sedentary sports rather than participative ones. I may imagine that you handle conflict through avoidance and that you are quite religious or spiritual in your life. I may believe that you enjoy the classics and that you have a few solitary but good friends.

The point is that by using only the information I have and my fantasy, I am to paint a thumbnail sketch of you that I will eventually share with you. Everybody will be doing the same thing. Obviously, there will be guessing based on minimum data. Our hope is that you will paint the best picture possible. Remember, the worst thing that can happen is that we are wrong. Since two of us will be painting the picture of each other person in the group, it will be most interesting to find the areas of similarity and difference in our descriptions.

One thing more; although this activity should be a great deal of fun, it should not necessarily be "comfortable." We are here to learn about leadership, and this is simply one source of important information that we rarely if ever have the opportunity to hear. So, now take out a piece of paper and for the next ten or fifteen minutes quietly observe the other two people in your group and paint your thumbnail sketches of them. At that time and before talking to anyone I will be back with one more set of instructions. Enjoy yourselves.

Almost without exception most individuals will begin the task with a mixture of trepidation and enthusiasm. After fifteen minutes or when most of the individuals appear to have completed their thumbnail sketches on their partners, the following set of directions is given.

I would now like each individual in the groups of three, one at a time, to take a walk around the room. For those who felt self-conscious when the two people in your group observed you, this should really do the trick. But, how we walk or present ourselves as we move about can often tell a lot about ourselves. Thus, the other two people in your group should observe how you walk and dig out any other information they can as they see you move around the room. This information can be added to what you have already gathered in your thumbnail sketches. You may find that you have different opinions, simply by watching the individual walk. Please watch only those in your group because this will be your only opportunity to observe them. Whoever would like to go first may now begin to walk around the room.

After everyone has returned to his or her seat and finished taking notes, the leader continues:

Now, the way we are going to make this activity work for you is to have two of the people in each group carry on a conversation about the third person as if that individual were not there. Rather than recite your categories as a part of a "laundry list," you will carry on a discussion with your partner about the third individual. Talk about how you view the person's childhood, family, interests, education, and whatever else has been incorporated in your observations. When giving the information, do not hesitate to explain why you see what you see, since the more complete the picture, the better for the individual who is listening. And, for you the lucky listener, please do just that—listen. If you need to jot a note or two for a question later, do so but do not interrupt as the two proceed to describe you. Listen to the possible differences or similarities. At the end of their discussion, which should take perhaps seven or eight minutes, you will have the opportunity to provide them with "truths" about yourself that support or reject the conclusions that they have reached from their brief observations and fantasies.

Remember, the importance of this activity is to help you find out what it is that people actually see and the impact you are having. In some ways the observers are providing you with a "gift" of insight. Even if they are "wrong," they are not really wrong—that is, it is important for you to understand the image you are projecting and why. Whether you wish to do anything about what you hear—are you flattered or disappointed?—depends entirely on you. Now enjoy yourselves, and we will see you in about twenty to thirty minutes. Please be very careful to hold yourselves to a total of ten (or fifteen) minutes per person or you will find that one individual will be shortchanged.

After approximately thirty to forty-five minutes, the leader can move quickly around the room and ask individuals to share one thing they have learned about the activity that they can take with them from the workshop. The incredible array of information that will be forthcoming will in itself suggest the value of the activity. In addition, the leader can ask how many participants found they were described accurately at a rate of at least 80 percent by their two partners. Interestingly, regardless of the group of people who involve themselves in this activity, rarely do less than 80 percent of those participating find their data less than 80 percent accurate. For whatever reason, most individuals have an incredible ability to see through us and to know who we really are from only a brief moment's observation. The shock is that we spend so much of our lives "hiding" or "acting" when people see through it all anyway.

Summary

This activity, in its use at the start of a five-hour workshop on leadership, follows some of the basic rules for effective design. That is, it is unexpected and disorienting, yet challenging and highly involving. It requires a shared risk by everyone in the room, and thus provides sort of an implicit permission for risk taking to occur. The situation is a "no lose" one in that if people describe you accurately, you will be amazed; if they describe you in a manner that is totally off target, you will have been given important food for thought as to the impression you really desire to make on other people. The process, furthermore, is data based; for example, it can be used in a variety of situations that might facilitate team building in a rapid and interesting fashion. Most of all, the activity is useful and fun. People tend to laugh uproariously as they hear about themselves—usually with incredible accuracy. Done well, this activity can have a group of two hundred people eating out of your hand and willing to be increasingly open and candid in their exploration of leadership issues during the remainder of the workshop.

Case 7: Microteaching—One Means of Influencing Specific Behavior Change

Whether they be teachers, sales personnel, speech makers, or group leaders of a hundred varieties, people who impose their style and personalities on those they work with should be required to receive information back concerning their own behavior. The idea of feedback first came into vogue back in the early 1950s with T-groups, encounter groups, and a variety of approaches to personal growth and development. The concept of microteaching was born out of the need for other methods to learn about our behavior and its impact on others. What has evolved is a "classic" design in which videotaping can be used as a vehicle for exploring alternate forms of behavior. This particular approach incorporates many of the characteristics of effective feedback, such as providing specific and immediate data that are descriptive in nature and open to possible change. Furthermore, the information received is verifiable from more than a single source, thus increasing the possibility for objectivity. The design has a potential for discovering discrepancies between perception of one's own behavior and the perception of that behavior by others.

Background

Ten sales managers have come together to accomplish two tasks: to assess their own styles of selling and to develop training techniques for their subordinates. Since they are not "trainers," it is crucial that any design they experience must be easily replicated in their back-home situation without the necessity of hiring outside personnel. Additionally, the benefits to them in their work need to be direct and relatively immediate.

The Design

As a group the managers define the most crucial behavioral criteria for effective selling.* Eight observable criteria are agreed upon in a thirty-minute session. These include such factors as direct eye contact, respect and good manners, knowledge of and belief in the product, personal interest in the individual, active listening skills, and a willingness to identify the benefits for the buyer. In addition, the participants are asked to develop four more criteria for themselves. They are then asked to rate themselves on each of the criteria, indicating the four that need the most improvement. Note that by doing this everyone in the room is given permission to be less than perfect as they focus on some of their own inadequacies. This in itself is a very "freeing" aspect of such a design.

The next step is for each individual to be given thirty minutes alone to develop a five-minute sales presentation to be delivered to the remaining nine people. At the end of the five-minute presentation, each person is asked to rate the individual presenter, based on the predetermined criteria. Similarly, the presenter is also asked to rate himself or herself based on his or her performance during the presentation itself. In addition, the presenter and the other managers are asked to name the two greatest strengths they each perceived in the sales presentation and two factors that might have limited the presenter's effectiveness in making the sale. Again, knowing that everyone is going to receive the same kind of information greatly diminishes the threat of being imperfect.

A brief discussion and clarification of some of the issues raised follows, although the intent of this part of the program is simply to explicate some areas of strengths and limitations. After the ten managers all have the opportunity to make a sales presentation and to receive both written and verbal feedback, they are requested to prepare a new presentation, making specific content and behavioral changes to improve their sales performance. Once more each individual addresses the group with a revised sales presentation, and once again each manager receives both written and verbal feedback from the others. On this second round, however, considerable focus is placed on the style and content that actually changed and how these changes either improved or detracted from the sales presentation itself. Discovering discrepancies between what the individual was trying to do and how the presentation is actually received is a powerful vehicle for learning. Obviously, if videotape is used, each presenter not only receives individual feedback from the group but also observes exactly what was seen and the impact it was having. By taping the second presentation, the difference created by the new behavior or new variables that affected the presentation and that had not been present originally can be seen.

---

*The same design can be utilized with selling being replaced by criteria for effective teaching, or counseling, or communicating. In this situation "selling" is the centerpoint for discussion and observation.

The aspects of this microteaching design that seem particularly beneficial include the following:

1. The participants can establish their own criteria for effective selling as a group and then personalize it with some of their own ideas. The idea is to reduce defensiveness and increase ownership of the total process.
2. The data gathered in the initial assessment of oneself prior to the first presentation gives each individual a "base line" of data from which comparisons can be made based on information received after both the first and the second presentation.
3. The discrepancy data can be a stimulus for an effective change and result from one's own perception or that of others, as well as from the video playback.
4. The feedback provided in the activity is descriptive, specific, and immediate.
5. The participants have an opportunity to practice their initial presentation and later to revise it in the hope of improving their performance. Again, this is based on data — not imagination.
6. Because ten individuals make presentations—not once but twice—each participant has the opportunity to come in contact with excellent examples of style and technique developed by other peers that can enhance his or her own repertoire of sales behaviors.

The entire design represents a highly intensive approach to the exploration of behavioral change based on data and geared to a person's "bread and butter," which makes the motivation to learn high indeed.

Case 8: A Life-Planning Module—A Pathway from the Intellect to the Emotions

Individuals are basically very self-protective. Within groups they tend to avoid conflict, intimacy, and self-disclosure. They often only play with intellectual ideas and suppress exploration of personal fears and emotions. In "family" groups (individuals with frequent contact such as experienced in the home, the office, a team, etc.), people often avoid such aspects of personal group life in order to minimize tension and stress they fear will not be resolved. In fact, many are concerned that opening issues will only increase the tensions. Thus, avoidance reduces individual vulnerability among the people we respect, love, or need, and that approach becomes a style. We avoid making decisions or plans until the last minute or on a pragmatic rather than desired basis.

Interestingly, groups of strangers often find it easier to deal with emotional issues since there is less to lose. But, at the same time, many people in a new situation are inclined to put their "best foot forward" and to appear strong, competent, and invulnerable. Trainers obviously need methods for breaking through these natural resistances and for giving individuals "permission" to deal with issues they normally would avoid because of their fear of appearing weak or inadequate.

Background

Thirty individuals have come together at a retreat center for two and a half days of a "life-planning workshop." Basically, they desire to explore where they are in their lives, where they think they might like to go, and what changes they will have to make to get there. While some come with a deep emotional commitment to explore their situations honestly, most approach the task from a safe, rather cognitive and rational perspective, with their intellects acting as buffers to their emotions. Because most personal growth and change is stimulated out of a "gut-level emotional need" rather than from neatly laid out intellectual ideas, these participants must be drawn rapidly into the emotions of the heart without embarrassing them or making them feel that their privacy has been violated.

The Design

Life-planning workshops are individually focused within a group context mostly because it is more cost effective and because others may have greater objectivity toward us as we move to a point of change. Thus, there is no need to create a cohesive community even though this often occurs as a result of the mutually shared intensive experiences that occur within small clusters and groups found in the workshop. Actually the two and a half days represent a series of developmental and closely related designs that are intended to explore values, hopes, dreams, and realities, which together form a picture of some depth that can allow individuals to gain perspective, clarity, and perhaps some new choices at a critical time in their lives.

At a point relatively early in the workshop and after the formulation of ongoing support groups of three people, the following design occurs. Each individual is given a large sheet of newsprint (approximately twenty-seven inches by thirty-six inches), along with several different-colored magic markers. The participants are instructed to go off by themselves for an hour to develop a three-part "time line" of their lives. The time line is to extend from the earliest point of remembrance to a point five years in the future. There are to be three distinct parts of the time line which can be depicted any way that each individual would like as long as it spans a spectrum of his or her entire life. One part, or "line," of the time line will record events that directly influenced the social and interpersonal aspects of each individual's life—for example, moving to a different house, the loss of childhood friends, the homesickness experienced in summer camps, the void of no friends during adolescence, or breaking off an engagement. There may be five, ten, or even fifteen of these events that we distinctly remember as having had a profound impact on our adjustments at any particular time. The second line should depict areas of achievement over the span of the individual's life. These are events or situations that surrounded experiences of major success or failure; for example, graduating from college may have been a major success, but a first job might have been a disaster. They are identified in relation to how each achievement influenced other aspects of our lives. In plotting these lines the person becomes aware of major events and critical incidents. Later, for each critical point on the relationship or achievement line, the individual should be ready to share the nature of the event and its impact beyond the moment of time. Finally, a third dimension of the time line should focus on five to ten critical events that do not fall neatly into either the achievement or relationship categories but that somehow had a profound effect on the individual. These are particular experiences that somehow helped an individual turn a corner, perhaps drew the person into a depression, or sent the person into a period of good feeling or prosperity. An inheritance, the death of a close friend, a spiritual experience, a sudden insight, or any of a thousand events might find their way into this particular category. The events must be crucial and dramatic in terms influencing the course of the individual's life.

Because the past is so personal, there is very little difficulty being involved. Also, because the task begins at the cognitive or memory stage, it is an adventure that few would refuse to take. Thus, although the building of the time line itself is not necessarily a happy experience, it tends to be one that is interesting and brings about the involvement of almost all the participants. After an hour, the participants are asked to report back to their small support groups with whom they now have some relationship and understanding based on other activities. One individual in each group is asked to share his or her time line by taking the other members of the group through it and explaining in some detail each point that affected his or her life. The other group members are to ask explicit and pointed questions to help the group understand exactly the impact of each event along the time line. The goal is to sketch as complete a picture as possible of the individual in areas that the person has chosen to look at. The time line suddenly becomes a road map into each peson's life and emotions as particular events begin to be verbalized. A natural unlocking of emotions occurs as individuals begin to feel the impact of the events—much more so than during the initial drawing of the lines themselves. Patterns and insights begin to evolve that have either been lost or never perceived. During the course of perhaps thirty or forty minutes (although an hour or more is not too long), a strong sense of each person emerges as the particular life direction unfolds along with patterns and rhythms peculiar to each. Thus, again, what starts out to be a rather simple but interesting task of "memory sharing" becomes a vehicle for exploring fears, concerns, and blockages to one's own growth and development as well as aspects of achievement and success that may provide the key to future progress and development. This design inevitably receives high marks from participants and becomes a source of reference for many of them as they move through the life-planning process.

Case 9: Developing Family Communication Skills

Parents and their children during adolescent years are separated by much more than age. Because they grew up in different environments, there are value differences, differences in personal histories and expectations, and literally a thousand other factors that affect existing relationships and result in communication barriers. Helping a "complex" family system, perhaps consisting of two parents and two children, overcome the expected sources of tension and poor communication and open the doors to more effective relationships is a challenge for any trainer. The trick is to reduce the need of individual members to defend themselves and to justify their previous behaviors while at the same time minimizing feelings of guilt, inadequacy, or blaming that might occur.

The first step is to provide a form of nondefensive listening. Then what can and should be changed should be diagnosed, and the problem-solving structure to facilitate that change provided. Building some kind of support system to ensure that something will actually result from their efforts is a critical part of this process. Without question, family workshops provide a true test for creative design.

Background

Eight families of three or four members each have come together for two days of listening, exploring ideas, and problem solving. They have come voluntarily either because they desire a remedy for a current problem within their family or are attempting to prevent a potential problem from occurring.

The Design

Placing blame is the most predictable outcome of pain within a family. Blended with self-justification or self-righteousness, blame can act to cut the heart out of the desire of family members to explore their relationships. This particular design works for the following reasons:

1. It is grounded on strengths that require no justification.
2. Past behaviors do not have to be explained away.
3. Participation brings about high involvement of both parents and children.
4. Because problems are shared with other families, each family's sense of isolation or belief that "we are the only ones who are feeling stupid, inadequate, or without helpful alternatives" is reduced.
5. Parents of children act as consultants with other families and are not placed in irrational or adversarial roles.
6. Eventually, parents and children share new ideas, many of which have been tried successfully in other family situations.

The design actually reflects a developmental process that incorporates a variety of designs—each related to the last. The workshop itself takes place on a Friday and Saturday in a classroom setting. On both days the program goes from nine until noon and from one until four in the afternoon, with an hour for a box lunch on each of those days. A three-hour follow-up is planned for one month later in one of the family's homes. This aspect of the design will not be discussed at this time.

Step 1. An invaluable and rather simple method for beginning a workshop in which the focus is on problem solving is to have the participants share their expectations and perhaps their concerns. One can assume that within any group of thirty-six parents and adolescents there will be plenty of ambivalence, tension, and anxiety at the outset. Thus, one way to begin is to have parents and children form into pairs with persons other than their own family members. These pairs are asked to take about ten minutes to discuss three questions and then to present their ideas and answers to the large group. The first question is, What do you want to take away with you after two days in this workshop in terms of feelings, skills, or perhaps attitudes? The participants are encouraged to be as specific as possible so that everyone, including the trainers, can reach a clear understanding of what exactly the people want. This information can be used later as a means of legitimizing certain activities that might otherwise appear threatening to the participants. The second question is, Is there anything you would not like to have in the workshop, either in terms of method or outcome? By legitimizing fears and concerns, this question also establishes a norm of openness among the participants toward the trainers and toward the workshop in general. The third question is, What are two or three factors that might prevent the workshop from being as successful as it might be? These factors might include issues of leadership, age differences, value barriers, or attitudes that might block the outcomes people previously mentioned.

After a period of about ten minutes, these ideas—a question at a time—are solicited from the participants and jotted down on large pieces of newsprint in the front of the room. The trainers now have the opportunity to discuss the nature of the workshop around the issues that the participants themselves raised, thus establishing from the outset what they perceive as possible or not possible given the design they have in mind. The goal is not artificially to squeeze the desires of the participants into the preconceived notions of the trainers, but rather to clarify expectations and, if possible, to adjust the workshop to reflect the particular needs of the group, which the initial design had not considered. Often the success of a workshop can begin with the honest clarification of expectations and the establishment of a climate of straight talk and open communication from the outset. This twenty-minute period of exploration also allows the trainers to become known to the participants and to place the workshop in a perspective of both seriousness and humor, each of which is essential if the program is to be successful.

Step 2. A workshop with such a diverse population needs from the beginning what we might call in the trade a "hooker." There needs to be an activity that will draw all the population into intense participation almost immediately and where age and background make very little difference to the success of the activity itself. One activity we have found quite successful in this kind of workshop is the one we describe as *Classic Design No. 6*. We begin by breaking the group into clusters of two parents and two children, in which the individuals are all unfamiliar to each other. Such an activity instantly establishes that if the program is to be successful, the participants must be willing both to risk and to listen, regardless of age or background. In addition to being a "hooker," this activity is also one that will tend to equalize participation. If the morning part of the workshop is to last three hours and the introductory-expectation part thirty minutes, then this part of the program could last a full hour and forty-five minutes. People would thus have plenty of time to consider each member of their small group carefully and to take the time necessary to feed the information back and discuss it. It also allows thirty minutes toward the end of the morning for people to share with the large group what they learned from the experience and what they might be able to take back to their own families. Obviously, such a wrap-up must be carefully designed so that all participants have an opportunity to discuss what they learned, perhaps in the safety of new clusters of three or four, before allowing those who would like to share some of their ideas to address the whole group.

Whatever design is used in the initial two or three hours of such a workshop, it must be capable of performing the following functions:

1. Equalize participation.
2. Be stimulating—interesting and hopefully fun.
3. Help establish clear norms of open communication, honesty, and feedback.
4. Provide the participants with an early success experience.
5. Help establish behavior that is uncommon in most families and yet may be critical to the success of good problem solving and communication.

Step 3. Having returned from lunch, the children and parents are again grouped in clusters of four, with no two people from the same family. The members of each cluster are asked to write down on a piece of paper two or three of the most positive traditions or activities that they do as a family (or once did). These are activities that they have most enjoyed and think other families might benefit from doing; they could include a certain kind of meal, a way of communication, certain kinds of games or activities, or even special events that have occurred only once but that they wish could happen again. Each person is asked to be as specific as possible in identifying exactly what it was about the activity, event, or tradition that was most crucial to its success and might be adopted by other families. When giving directions for this kind of "show and tell" experience, make it clear that ideas that are to be shared must be quite specific, simple in their transferability to another family, and capable in some way of making the family more of a family. The ideas can be simple or complex.

After five or ten minutes, individuals are asked to share, one at a time, the ideas they wrote down. Each individual gives a single idea, waits for questions to be asked for clarification, and participates in a brief discussion of the idea. Then the next person continues in the same fashion with a new idea. In this way everyone is encouraged to contribute, and full participation becomes the expectation. In addition, this method prevents a particularly vocal person from taking over or a shy individual from hiding behind the ideas of others. This brief design legitimizes full participation and is built on the belief that even families "in trouble" have developed over the years useful experiences that can be shared and valued by others. With only five to ten minutes to delve into their personal family histories, each group of four will generate from nine to twelve ideas, and the total group often generates somewhere in the neighborhood of eighty to one hundred ideas.

After about thirty minutes of sharing, each cluster of four is asked to select three or four ideas that seem the most unique but, at the same time, most easily transferred to other families. The groups are given twenty minutes to decide on these "best ideas" and to modify them in any way that might make them more easily adaptable by another family. Again, specificity and transferability are stressed. At the end of fifteen or twenty minutes, each cluster of four is directed to meet with another cluster and to share with those four people the ideas that have been developed. Thus, from an initial group of twenty-four ideas that would have been generated by two clusters, only the best six or seven ideas are shared with this new group of eight. The new groups are not to argue or discredit any of the ideas but rather are to ask questions of clarification to make sure that each of the ideas is clearly understood. People are encouraged to take notes since they will be expected to share these ideas with their own families before the end of the afternoon.

Quite often there will be some similarity among one, two, or perhaps three of the ideas shared between the two merged clusters. This leads to a reinforcing and strengthening of some of the ideas. At the end of about twenty minutes of sharing, individuals are asked to return to their own families. Even though a family member or two may have been together in the groups of eight, usually half of the family members will have been in different groups of eight. Thus, typically, a family of four will have received at least twelve ideas for improving family life. These ideas have been screened as being the most interesting, unique, and transferable. The process gives credibility to the various ideas and reduces the need for any individual family member to "sell" an idea as being worthwhile, for adults and parents have already conceded that the idea is worthwhile or it would never have reached this point. Families are asked to share the ideas they have heard and to come to some agreement over three they believe might add to a positive family atmosphere within their own family. For every idea they choose, each family is asked to make a contract indicating when the idea will be attempted, what must be done to make it successful, and, finally, how to determine whether the idea has been successful and should in some way be continued. This part of the design usually takes somewhere between thirty and forty minutes to complete.

The total design for the afternoon session will take about two hours. We feel its value lies in the following factors:

1. The process evolves so that all participants have the opportunity to contribute and in some way be experts.
2. The methods of selecting the "best" idea are created without minimizing the efforts of any individual.
3. An atmosphere of listening and creativity is encouraged.
4. Each step in the design allows for a successful experience to develop.
5. Each person is stimulated by new ideas and new ways of thinking about his or her own family without having to be defensive or to justify particular actions.
6. Individual families are finally challenged to use some of the "good ideas" that have been developed by other families; by this time these ideas do not seem as strained or radical. Being forced to come to agreement on three of these "good ideas" can be a positive and rewarding experience for family members who so often do not listen or make constructive decisions about their own process of living together.

Up to this point the key to the entire design has been not to probe into the problems of each family, but rather to allow a positive and rewarding experience to occur so that when problems are looked at, there will be less resistance. Also, hearing ideas from other parents and children tends to enable people to listen more positively to the ideas of their own parents or children, who in the past have been perceived in a more adversarial role. Before going on, people will need a ten-minute break.

Step 4. After the break the thirty-two participants are told that having generated a wide variety of ideas for helping families have more fun or work better together, they will now take a serious look at the factors that actually block families from being as effective as they might be in living together. The large group is again broken into clusters of four, but this time two of the four-person clusters will be made up of children, two of parents only, and four, a mixture of parents and children. Again, family members are requested to find their way into separate groups as much as possible. A large piece of newsprint and a magic marker are given to each cluster. Then the following directions are given:

You will have a total of eight minutes to generate a list of at least fifteen blockages to family cohesion and harmony. These are blockages that occur frequently and tend to disrupt the positive nature of family life. The only ground rule in identifying these blockages is that they should not be tied into a single individual's neurotic or disturbed behavior that is out of the control of the others (drinking, carousing, etc.). Obviously, you have a wide avenue of choices. I might suggest that while listing your fifteen or twenty blockages in the allowed period of eight minutes that you do not take any time to discuss the various ideas; you will be given time for this later. Simply have one person record and write down as many ideas as you can as fast as you can. Again, save your talk until later.

During the eight minutes the facilitator actively encourages, coaxes, cajoles, and humors the various groups into producing as many blockages as they can using the pressure of time as a prod to their own idea development. At the end of eight minutes the clusters are told that they will have fifteen minutes to come up with the four blockages that seem to be common to most families and that seem to be most correctible or changeable. The clusters are encouraged to be as specific as possible in their identification of these four blockages. For example, "communications" is not specific enough. Finally, the four blockages that each cluster eventually chooses should in fact represent and be supported by all members of that cluster. Half sheets of newsprint are handed to the clusters, and they are told that the fifteen-minute deadline will be enforced.

At the end of fifteen minutes (give or take perhaps five minutes depending on how well the groups are doing), a new set of instructions is given:

We are now going to ask the two "children" groups, the two "parent" groups, and the two pairs of mixed groups to join together for a period of twenty minutes or so. During this time you will share the four blockages of your cluster, listen to those of the other cluster, and as a group of eight choose four that would be the most important to solve if families are to be more effective together. Again, specifying the exact nature of the problem or blockage is critical, for it should be one that is present in a wide variety of families. At the end of twenty minutes each group of eight can support the three or four blockages that it is going to share with the total group of thirty-two.

At the end of twenty or thirty minutes, depending on how successful the groups are in completing the task, the total group reconvenes, and each group of eight shares its four blockages with the total group. The facilitator stands in front at an easel with newsprint and solicits one blockage at a time from each of the groups, thus moving around the room from group to group until as many ideas or blockages—without any repetitions—are written on the newsprint. Instead of sixteen ideas, there will tend to be perhaps, eight, nine, or ten. The overlapping of ideas among the groups of very different constituents will lend a certain credibility to the process and make clear the universality of many of the issues.

Once the issues are on the newsprint, the participants are told that they will all have an opportunity to vote on the issues they believe to be most critical—those that the group will be problem solving the next day. Each person is allowed ten points when voting for the issues that have been placed on the newsprint. Thus, an individual could place all ten points on a single issue and have no votes left for anything else; or participants might place one or two points on a variety of issues, thus spreading their influence but weakening their ability to impact the final selection. Again, the group is told that the next day's activities will focus on the problem solving and will be based on the blockages most favored by the total group. A few minutes is allowed for participants to think about how they are going to distribute their ten points and also to ask clarification questions concerning any of the issues on the newsprint. The vote is then taken. It adds a powerful ending to a day that has been keyed to collaboration and idea development. It allows the group a clear understanding of what is to occur the following day, the impact being that tomorrow's agenda will be the result of its own deliberations and concerns.

Step 5. Usually three or four, at the most five, of the blockages gain the predominant number of points. Also, any of the issues that are among the top vote-getters are acceptable to almost everyone present. Between the sessions the facilitator must take each issue and make sure that it is specific, understandable, and stated in a manner suggesting the possibility of change.

As a bridging activity the following morning, the group is asked to sit in a large circle. The participants are asked to think for a moment about something positive that they were able to take away from the previous day's workshop that gave them some reason for hope in terms of their own families or what they might do to make their family situations better. This sort of "whip" activity should be done quickly by moving around the circle and accepting only brief statements from each individual. The result is a very positive experience; at the same time, it allows a legitimate review of much of what happened the previous day.

This warm-up or transition activity is followed directly by the problem-solving session that had been announced the previous day. A list of the top four blockages or problems affecting a family is displayed, and the group is told that the major part of the day will be spent developing a variety of clear alternatives or actions to help alleviate these blockages. Again, note that presenting the blockages this way reduces the need for families to feel embarrassed or inadequate for having the problems and legitimizes people's having to look for solutions to alleviate them. Thus, we immediately remove some of the greatest blockages to change—the needs for self-justification, denial, rationalization, and an unwillingness to "own" the problem. It is fairly safe to assume that perhaps three, or even four, of the blockages are undoubtedly the issues that face most of the families present. The participants are then involved in a rather tried and true approach to problem solving, which again encourages the generation of a variety of ideas that will allow the group to see new alternatives and possibilities for change within their own families.

The participants are once again asked to form groups of four—two parents and two children in each group. Individuals are encouraged to work with people they have not worked with previously and to avoid parents or children from their own families. The four blockages or problem conditions that were identified earlier are distributed among the eight groups so that two groups have the same problem. Each group is given five to ten minutes to clarify the problem and to make certain that the group agrees on what the problem condition is so that everyone is starting from the same point.

The second step is for each group to answer two questions that will form the diagnostic base upon which the problem will eventually be solved. The first question is what resistances have prevented the present situation from being altered or have kept change from occurring in the past. The second critical and closely related question is what actual benefits are to be gained from not changing the present situation, for not improving the condition within the family. Clearly, without understanding the resistances or blocks to change and without understanding what real benefits there are to not changing, developing workable strategies for improving the situation will be almost impossible. One suggestion is that each group make a list of such resistances and benefits without much discussion except for clarification. The idea is for participants to gain a clear view of exactly why the problem tends to be so difficult to change within a family context. In our experience the "benefits" question produces dramatic understanding and places the problem solving in a perspective of seriousness, for clearly if there were no real benefits to not changing, the problem would have been resolved much earlier. For example, the explosive use of anger by one or more people within a family has the clear benefit of intimidating and forcing the other member or members into acquiescing. The angry party wins each time, so why stop? Similarly, failure to define limits of authority can give parents almost unlimited power to demand what they would like and makes the children almost totally dependent on the whims and arbitrary decisions of the parents. On the other hand, children who continually are unwilling to abide by certain rules or who flaunt time expectations have the real benefit of paying parents back and exercising their own power and control. The point is that the most effective problem solving demands that both parties give up some of the benefits they have previously reaped from the old system.

Once a list of the benefits and resistances has been clearly defined (this usually takes about twenty minutes), each of the restraints or benefits has to be weighed and assessed in relationship to those that the group believes can be effectively altered by the family and those that are most essential to change if the problem condition is to be resolved. This step is crucial prior to developing alternatives since we often spend too much time spinning our wheels looking for solutions to issues we simply can't change. Thus, of the list of perhaps eight, ten, or even fifteen resistances and benefits, the group may decide that only four or five can and must be changed. This brief task will take only ten or fifteen minutes.

Up until now, the small clusters of four have been working on the problem for about forty-five minutes. It is critical that this initial period not be used to solve the problem prematurely. So often, the mistake in most problem solving is to leap into solutions without having considered all of the implications or all of the factors that make the implementation of solutions so difficult. But, having gone through our own diagnostic process, it is now possible to begin to search for effective alternatives.

One way to come up with suitable alternatives is to place each of the resistances or benefits on a half piece of newsprint. Then the participants in their groups of four—without discussion—are instructed to develop a list of at least three sensible, conservative alternatives that would have a positive impact on changing the present problem condition. These solutions should be rational and easy to control and monitor; they should make sense and fall easily from the nature of the problem itself. In addition, for each one of the major resistances the groups are also instructed to generate at least three relatively creative, innovative, even wild solutions; these would by their nature force a family into a different set of responses to the situation that is creating the problem. The facilitator must legitimize as essential the creative process of developing unusual and even fun approaches to removing serious blockages. After generating the four or six different strategies around a particular resistance or "benefit," the group is requested to consider a variety of other alternatives or strategies for each of the other resistances or benefits without spending too much time in overall discussion. The idea is to generate lots of alternatives and strategies and to free the group from just thinking in traditional ways.

Note that if this process is carried out even halfway successfully, the group will generate anywhere from twelve to twenty-four ideas. Next, some concrete, workable strategies that could be implemented within a family must be developed from all the ideas that have been generated. Such strategies have to include details of how they would work, what kind of cooperation would be demanded, how often and under what conditions they should be utilized, and, finally, how the family can be accountable through some kind of a monitoring process in order to know whether or not a particular strategy is working. Thus, the first four steps of the problem solving will take around two hours, and the last step—that of finalizing a concrete, workable proposal—could take another hour. The way to stimulate a sense of urgency and responsibility on the part of the participants is to have them develop the best possible strategy and the best possible plan for implementing such a strategy within the family. Inform each group of four that after an hour of attempting to integrate and concretize the various ideas they have developed, they will be expected to "sell" their ideas to another group. The job of the other group is to make sure that the proposals being presented are workable and that all of the consequences of the plan have been thoroughly discussed. If on the second day the workshop began at nine o'clock in the morning, by eleven o'clock the eight small groups would have been given the task of integrating their ideas into concrete proposals; they would be expected to present these proposals to the other group working on the same problem at one o'clock. The two hours between eleven and one would also include time for a box lunch so that the four-person problem-solving groups could have "working lunches" if necessary. The job of the facilitator is to create a climate of enthusiasm and responsibility so that each of the small groups takes its job seriously and prepares the best possible set of solutions.

At one o'clock the two groups come together to help each other clarify and understand the consequences of the solutions they have both developed. The four groups of eight are told that at two o'clock the whole group of thirty-two will meet. At that time the solutions that each group believes are interesting, creative, and practical enough actually to work within a family will be presented. In order to prepare for this presentation, each one of the four-person clusters within a group of eight should present its ideas to the other cluster, with the other group first listening and then asking questions to help point out areas of concern or lack of clarity. This session is not meant to be a debate but rather a helpful process to make the various solutions of the one cluster more understandable or acceptable. The second cluster then repeats this process. After both clusters have presented their ideas, the group of eight should have a discussion to decide which of the ideas are the most usable and should be presented to the entire group at two o'clock. What usually happens in the various groups of eight is that there will be some startling overlaps of similar ideas. There will also be some ideas that are simply qualitatively much better than others. The hope is that the groups of eight will present an integrated set of proposals to the large group. The facilitators must be careful that a "win-lose" mentality does not develop between the clusters of four, which obviously have some vested interest in their own ideas. With the proper coaching and support, however, the groups of eight can be guided into developing their own support systems with a goal of presenting the best product for the whole group rather than just sharing ideas because they were registered by one cluster or another.

At two o'clock a representative from each group of eight is allowed ten minutes or less to present a clear and incisive description of the problem as well as the specific solutions that were developed. The key here is that solutions are to be stressed rather than long explanations over why the problem is a problem or over the restraints or benefits generated in the diagnosis.

The Final Step. It is clear by now that the great percentage of time during this two-day workshop has been spent in listening and developing new ways of thinking about old problems. By taking an in-depth look at a few problems with some creative solutions, the participants, usually working independently from their families, begin to get enthusiastic about the ideas developed in their own small groups and soon to be taken back to their families. The fact that a group of eight people agreed on a set of solutions gives support to the possible use of such solutions within a family context. Family members interested in a particular idea do not have to feel that they stand alone in trying to persuade their families into trying it since clearly as many as 50 to 75 percent of the workshop participants would probably agree that the idea was useful.

At this point there is still an hour and fifteen minutes or so left in the workshop. After a brief break, the family groups reconvene. They are then asked to develop in the next forty minutes a concrete set of plans for implementing one, two, or more of the strategies that were presented earlier in the day. To accomplish this last task they must obviously come to an agreement on a particular problem area and on a particular set of strategies. To keep old family patterns of communication from debilitating the process, the facilitator can suggest that each family member express two areas of concern that he or she believes the family should be dealing with and decide which of the strategies developed in the workshop might be valuable to implement. This simple device keeps one dominant family member from controlling the conversation and expressing all the ideas; thus the group itself usually discovers common concerns and some common interest in certain solutions.

As a part of the closing activity we suggest that each family briefly describe at least one concrete strategy that it will attempt to implement as a result of the workshop and how family members hope to maintain the open communication that has begun. Part of the facilitator's role is to summarize briefly how the various problem-solving strategies and diagnostic methods could be implemented in the home when certain problems arise and a more objective approach is needed. For example, a mother and son could work on the solutions to one set of problems while the father and daughter work on another problem; then they could come together to negotiate their ideas for improving a particular situation. The problem-solving structure tends to lend objectivity and a greater sense of fairness to the total situation.

Summary

Clearly, the function of the workshop is not to solve all of the families' problems or to provide in-depth therapy. The intent is to facilitate people's listening skills, to develop new ways of generating ideas, and to help diagnose problem conditions. By providing the model for structured problem solving and by helping the participants to experience some degree of success, we hope to encourage families to begin utilizing themselves as resources in a more effective manner. The theory behind keeping the families together only two hours out of twelve is that while much work remains to be done in the home, the families can take with them a different approach and a possibility of some follow-up to the structure established in the workshop. The various family groups are encouraged to sit down together periodically over the next few weeks to continue working on implementation of the various ideas and to monitor their success. The extent to which they actually do this is the measure of success of the workshop.

Case 10: Team Building—Sensible Is Not Always Sensible

Designing for team building is a much abused and misused process because it involves so many levels of attention and demands a clear understanding and sensitivity toward the various members of the team itself. For one design or series of designs to create mutual respect, cooperation, interdependence, enjoyment, and an increased level of trust represents to us state-of-the-art designing. All too often what is called team building is merely some "canned" program or series of activities using a similar approach for any group of people that would like to call themselves a team. The fact is that team building should differ dramatically according to the particular needs of each team, its readiness, and its past experience with similar activities. In its simplest form team building occurs when members are able to experience each other in a wide variety of situations. Such experiences can be either task oriented or focus more directly on maintenance or process dimensions of group behavior. Also, team-building activities by their nature provide permission for a group to look at its own behavior and also to explore new ways of approaching problems in order to be more effective. This self-analysis, in turn, has the potential for opening new doors and breaking restrictive norms of patterns of group behavior.

Background

Often facilitators limit themselves because of stereotypes and untested assumptions they carry about the groups with whom they work or about certain participants who are members of a group. In this particular case an executive team is being formed. Three of the members are sixty-three years old, including the president and the executive vice-president. Another individual is forty-five, with a military bearing and businesslike demeanor; informal rumors are that he will be the next president. In addition, there are two men in their early forties, one of whom is the business manager, and a thirty-five-year-old woman, recently elected to the management council. Basically, the group is conservative, highly motivated, time conscious, and serious; the members obviously hold some common worries and concerns about the nature of the two-day program they are beginning.

Just prior to this workshop consultants had gathered some rather disastrous-appearing data on the organization and especially on the performance of the office manager. Everyone is aware that the data will be reviewed in depth at the sessions, but there is quite a bit of concern that the workshop might turn into an affair to be likened to the old encounter or sensitivity sessions in which people were sometimes scapegoated and blamed in front of their peers. Thus, the group, although conscientious and desirous of positive change, is highly concerned about the potential impact such a meeting might have on the individual players and on the organization as a whole.

The consultant-facilitators are respected but somewhat unknown commodities to the group. The two facilitators—a man forty-five and a woman thirty-five—after assessing the factors of age, background, expectations, experience, threat of the data, and lack of cohesiveness of the group, wonder if they shouldn't tread carefully, expecting little enthusiasm from the older members and some defensiveness from the others. Happily their attitude of "reason" does not prevail. Instead they decide to risk a bit—to throw the participants off balance, to demand new behavior, and to reveal (if the design is successful) the potential held within the group for flexibility, hope, and creative change. For the facilitators it is an occasion for horseshoes and prayer beads.

The Design

At the exclusive "pedigreed" conference center, there is great concern and expectation on the part of all the participants toward the data. It is a looming cause for anxiety. The trainers, however, figure that unless the individuals have greater trust and hope in themselves as a group, even the most objective data feedback will result in predictable defensiveness, rationalizations, and justifications.

First, the members are asked to go outside on the conference center grounds and collect three objects that represent their own personal strengths and two objects that represent any weaknesses that might get in their way as this group tries to formulate itself into a team. To the facilitators' surprise, there is virtually no resistance to the task whatsoever. There are innumerable questions as the members attempt to gain clarity and further understanding of their strange task. Some individuals even registered signs of enthusiasm at having been given permission to do something so out of the ordinary.

After the participants have returned with their material, everyone is asked to look around the room at the other participants and to consider two strengths and one possible blockage that the others have that might help or hinder them in their efforts to become a team. At this point an individual is asked to share the objects collected in nature and to discuss how they represent his or her strengths and limitations. To the surprise of the facilitators (so much for another stereotype) one of the more conservative sixty-three-year-olds volunteers with enthusiasm and enters into a most delightful description of himself with candor, feeling, and obvious self-awareness. When he finishes, the others are asked to share their perceptions of the gentleman's strengths and potential blockages as they might relate to the team-building task that lies ahead. All but one individual enters the task with relish, and it seems as if the whole group has been "let out of school." There is laughter and bantering, and very specific information is passed to the individual. The group obviously knows each other well and had simply never been given permission to give each other anything other than superficial praise. The facilitators attempt to keep the participants using descriptive information and find they have to do little monitoring indeed since the group internalizes that process immediately.

Finally, after two hours of the most interesting, stimulating, and candid conversation (originally only forty-five minutes had been allotted for the activity since it was assumed the level of involvement of the participants would not be very high—so much for assumptions), the group is asked to do one more task. The participants are requested to take the various objects collected earlier and to make a collage of the group's greatest strengths in an integrated fashion. The collage is to represent what the group can give to the potential team it is trying to create and what will represent the backbone of its possible success. What the facilitators thought might be taken as a silly or nonsense activity is received in deadly earnest but with the same candor and humor evidenced previously. As one person later says, "The group is having such a ripping good time that nobody wants to stop."

Summary

The facilitators' own fears and concerns, drawn from their stereotypes and untested assumptions about the group, had almost deprived the participants of a stimulating and freeing experience that proved to be a perfect kickoff for team building. The early candor laid a foundation, which later allowed participants to take the serious data with a grain of salt and some much needed humor rather than with defensiveness. Even though many of the participants had worked together for years, the norms of the system rarely allowed them to express honest opinions of good feeling or appreciation. Again, given permission to be candid, forthright, and positive, a wealth of feelings emerged from the group in such a spontaneous fashion that the basis of trust that had always been there swelled into much greater proportions. This camaraderie allowed the "bad news" of the data to be taken with some equanimity. Upon later reflection, the facilitators could only wonder how many times their own apprehensions had limited their creativity and willingness to risk, which in turn had limited the fun and creativity that have been shown in this brief example.

Case 11: Bringing Magic into a Lazy Sunday

Increasingly facilitators are expected to have a variety of design activities that can explore the impact of a person's behavior on others. Although sensitivity sessions, the "hot seat," and encounter groups have gone out of vogue, there is still a need and interest for people to realize their impact on others. The belief is that by having a clear picture of their own behavior and its influence on those around them, people will have an opportunity to choose whether to maintain that behavior, discard it, or alter it in some way to make themselves more effective. Sitting around a circle and "encountering" each other or taking turns giving feedback is not particularly creative or stimulating and often produces considerable defensiveness among participants. Therefore, many trainers are continually searching for designs that give people meaningful information about themselves in an interesting and enjoyable manner with the participants remembering both the feedback and the situation.

Background

The sixteen participants have spent a week exploring the fundamentals of effective leadership and supervision. They have received data on themselves in a variety of ways and have had the opportunity to develop change strategies both for themselves and for their areas of back-home responsibility. Thus, the workshop has had both a personal and organizational direction. The program is being held at an offsight retreat center, and the group has had a late and very "successful" party the previous evening. They are now faced with a nine o'clock Sunday morning session, with the workshop program concluding at three or four o'clock the same day. As one member puts it, "It would take a miracle to interest me this morning." The members drag themselves into the workshop and with bleary-eyed goodwill sit in what one person describes as an "attentive stupor."

The Design

We have a situation in which the members of a group have developed some level of trust and understanding and are, to some degree, open to feedback. This particular activity is designed in a way that will almost guarantee a stimulating, challenging, and humorous experience. At its core is serious feedback, but its process is thoroughly involving and fun. Past experience had indicated that this design will not only remove the group from its stupor, but also provide participants with one of the more stimulating experiences of the entire week.

The sixteen participants are divided into groups of four—Group A, Group B, Group C, and Group D. Group A is told that they will design for Group B, and B for Group A. Similarly, Group C will design for Group D, and D for Group C. Each small subgroup of four members is given one hour to develop a thumbnail sketch of each member of the other group. Thus, Group A is to look at each individual in Group B and describe the person as quickly and as thoroughly as possible. Someone taking notes might write about "Tom" in Group B, based on the ideas that flowed from a discussion about Tom. Thus, the notes on Tom might read as follows:

- Quick to act
- Certain
- Aggressive
- Takes charge, often to a fault
- Hears, but often doesn't make people feel listened to
- Serious; has a sense of humor but seldom shows it
- Dependable
- Practical

The idea is to develop as clear and as comprehensive a picture of Tom as possible in a short time, including behaviors perceived as particularly effective and those that he tends to "overuse," as well as behaviors that he might develop to be even more effective. In the meantime, the members of Group B are preparing the same profiles of all the members of Group A. (The same process is occurring between Group C and Group D.) As much as possible the descriptions should be behavioral in nature and relate directly to the individual's leadership style or ability to deal effectively with other people.

Once each individual has been adequately described by the particular design group, the task of the design group is to develop a vignette or skit for each member of the other group. Thus, Group A is to develop four separate skits for the four individuals in Group B, with each skit or situation lasting several minutes. The skit or vignette is designed so that an individual has to respond spontaneously to the events of a particular situation—for example, answering the telephone, leading a meeting, talking with a subordinate, or simply following directions. The situation should be such that each individual will have to respond without time to plot a strategy. The skit should provide the person with a chance to be effective but in a situation that might cause the individual to revert to less than effective (and sometimes predictable) behaviors. In the course of preparing these skits, the planning group should take the following steps:

1. Develop the props and other roles necessary to carry the skit off.
2. Write a prediction as to how the group believes the individual will respond behaviorally to the stimulus situation or skit.
3. Be ready to stop the skit once the person has either acted in the predictable manner or chosen another course of action.
4. Discuss how the individual felt, how those observing felt about the behavior of the individual, and what was useful and what was not helpful in the individual's behavior as the scene was played out.
5. Finally, share the prediction with the individual as a source of direct feedback.

Once the hour-long planning session is over, the total process of structuring the skit, as well as the ensuing discussion for each individual, should take no more than about fifteen minutes for each participant. Thus the total design time from beginning to end is about three to three and a half hours. In this particular design, two groups of four (such as A and B) meet and work in one room while the other two groups (C and D) work in another.

Clearly, the point is to focus either on a behavior that an individual overuses or underuses in a situation in which the individual is forced to use or at least consider some new or more appropriate behavior. By providing a slight structure to the discussion following each of the vignettes, the shared information can be of tremendous value to each individual. Seldom does the individual forget either the feedback or the skit. There is an opportunity to be sensitive and yet creative in virtually every skit. In this particular design, creativity and fun usually join hands, especially once those in Group A hear the laughter from those in Group B who are planning a unique experience for someone in Group A. Group A's adrenaline tends to start pumping as it too attempts to design a useful yet involving and interesting skit for the individuals in the other group. The combination of challenge, apprehension, and curiosity among the participants, along with the demands on them to be both sensitive and creative, results in an extraordinary experience, regardless of how exciting and tiring the party was the previous night.

The following examples of some successful skits or vignettes might give you an idea of the range of experiences that people can have.

Example 1. In one of the groups is an attractive, middle-aged woman who comes across as prim, proper, and almost perfect in every respect. Although she is intelligent and skilled in much of what she does, she has a way of putting people off because she finds it difficult to relax or be casual with others. In her role as a leader and trainer, she thus tends to appear distant, aloof, and, for some people, even slightly conceited. When people get to know her, they realize this is not the case. However, since first appearances are critical, the group feels it is important for her to find out through a vignette how essential it is for her to give herself permission to be more revealing and casual about herself in her style. They have her sit by herself at a table, and she is told that when the make-believe telephone rings, she should pick it up and answer as she sees fit. At this point, two people stand by each of her shoulders. The telephone rings and she answers by saying hello. A voice on the other end says, "Who are you?" She gives her name. The voice again says, "Who are you?" She says, "What?" The voice replies, "Who are you?" She looks flustered and annoyed. She looks around ruefully and gives her name again. The voice answers, "Who are you?" At this point, the person standing next to her right shoulder says, "Don't be foolish; don't let the person know who you are—you certainly don't want to let the person know who you really are." The person on her left shoulder says, "It's alright, let the person know . . . be yourself . . . relax, they'll like you just the way you are." She looks slightly dazed. The voice on the phone says, "Who are you?" She appears exasperated. The voice to her right says again, "Don't say anything, don't let them know, don't reveal yourself." The person on her left says, "Go ahead, it's alright, have a good time, let them know the real you." The voice on the phone says, "Who are you?" The woman slams down the phone. The person directing the vignette halts the action. At that point two questions are asked. What did she feel and how did she see herself reacting to the frustrating situation? After she explores these in some depth, the people watching in both Groups A and B are asked to give their views. A tremendous amount of interplay follows as those watching expressed their feelings of frustration and hope for what the woman should do as well as their sympathy and concern for the predicament in which she found herself. Finally, Group A reads the prediction that the members had made of what the woman would actually do in the situation. Their prediction to the group says, "You will become frustrated and agitated and then annoyed at the situation and the demands being placed on you. You will control the situation by either hanging up the phone or acting as if what is being asked for is not clear. You will find it difficult to face the question that you are being asked, which underlies the purpose of the vignette.'' Again, the reading of the prediction generates more enthusiatic talk from the woman as well as from individuals in both Groups A and B.

Example 2. The young man for whom the skit is being designed is popular, charming, witty, and in every respect well liked and a decent human being. What strikes the group particularly in their efforts to design the vignette for him is that he continually gives a piece of himself away as he tries to please everyone—he finds it almost impossible to say no or not to do what is being asked of him. He avoids conflict at all costs and finds it difficult to confront people or be negative, even when it would be appropriate. In setting up this skit the following occurs. He is asked to stand in front of the room in a cleared spot. One person directs the scene. He says to the young man, ''Please do exactly as I tell you.'' He gives no reason or any other instruction. He then says, ''Please lie down on your back on this spot on the floor. Now, we are going to cover you with these large pieces of cardboard.'' Three very large pieces of heavy cardboard are placed over him so that he is completely covered. The director says, ''What you have provided us with is a small bridge. And what each of us in our team is going to do is to use this bridge to get to the other side. What we need from you is your cooperation to lie very still in order to accomplish our task.'' With this the four members of the planning or design group walk very carefully up and over the cardboard on top of the young man. After each has ''walked over him,'' the director indicates that the skit is over and open to discussion. He first asks the young man how he felt and what the message was that he received while lying on the floor under the cardboard. Next, the audience is asked how they felt as they saw the man being walked over. Those walking over the bridge are asked for their feelings. Finally, the prediction is read, which says, ''Without a doubt Joe will allow himself to be walked on by the members of the team and will never even show a sign of objection. This reaction will be totally consistent with how others tend to use him and how he is often unwilling to take care of himself.'' Again, the reactions to each of the questions, the interactions and feelings expressed are enormous. The young man indicates he never in his life believed that his attempts to be positive might in fact act as a hindrance to him and his effectiveness as a leader.

Example 3. In this situation a very different kind of vignette or skit is constructed for a problem similar to the previous one. The woman for whom the plan is being designed is seen as quite simply being unable to tolerate conflict and will avoid it at all costs. The group sees this as getting in the way of her general ability to be effective as as leader and also her willingness to enter into long and meaningful relationships, since any good relationship is often plagued with a certain amount of tension that needs to be looked at periodically and resolved if the relationship is going to flourish. By avoiding any conflict, the group also sees the potential of avoiding intimacy as well as being involved in authentic, real relationships. Thus, the woman is asked to stand in the middle of a circle of the other seven participants from Groups A and B. She is instructed to "stand in front of each person in the group for a moment and tell each one specifically one thing he or she should do in order to assure a good relationship between the person and herself. Second, the woman is to tell one thing that each of the others might change in order to improve the effectiveness of his or her present relationship with her.

Clearly there is a different kind of discussion based on this kind of experience. Everyone in the group has strong feelings about the event itself and how the individual carries out the task. They had predicted that the woman would be less than candid and direct and would spend most of the time with the first part of the task—telling the person in front of her what could be done to maintain the relationship rather than being specific and facing the individual with what might be inhibiting the effectiveness of the relationship. What in fact actually happens is that the individual is very direct and specific once she received "permission" to be direct; she became open and confronting and accomplished the task with skill and apparent relish.

Thus, while the prediction is not accurate, the feedback the prediction allows is marvelous, and the individual receives a great deal of support and positive reinforcement because of the skillful way she handles the situation.

It is clear from these three examples that there is no end to the creative ways that skits, vignettes, or activities can be constructed to place the participants in situations of spontaneous action, from which they can receive feedback in the best possible way.

Summary

Clearly, this design is complex. In many ways it is a design within a design. It should only be used with groups that have developed some trust and understanding and that have some understanding of the concept of design itself. But, with this in mind, the activity will be an almost guaranteed success. Some of the reasons are as follows:

1. The design is "reciprocal," with those designing for one group also being "designed for" by the other. Since both groups know this, they are both extra sensitive but also creative and humorous in ways of expressing themselves.
2. The situation is inherently competitive but in a most constructive sense. The competition itself stimulates creativity and risk taking among the participants.
3. The design promotes skillful giving and receiving of feedback.

4. The feedback is provided along several dimensions, including the prediction itself, experiencing the skit and one's own interpretation of it, and, finally, the observations and feelings of the other group members to the individual's reaction to the situation.
5. For participants who are interested in the concept of design, the overall activity is a good example of a highly complex design. It provides an example of how specific instructions and structure can be provided for the group while still giving them a maximum amount of input and investment into the process.

By having the participants first "diagnose" each of the participants in their sister group and then "design" in light of the data, there is an excellent opportunity for them to experience exactly what good design is all about. Thus, at the end of the three- to three-and-a-half-hour design, it is helpful to spend a few minutes with such a group discussing why the design was successful and how it was possible to take a rather passive and sleepy group of individuals and stimulate them into creative action. It is this lesson that may be as important as any in terms of the value of the design.

Conclusions

Perhaps the best way to grasp the significance of this chapter is to review the meaning of *classic designs.* Rather than meaning they were the best, the term suggests they were ultimately appropriate for a given situation. Each was unique and seemed to be successful because of the way a particular situation was diagnosed. In other words, the design was created from the diagnosis. All too often an interesting design is forced into a situation with satisfactory but rarely outstanding results compared to those achieved when the design falls literally out of the diagnosis itself. One should never be afraid of using a tried-and-true design or activity, but it must fit into an overall design puzzle, like a perfectly matching piece.

Situations are fluid-forming creative moments that a skilled trainer can take advantage of. Effective designs require an understanding of the demands and needs of a group and the individual participants, the realities of time, the resources available, participant readiness, and the degree of risk participants can handle.

It is true that even the most effective trainer-facilitators occasionally experience failure and imperfect designs. But, these failures occur less and less frequently as one is increasingly able to predict the consequences of certain types of interventions and as one is able to respond creatively to the immediate needs of a group.

6

Specific Interventions for Conflict Situations

In our society conflict is considered natural. The absence of conflict in organizations should cause nearly as much concern as its presence, since conflict arises from common organizational shortcomings, such as unclear goals; overlapping or ill-defined roles; differing expectations; arbitrary, overly demanding, or vague use of authority; irritating personal styles; and questionable use of personnel, materials, money, or other limited resources. The issue is not whether conflict exists but, rather, how to resolve conflict in the most constructive manner when it does arise.

Most people seek to avoid pain and to attain some level of comfort and predictability in their lives. Since conflict usually brings pain, discomfort, instability, and often the need to change, it is not difficult to understand why people avoid, deny, or minimize the importance of conflict situations. Further, people see conflict itself as a problem rather than as a symptom that tends to accompany unresolved problems.

This chapter is not intended to be a definitive examination of conflict resolution; rather, it aims to explore how the concept of *effective design* can be used to reduce conflict in a wide range of areas that affect the lives of people who live and work in families and organizations. Over the last several decades much has been learned about the nature of conflict and handling it more effectively. For example, conflict is increased when people believe that:

1. They are not being heard;
2. Their feelings aren't accepted;
3. Others are closed to new ideas;
4. They are blocked from necessary information that they lack;
5. They are out of control and powerless to influence their present situation.

Each of the designs that follow brings out certain questions that should be asked by group facilitators before they attempt to create an intervention for reducing a particular conflict situation. The quality of the answers to each of these questions influences the effectiveness of the conflict resolution process. This method is not a panacea for all conflict; it simply provides a way of thinking, some questions for focusing attention on the problem, and some sample designs that have worked in the past and that seem to bring out some interesting ways of viewing conflict resolution.

The following questions are the "tough ones" that facilitators should ask before attempting to create a design to reduce a particular conflict situation.

Tough Questions to be Asked When Designing for Conflict Resolution

1. Have we listened clearly and attentively to the other parties, and have they been able to recognize our understanding of their concerns?

2. Have we been able to acknowledge the position of the others and to show acceptance of their feelings even if our own ideas may differ from theirs?
3. Have we made a serious and conscious effort to assess our own biases, stereotypes, and vested interests, which may distort our own ability to resolve the conflict?
4. Do we know as much as we can and need to know about the conflict situation? In other words, have we diagnosed the nature of the conflict and whether it stems from differences in style, goals, or roles; lack of information; or the methods used in problem solving or *processing* the issue?
5. From our attempts to clarify the nature of the conflict, have we been able to identify specific rather than general issues?
6. Are we aware of what has been done previously to remedy the conflict situation, and do we understand why such efforts have not succeeded?
7. Are we clinging to preconceived solutions without allowing a more creative process of conflict resolution to occur?
8. Are we truly open to new alternatives, and are we creating a process that will allow them to arise?
9. Are we willing to ask tough questions of *consequence* as a result of our conflict resolution efforts?
10. Will our actions reduce conflict, or will they actually increase the adversarial nature of the situation?

Conflict resolution is the most difficult when individuals are locked into old patterns of thinking or into predetermined solutions. Successful facilitators seek to provide individuals with the opportunity to open themselves to new ways of thinking and relating to the conflict itself. Again, the task of designing specific interventions can be likened to an artist taking a variety of unrelated colors, mixing them, and applying them to a canvas in a manner that creates a desired effect or outcome. Facilitators are influenced directly by the kinds of questions they are willing to ask, which again can be likened to how the artist must think before applying brush to canvas. Often what goes down on the canvas itself is less important than the creation of the concept, the mix, and the eventual application. In other words, the prework or preparation stage of a design is what ultimately determines the success of the application.

A number of designs that have dealt successfully with issues of conflict and that have helped to resolve actual conflict situations that have arisen between individuals or within organizations are described in the following cases. Although many of the designs relate to a particular situation, the thinking that has gone into each of the designs can be transferred to other similar yet individual situations.

Case 1: Sensitizing People to the Issues Inherent in Conflict and Change

When bringing groups together to deal with differences, and if time allows for a period of preparation, the facilitator can design an intervention that allows the participants to consider how they respond to conflict as individuals. This approach can educate the group to ways of thinking that may well reduce the inclination to use unproductive approaches to conflict resolution.

The Design

This activity, which can take anywhere from thirty to sixty minutes, aims to draw participants into thinking about the nature of conflict and how to minimize defensiveness, thus reducing their natural tendency to resist change. The facilitator first arranges clusters of three or four people who talk for five or ten minutes about the most prevalent sources of conflict in their personal experiences or within their organization. At the end of this period of time, the facilitator asks them to construct a list of five or six of these sources of conflict to share with the large group. Having to produce even a minimal product like this to be shared with the whole group will increase the level of involvement and result in a feeling of seriousness among the participants. Whether there are five, ten, twenty, or even more groups of three does not matter. At the end of ten minutes, the facilitator simply moves around the room and asks for a single source of conflict from each group. By taking only a single issue from each group and not allowing overlapping ideas, original ideas will usually peter out after ten or fifteen have been collected. In fact, seldom are more than twenty ideas drawn from all the groups. The collected ideas are written clearly on a board or large sheet of newsprint. Out of one group came the following list:

- Feeling overpowered
- Feeling out of control—unable to alter the situation (forced or compelled)
- Needing to choose between several positive alternatives
- Needing to choose between several negative or unsatisfactory alternatives
- Feeling taken for granted—unappreciated—minimized
- Feeling guilty
- Reacting to someone's personal style (the person's arrogance, insensitivity, or perhaps coolness)
- Feeling dependent on authority
- Feeling inferior—inadequate in a given situation
- Feeling rejected—being disliked or unacceptable
- Failing to act honestly out of the fear of possibly altering a friendship or relationship
- Feeling insensitively treated—hurt or abused

- Not feeling understood or heard
- Feeling manipulated—not being informed or privy to important information
- Feeling uninvolved in problem-solving issues that affect daily lives

The participants are then asked to decide which of the fifteen items usually create the most tension or conflict within them, and to prepare to vote on these. Each person is to vote on the five he or she feels have created the most conflict or tension. After the vote in the previously mentioned example, six out of the fifteen items stood out rather prominently:

- Feeling out of control—unable to alter the situation (forced or compelled)
- Feeling taken for granted—unappreciated—minimized
- Reacting to someone's personal style (the person's arrogance, insensitivity, or perhaps coolness)
- Feeling inferior—inadequate in a given situation
- Feeling misunderstood or unheard
- Feeling uninvolved in problem solving the issues that affect daily lives

At this point, each person present is handed a list similar to the one below:

Fourteen Methods for Dealing with Conflict

1. Be indirect—only hint at feelings or a problem bothering you.
2. Find something to blame the situation on—something outside of yourself.
3. Use sarcasm in dealing with the situation when talking about it with others.
4. Seek a specific scapegoat.
5. Make an active effort to smooth the tension over or to live with the situation, even if it may be negative.
6. Blow up—let off steam—let people know just exactly how you feel or how angry the situation makes you.
7. Hide your feelings at the moment and only reveal them later to friends or confidants in private—don't deal directly with the situation.
8. Attempt to seek clarification and more information about the situation.
9. Sublimate your feelings—put your energy and attention into other unrelated activities or interests.
10. Spend time listening and gathering additional information by talking with those involved.
11. Back down under pressure—capitulate or acquiesce rather than deal with the conflict itself.
12. Make an active attempt to compromise.

13. Complain to others about the unfairness of the situation.
14. Make an effort to seek creative alternatives to the situation—a new way of approaching the conflict.

The following instructions were all given for using the fourteen statements.

First, keeping in mind the sources of conflict you have identified as being most problematic to you, take the list of fourteen ways of handling conflict and put an X by the five methods that you truthfully *find yourself using most often. Your answers will be kept anonymous so please take a hard look at yourself and be as honest as possible.*

Now, place a check next to the five ways of handling conflict that you find being used most by other people in your organization. Of course, you are looking for the general pattern of response since clearly individuals vary greatly. Again, think back about how conflicts are resolved in your organization and then mark the approaches that seem to be the most prevalent. Please do not sign your names to these sheets; they will be collected in a few moments, and we will use your responses as part of our final activity.

The next part of the design requires the group again to break into clusters of about four people in which they are asked to consider the six sources of conflict that the group had earlier found to be most difficult. This time they are to generate two or three specific methods that they believe could reduce one or more of those sources of conflict. Participants are requested to be as specific as possible so that any suggestions can actually be utilized.

In one problem-solving workshop in which this design was used, the thirty participants working in six groups came up with seven rather specific examples of "rules" for reducing conflict. For example, one suggestion was that when differences were being discussed, individuals should be required to "paraphrase" the thoughts of others before they could give their own idea to make certain that people felt heard and understood. Another suggestion was that individuals should present their ideas in descriptive terms rather than those tainted with judgments of "good or bad." Thus, an individual who was talking about an idea that differed from somebody else's would state the idea specifically without embellishing it with value judgments or trying to "sell" the idea during this part of the discussion. A third and rather creative idea had individuals place a twenty-minute time limit on a discussion over a rather volatile topic. Each participant was given ten slips of paper. Every time an individual talked, he or she had to turn in one of the ten slips; speaking more than thirty seconds would cost another slip of paper. The belief, of course, was that people would be forced to be more considerate in what they said and more succinct in how they said it.

The outcome of this part of the activity was that the participants were left with some good ideas for working as a group. They also provided themselves with ways of ensuring greater consideration for each other during the rest of the day, which was to be spent focusing on problem solving of ideas that previously had been sources of conflict among many members of the group.

The final part of this design is the presentation by the facilitator of the tabulation of the data drawn from the fourteen statements of how conflict is resolved. Look, for a minute, at the nature of the statements themselves. Statements 1, 3, 5, 7, 9, and 11 are all "passive" ways of handling conflict; conflict is either avoided or denied—certainly not an active resolution of conflict. On the other hand, statements 2, 4, 6, 8, 10, 12, 13, and 14 are all "active" approaches to conflict. Yet only items 8, 10, 12, and 14 can be considered positive approaches to the conflict in that they are not punitive or negative. Interestingly, the data from the thirty-person workshop we continue to refer to had twenty-two people seeing themselves in a "positive-active" category with some of their responses. However, only eight of the thirty saw others in the organization using these same approaches. The group saw others in the organization tending to be much more negatively active in their responses to conflict. Thus, blaming, scapegoating, and blowing up were all higher than any other single item on the passive list.

After reviewing the data, the group is asked to make some statements to explain the discrepancy between how people see themselves versus how they see others in the organization handling conflict. The obvious tendency for members to project negative attitudes on their peers but not on themselves causes both laughter and concern. It also becomes clear that by identifying the high tendency to blame and scapegoat, it is now possible to create a "norm," if only for the duration of the workshop, in which such behaviors are not acceptable. It is also stated that people do not like the implication that they withdrew from conflict many times rather than taking a more positive view of confrontation and resolution. Again, it is easy for the facilitator to use data as a framework for establishing a norm of openness and candor rather than passivity.

Summary

This total activity takes no more than one hour and yet can provide a group with a foundation for handling problem solving during the remainder of the day. In its own way the design models the necessary processes of data gathering, listening, and reflection, which are so critical to any rational problem solving. By developing new ways of thinking about conflict resolution and by establishing new ground rules—some developed by the members themselves—the rest of the day can become a positive affirmation of this first activity.

Case 2: The Prussians and the Leisure Class

Designing for the resolution of conflict between two groups working in an interdependent fashion will test the mettle of any trainer. Usually such tensions are only handled on a crisis basis—being allowed to smolder until they burst into flame. Prevention is rarely the rule. One reason groups seldom work until a crisis occurs is the implicit fear that any such "dealing" will result in expressions of anger, confrontation, or showdown and also will waste important work time. In addition, having to "deal" with such conflict issues suggests that something is wrong. Since almost everyone tries to at least appear to be in good shape, if not "perfect," it is the unusual individual who is willing to look at a problem as it is evolving and before it reaches the crisis state.

Perhaps more than anything else, conflict between two groups is predictable; in the eyes of many, bringing them together creates a highly volatile situation with few apparent controls and a lurking sense of the pending catastrophe. This is exactly why facilitators grow beards and retire early. And it is exactly why diagnosis becomes an art, quickly separating the "bag people" from creative individuals who are able to diffuse such volatile situations and leave a reservoir of goodwill necessary for future productive work between the two groups. Individuals dealing with such groups should be able to:

- Prevent further polarization around highly charged issues.
- Induce collaborative activities.
- Reduce the inclination to "pay back" the other group and further increase hostile feelings.
- Begin to build a history of positive and productive experiences.
- Reduce stereotypes, which provide negative views for one group or the other.
- Expand the group norms to include appreciation and perhaps even enjoyment and fun with the other group.
- Develop ongoing monitoring mechanisms for use in the future to reduce the tendency to put off negative or conflicting issues until they reach crisis proportions.

Background

A world-reknowned engineering construction group has been hired by a large local public utility to build a billion dollar nuclear reactor. A key steering group selected from each organization and comprised primarily of experienced engineers is to coordinate the entire program. The consulting organization itself has a reputation for being efficiency-minded and cost conscious, and for having a no-nonsense—even "Prussian-like"—attitude toward clients with whom it works. The organization is recognized as the best in the field. Quite often, its consultants have exhibited a patronizing and even superior attitude toward people from the hiring company. In this particular instance, the consultants view the engineers at the utility company as leading a rather "leisurely" life, an unpressured existence in the public sector. Clearly they are individuals who sacrifice higher pay and competition for a work environment of security and comfort.

On the other hand, the public utility engineers have tended to react to the lack of respect and the apparent arrogance that the consultants often display by ignoring them as much as possible. They have reacted passively to job requests, to information sought, and to meetings demanded. Communication has begun to deteriorate, and the cost ratio to soar for the consultants. To make matters worse, the headquarters for the consulting group is in California, and the utility is on the East Coast. Unquestionably, something has to be done before the problem reaches astronomical financial proportions. Trainers representing both organizations meet and decide on a two-day program, which is composed of six major designs, each dependent on the success of the previous one. Our goal here is to give you a sense of the "flow" of the overall program and individual designs without going into too much detail.

The Design: Phase 1

Given the high degree of anticipation and anxiety by the thirty participants (fifteen from each organization) and the expectation of an all-out war and confrontation that has developed over the weeks preceding the workshops, the facilitators decide to ease into the program without being too dramatic and without letting the serious nature of the event act against its very success. Thus, the facilitators allow some time initially to let individuals introduce themselves and describe their function in the construction project. The facilitators realize that most people will only remember a few names and faces, but they believe the activity will provide some sort of ego identification by matching a few key names with faces. Then, in groups of four—two from each organization—the facilitators ask the participants to answer the following questions:

1. What outcomes do they want from the two-day session for the project as a whole?
2. What outcomes do they want for themselves as individuals?
3. What do they not want from the two days or how might the two days pose problems or cause blockages to the total process?

These simple questions provide a much needed additional focus and give the trainers some basis for understanding the places from which the various participants have come. It also allows the facilitators to begin working on the participants' concerns rather than having to "lay on them" a set of the facilitators' own goals. Perhaps, most important, these few questions provide individuals with an opportunity to air their concerns and apprehensions about the two days and allow the facilitators to legitimize these concerns through their recognition and acceptance.

At the end of this short period of time, the facilitators compare their expectations and hopes with those of the participants and begin to create some base of reality. At the same time, the facilitators begin to lay to rest some of the myths and fantasies that have engulfed the workshop.

The Design: Phase 2

After the first arrival of participants the facilitators clearly recognize that the atmosphere is "too heavy"; something has to be done to put things in their proper perspective. If something is not done, tensions and antagonisms will undoubtedly flare and lead to blaming and scapegoating of a most unproductive nature. The fear of creating further polarization among the antagonists is central in the facilitators' thinking. The key is somehow to "disorient" those present without reducing the importance of their feelings or concerns. For this reason, the facilitators divide the group of thirty into six groups of five, with each small subgroup comprised of individuals from their own organization. Thus, there are three groups from the consulting organization and three from the utility.

Each group is asked to take thirty minutes to paint a verbal picture of the other organization. Thus, the three consulting groups are to each make a list of all the characteristics, traits, or stereotypes that describe the utility. There are to be no holds barred; exaggerations are all right as long as the essence of the description is true. Similarly, the three groups from the utility are to create a verbal picture of the consulting group and how they view the consultants as operating within the utility. Again, there is to be no holding back of the feelings and impressions generated in those from the utility as a result of the behavior and actions of the consulting organization.

One can only imagine the joy of the next thirty minutes. Uproarious laughter from among the six groups floats throughout the room as each of the groups identifies its own perceptions through the use of serious examples, which somehow in retrospect are proving to be rather hilarious. At the end of thirty minutes, the groups are told they have an additional thirty minutes to create a presentation for the total group. The presentation is to represent the description of the other organization that has evolved from the descriptive words developed in the previous work period. The groups are encouraged to be creative and to use humor in the presentation. The only "rule" is to make certain that the points that need to be made are made. Groups are free to use skits or vignettes, construct fairy tales or stories, write a poem or create a song, develop a game, or even create a picture—whatever medium each selects must somehow be reflective of the truth that is perceived.

For a second time uproarious laughter and joking prevail as the groups prepare their presentations and discard those that are perhaps too risky but enormously funny to consider. It should also be noted that in addition to legitimizing candor, the design also stimulates a certain healthy competition among the groups. Hearing those from "the other side" seeming to enjoy the apparent frailties of the other is all that is necessary to encourage truth, creativity, and a dash of outrageousness in each of the presentations. The facilitators are amazed at how much the atmosphere has changed and how much the participants are obviously enjoying themselves and letting down their hair. The facilitators only hope that the presentations will maintain some degree of propriety. Interestingly, however, this is usually not a problem since most designs have a built-in protection owing to the individual groups tending "to do unto others only what they would hope will be done unto themselves." Generally, a certain guarantee of self-protection exists in these situations.

The six presentations take approximately forty-five minutes, and one can only say that the pain comes more from laughter than from anything people say or display. There are three skits, two songs, and a large picture with a poem attached. The engineers from both the utility and the consulting organization outdo themselves. It is a roast to end all roasts. Of course, the reason it is so funny is that behind every barbed word and humorous statement lies the underlying reality of truth.

The session ends with a break for dinner; the participants are encouraged to sit with members of the opposite organization. The good humor resulting from the shared "initiation rite" of the presentation acts as a bridge toward building better relationships.

The Design: Phase 3

Having reduced the initial anxieties of the two groups and legitimized through humor the expressions of frustration and even hostility that had existed, there is now clearly a need to draw the two groups into a better working relationship—again building a foundation that will last well beyond the two-day workshop and into the months ahead. The facilitators are quite sure that the group is still not ready to confront the problem blocking their ability to work more effectively together. The buffer of goodwill and trust that has begun to develop through the presentations of truth and humor is precarious indeed. The fact that one organization tends to be direct and confronting in its approach to conflict while the other is passive and constrained worries the facilitators; they fear that prematurely putting the groups together into a mutual problem-solving situation might reverse the gains made earlier and result in the kind of intimidation and "games" that will be played out based on the previous history of the two organizations. Thus, during this third phase, the facilitators decide to draw the two organizations together by means of a shared problem-solving simulation that has nothing to do with work but allows the various members to utilize each other in positive and constructive ways and to share the benefits of a creative problem-solving experience. It is important to note that the nature of the individual simulation activity is important only in that it allows certain kinds of interaction to occur. The situation demands the following design:

1. A stimulating problem that will draw on the intellectual resources of a group of engineers;
2. A problem far enough removed from the "work reality" that individuals will not get caught into back-home roles and expectations;
3. A simulation real enough that the "players" can see the relationship between the staged situation and the reality of their work life;
4. An activity designed in such a way that a high degree of participation and interdependence can be ensured by those involved.

The problem selected is an army tactical game of war in which a situation is presented that requires overcoming certain natural obstacles and allows the participants not only to use their background and training but also their creative talents if the problem is to be resolved at all. Heterogeneous groups composed of members of both organizations are assembled. The simulation is such that a certain element of competition evolves, which lends an air of reality to the total problem.

The simulation activity takes an hour and a half, at the end of which the two organizations come to the following realizations:

1. They can work productively together.
2. They can experience success together, which is critical in this stage of their development.
3. They can begin to see strengths in individuals from the other organization as a result of working with them in the problem simulation.
4. For the second time in a relatively short period of time they are able to enjoy each other's company, yet in a manner that is very different from the first time.

Experiencing a second success in an atmosphere of increasing goodwill literally opens the door to the group's ability to solve its own organizational problems, which somehow have now taken on a very different perspective in a very different problem-solving climate.

The Design: Phase 4

So far in the two-day workshop, almost one full day has been devoted to getting the two organizations ready to face their own real problems. Although this amount of time might seem extravagant to some, the facilitators are looking toward the long-term building of relationships among the two groups; they believe that the seven to eight hours involved in the presentations and simulation activities, as well as in "breaking bread" together, have provided the solid foundation needed to tackle the more serious problems. The earlier anticipated hostile confrontation is simply not going to occur because the participants are suddenly respecting the talents, skills, and humor they have identified in the "others." Most of the stereotypes had been dispelled or at least recognized and put into perspective.

During the final three phases the facilitators are able to use a rather traditional problem-solving model consisting of a period of problem diagnosis, a period during which specific action alternatives are generated, and, finally, the creation of a means of monitoring and follow-up so that the progress gained in the workshop will not be lost as a result of time and distance. Thus, phase 4 is handled by a brainstorming activity that allows mixed groups of four participants each to identify a list of every block or restraint that has kept the two organizations from working effectively together. Time is then allowed for the groups to consolidate these twenty to thirty issues and to focus on those that *can* and *must* be solved. The problems identified are placed in the following categories: (1) those the group has little or no control over, (2) those that affect the life of the group in the short run and need to be given immediate attention, and (3) those that are described as "long run" in nature and might take three to six months or longer either to be resolved or in some cases to surface as problems. Most of the issues identified have an organizational flavor to them. Many involve specific problems of management and supervision. Certainly communications is a major area, as well as problem solving, decision making, and span of control. A process for synthesizing and creating priorities out of the three categories of issues is established.

The Design: Phase 5

A list of six problems—three short-run and three long-run—are identified by the two organizations as being most essential for problem-solving attention during this workshop. Other problems are identified but placed in a hopper for later action. Next, new groups of five are established; each new group has at least two members from each organization. One of the facilitators' goals is to move people into contact with as many participants from the other organization as possible—a total of five opportunities for this are created during the course of the workshop. Each of these five-person problem-solving groups is given one short-run and one long-run problem. At this point we will bypass the details of this kind of problem solving, but generally speaking the following scenario occurs during the next four hours.

One hour is devoted to a series of brainstorming and creative problem-solving approaches to the short-term problem. The participants are encouraged to create a variety of solutions that are specific and cost-effective in nature. A joint committee of three members from each organization is assigned to screen the various proposals and take them to the next step of implementation. It is agreed that the group will be both a screening and a decision-making body unless large amounts of money, work priorities, or legal issues are involved. Clearly, the committee is to consult with the management, which is also represented in the group.

A three-hour block of time is devoted to the three long-range issues—again two groups having the same issue. The problem solving is structured in a way that establishes clear time boundaries and assists the groups in looking at each problem in relation to the following factors:

1. The problem condition at the present time;
2. What an ideal situation might look like without worrying about solutions or "how to" responses;
3. The resistances to change, including structural and functional blocks as well as the presence of actual benefits for maintaining the status quo and not allowing the problem to be resolved;
4. The generated/creative alternatives;

5. The integrated strategies created for solving the problem;
6. An assessment of the consequences of those strategies;
7. Detailed specific steps for implementing solutions.

Working through the various steps of the problem-solving process on the long-range problem takes each five-member group a little over two hours. Toward the end of this time each group is told it will be expected to present its rather specific proposals to the other group that is working on the same long-range problem. The other group will then, in turn, present its ideas. The two groups will next (1) search for areas of common agreement, (2) select the best parts of the two proposals, (3) add additional parts to mesh the two ideas, and (4) develop a single, integrated set of strategies that will be presented to the entire group. A critical part of this activity is setting it up in a manner that is collaborative and not "win-lose," thus reducing the need for each group to sell its own ideas. Participants must realize that shared success will be advantageous to both organizations.

Summary

The real challenge with conflict management workshops other than avoiding further polarization of already hostile problems is the need to ensure that gains made during the program are maintained after the workshop ends. The tendency is to regress into old patterns of behavior at the first sign of noncompliance. Thus, many workshops have been written off later as having been interesting, but unrealistic or artificial when they came down to the implementation phase. Thus, a strong rule for any trainer is to make certain that some legitimate body is created out of the workshop to monitor, evaluate, and maintain the gains carved from the problem-solving sessions. In this particular workshop, the six-member implementation group becomes the natural vehicle through which the various solutions generated in the problem-solving phase can be submitted for final reality testing and implementation. Always remember that even excellent ideas, generated by a group of well-intentioned individuals, can fall apart at the implementation phase. The reason, of course, is because until that time, nobody really has to do any changing, and it is the changing that causes discomfort and pain. Thus, we have learned over time that without proper and powerful monitoring, the chance of success in such a workshop is minimal indeed.

Case 3: Of Kings and Queens and Fairy Tales

Organizations that are part of large state bureaucracies and thus part of complex financial and political systems often breed conflict. Much of this conflict can be attributed to feelings of hopelessness or impotence that many people have regarding their ability to influence the system or bring about creative and necessary change. However, such an organization often can do a great deal that is positive and can make a real difference in providing a satisfying environment.

The problem, of course, is finding the necessary time and structure to create a "design" to make that improved environment a reality.

Background

In this particular case, the organization is a large state mental health institution that has become caught in a bureaucratic financial squeeze. Many of the staff are feeling both helpless and hopeless about not being able to do anything to improve their working conditions. Such an attitude is destructive in itself and creates frustrations among staff who are more and more often turning their own sense of impotence onto themselves. The result is an almost constant flow of interpersonal conflicts and antagonisms. The problem for the facilitator is not to become sucked into the "symptoms" (interpersonal conflicts, backbiting, cliques), but rather to provide the group some hope by having people flex their own creative muscles in a constructive and positive manner.

The facilitator has designed a seven-hour, on-site workshop. Fifty-seven staff members, ranging from the director down to a sampling of the day-care workers, are in attendance. Watching the staff filing into the large work room area, the facilitator realizes that a very long day lies ahead. The participants sit in small clusters, many with arms folded and legs crossed; most of them have a decisive "so you think you can do something about this mess?" attitude.

As in other situations of this type, the facilitator's inclination is to leap directly into problem solving since time is so limited and clearly so much has to be done. However, fighting that inclination is incredibly important; take a step back and ask yourself what you can do to give the group hope, to reduce the negativism, and to turn their expectations of a dull, useless workshop into an experience of hope and enjoyment. Often, under the negative pressures generated by the kind of participants we are describing here, a facilitator who also has a need to be liked and appreciated will revert to a conservative design, which may be exactly what the situation does not require. An analogy might be an organization that is on the verge of bankruptcy with few capital resources at its disposal being told that in order to save itself it must spend a large sum of money in advertising and public relations. At such a time, it is very difficult for management to consider such a proposal. There is often a tendency to reject it outright. Similarly, a facilitator's inclination may be to move toward the "tried and true" and shy away from the creative design that may be exactly what the doctor ordered.

The Design

The participants are asked to count off into five random groups of approximately eleven members each. Obviously, the grouping is done to help break up cliques, who find resisting an activity or program "among friends" is easier than in new groups. The five groups are given the following instructions:

You are to imagine that this organization is a kingdom in a land of make-believe. Like all good kingdoms, this one has kings and queens, princes and princesses, dragons and witches, castles and spells, goblins and fairy tales, and everything else that any good make-believe kingdom should have. In a period of thirty minutes each group is to weave a tale explaining the situation in which this kingdom (or organization) finds itself. The stories must be couched in truth, with all the flamboyance and romanticism that would be true of such a fairy kingdom. Each group's tale will be read back to the total group. Your tale should take no more than five minutes. Thus, it is essential that what is most important be said and the most explicit picture that is possible be created and shared in that relatively short period of time.

The task itself is so disorienting that even the greatest skeptics have to laugh. By utilizing the vehicle of a fantsy land, with all the villains and heroes and hopes and dreams, the facilitator has given the participants an opportunity to express a broad range of feelings—a catharsis if you will—in a legitimate way. They have permission to say what is on their minds. At the end of the planning period, the facilitator gives them five additional minutes for one more task: they are to make three magical wishes, which, if achievable within their own organization, will not depend on sorcerers, magicians, or even state officials to come true. The three wishes are to help make the organization a better kingdom in which to live.

Before each group shares its tale, the participants are given pieces of paper and asked to jot down common themes from each of the stories. What follows are thirty-five minutes of the funniest, wittiest, and most creative moments imaginable. Each tale has its own twist, its own style, and its own special cast of characters. But the frustrations and problems leap forward in the form of demons and dragons and spells, to which everyone can relate. At the end of each story, the group's three wishes are posted. Then the participants are split into groups of five, with one person from each of the five original groups comprising new groups of five. The participants are asked to take the themes common to the five presentations and turn them into problem statements that are in the domain of the organization to do something about. Such problems might range from their own internal communications and problem solving to methods for influencing external sources of power. The eleven groups of five are each asked to generate at least six such problem statements and to be as specific as possible.

At the end of thirty minutes, the total group again reconvenes. The facilitator has taken the fifteen wishes and translated them into a very concrete paragraph that seems to represent the desires of a group for a more ideal organization. The facilitator then suggests that the problem statements, which are about to be shared, represent blockages to this ideal, and that the rest of the day will be devoted toward removing some of those blockages. The goal is for the organization to function more effectively, even though there are many factors over which it has no control. The facilitator moves around the room and takes a single problem statement from each of the groups, avoiding overlap. A total of thirteen independent problem statements are thus identified.

At this point the participants are given a break and told that upon their return they will be asked to vote on the issues toward which they think their group can and should focus their energies in problem solving in order for the day to be a success and for them to gain the most benefit from their problem-solving efforts. Thus, in a period of less than two hours, a resistant group of people with many internal conflicts have enjoyed themselves together, have developed a sense of their "ideal" organization, and have identified a variety of specific, solvable problems. Having experienced some short-term successes, the members are now looking forward to the remainder of the workshop, with at least some minimal newfound hope. In this particular case the conflicts are with the facilitator's presence, with the management of the organization, with external authority that so influences the life of any system, and among individuals within the organization. The initial design and the problem-solving activity have created positive movement in three of the four conflict areas without creating unreal hopes or expectations.

Case 4: The Marvelous "I Gotcha" Design

For anybody who takes time to observe life's journeys, it is difficult not to realize that much of life is spent coping with the games of others and with those we perpetrate on ourselves or on people around us. We constantly fool ourselves into believing that what we do is good for us; we rationalize that our choices are appropriate, and we often justify a course of action without really looking at the alternatives or assessing the consequences of our actions.

About thirty years ago the notion of "feedback" spread across this country like wildfire. Feedback was simply an attempt by individuals to give other people specific and descriptive information about how they were perceived as acting and the impact their actions were having on the individuals providing the feedback. The belief was that by receiving feedback from an individual that was in some way verified by others, the recipient of the feedback would have a clear picture of the impact he or she was having on the world. With feedback, a person theoretically had a choice as to whether to accept what was said or whether to change as a result of what was said.

The vehicles for this type feedback were numerous and included T-groups, sensitivity training groups, encounter groups, and a wide range of spinoffs, all of which gave people the legitimacy to say to others what was on their minds. The problem, of course, was that people tend to be protective of themselves, to the point of being defensive when they hear what they do not wish to hear; furthermore, feedback was often presented unskillfully, with lack of sensitivity and often for the wrong reasons. For many, feedback became a license to say to somebody what they had always wanted to say (usually negative) but had not had the courage. Now, with "permission" to give feedback, people could say what they wanted to say with the hope that the receiver would accept the advice and hopefully change.

Such manipulation and ill use of feedback disturbed many people in the field. Just as disturbing was to see individuals in a group placed on the "hot seat" as the group members poured out feedback. The impact of this barrage was often negative, defense producing, and even traumatic. Rarely did it create real alternatives for the individual or offer the prospect of change.

But, what can be done for people who have worked together over the years and have built up considerable negative feelings toward each other? How can these negative feelings be shared and the air cleansed so that work can be more productive? How can the idea of feedback work in a constructive and supportive environment so that it can be a true gift to individuals who see it in the context of support rather than attack, manipulation, or criticism? Most of us who have worked in groups for any period of time are all too conscious of the "unfinished business" that keeps relationships strained and creates tension and conflicts among members and inevitably affects the quality and quantity of work produced among the group. Positive and constructive ways of reducing these conflicts must be developed so that trust and support flourish among the group rather than defensiveness and mistrust. The following design has been used many times on groups in which members have been overtly hostile with each other. This is one of those rare designs that seems to work nearly every time. It is used in situations in which the parties involved have a real interest in reducing the conflict and building the group into a more supportive and effective team of people.

Background

In this particular situation, six executives regularly meet to solve organizational problems; the group includes the president, the executive vice-president, and four vice-presidents. The six individuals spend most of their time working autonomously, although there are many organizational problems for which they each have a mutual vested interest. Although these individuals are skilled in their own right, they are limited, as one might expect, in their own range of experience, their own qualities of leadership, and in their own personal styles. The predominating norm in the group is to be problem oriented and to avoid issues of an interpersonal nature. Thus, over a period of five years a number of unresolved differences have accumulated. There virtually is no legitimate avenue for feedback among the group and only in periods of crisis do emotions flare, at which time the depths of some of the antagonism become apparent. Although individuals are superficially friendly and well mannered most of the time, one has the feeling that the group is constantly sitting on a powder keg of emotions that block effective communication and problem solving among the group.

In many organizations the inability to handle interpersonal conflict is a major block to organizational effectiveness among key problem solvers and decision makers.

Most executives are opposed to dedicating any time to their own "maintenance"; they are expected to have a certain amount of interpersonal skills. The problem, however, is that people in such positions of authority receive very little feedback. They seldom have access to effective supervision; furthermore, their peers and subordinates are not in a position to provide them with the kind of information they need concerning their own behavioral impact on the organization. Subordinates often tend to accommodate the needs and interests of their bosses; to their faces subordinates will protect and support their bosses' ideas. In addition, they often go out of their way to protect themselves and keep to themselves information that could make them look less than favorable to their bosses. Thus, in most organizations there is an unspoken collusion between subordinates and bosses that produces the opposite of what a good supervisory process or a system of feedback might contribute. It is a process we call "the seduction of the executive," and it is one reason that organizational and individual feedback systems are crucial to the health and well-being of any effective organization. It is also why we demand enough time to do the job right when we are asked to help such executive groups improve their effectiveness in working together.

In this particular instance the facilitator asks for the equivalent of two days—from 9 A.M. until 10 P.M. on the first day and from 9 A.M. until 4 P.M. the second day. If executives are not willing to give this much time to their own operational effectiveness, then it is doubtful whether they are very serious about the process or with dealing with the issues that are bound to arise.

The "Inner-Outer" Design

Rarely is it possible to initiate a feedback process without time for the group to warm up and gain a greater sense of familiarity and trust with each other. In this particular situation, the facilitator uses a variation of the "inner-outer design" by asking the group of six executives to complete a very specific task in a forty-minute period of time. The time itself is broken into five, seven-minute periods, with a minute break between each working period. During the break the participants are asked to move themselves physically in their group and not to work on the task at all. (See Case 1 in Chapter 5.) The group is asked to generate a list of no fewer than ten specific problems that have kept the group from functioning as well as it might (excluding personality issues) or problems that have seemed to influence the total organization in which all the members present have some sort of vested interest. These problems are the ones the group will involve itself in problem solving.

The participants are asked to rank order their top ten problems in terms of those issues that can and must be solved as soon as possible. The task, a very real one, catches the interest of the group and gives the facilitator an opportunity to understand their dynamics as a working group as well as how each responds as an individual. In addition, the process is diagnostic in that the participants are able to perceive the issues that most block their own development. The information they generate during the task, however, is put aside during this particular activity, and the participants become involved in a lengthy "process" analysis of how they have worked as a group during this period of time (again, refer to Case 1, Chapter 5). Each of the three pairs of the participants are assigned some aspect of group process to analyze such as leadership, decision making, membership, norms, or goals and communications. Each pair is expected to provide specific examples of what behaviors actually occurred that were helpful or not helpful to the group in accomplishing the task in each of these process areas. After each group has reported its findings and time has been allowed for a general discussion, each individual is asked to write in private three statements that are based on what has occurred during the task activity and that seem to be characteristic of how the group usually works and what the group might do to become more effective in each of the areas. Among the eighteen recommendations that are generated in a five-minute period of time, there is, predictably, an enormous amount of overlap so that the group ends with five or six recommendations that have strong agreement across the group. These areas of agreement, plus several other recommendations, are then put aside with the group's promising at a separate time after the two-day program to develop specific strategies to improve its performance on task activities in the future.

Thus, in less than two hours the six participants have:

1. Experienced several successes, including the completion of a number of specific tasks that would benefit them in the future;
2. Been able to be specific and personal with the information concerning how they perform as a group and how they might be different in the future;
3. Developed a relatively clear picture of how they operate as decision makers and legitimized the fact that they are indeed imperfect and might benefit from change. Indeed, they have experienced the fact that candor, directness, and openness do not have to be particularly painful, and, in fact, can be accomplished with humor and goodwill, as long as a working situation is structured and time bounded in a manner similar to what they have experienced.

All of this activity, of course, is very important to the facilitator for another reason. That is, the facilitator now has an enormous amount of information about how the group responded to the task and to the opportunities for feedback. Based on this, the facilitator must now determine whether the group is indeed ready for the classic "I gotcha" feedback design. Unless the facilitator sees support, trust, and candor exhibited during these sessions without people getting hostile and defensive, undertaking the following design will be inappropriate. Thus, this particular design assumes some level of trust, openness to change and feedback, and the group's willingness to work together in relation to the members' own personal development and growth. The design is built on the assumption that these individuals influence the lives of their subordinates, and unless they are willing to scrutinize themselves carefully and maximize their own individual development, they should have second thoughts about being in positions of influence over the lives of others.

The "I Gotcha" Design

The six members of the group are each given two large pieces of newsprint and a magic marker. They are told to divide each sheet into two long columns. On the first sheet they are to list eight to ten of their greatest strengths as people and as managers-supervisors. They are to be specific, with each strength hopefully defined in terms of some kind of behavior. Furthermore, they are to include one or two specific examples of how they see these strengths being utilized. In the second column on the same sheet they are then asked to make a list of the eight to ten strengths they think their other five associates see in them. They are told that it will be quite legitimate for the two lists to be substantially different, since what we believe are our strengths may not be as visible or obvious as the ones we believe others may see.

On the second sheet of newsprint the participants are asked to list in the first column eight to ten areas in which as a person or as a manager-supervisor they feel they need to grow or develop to become even more effective. With some humor it is suggested that if they cannot find eight areas of needed growth, they probably aren't alive. Again, they are encouraged to identify specific behaviors and wherever possible to have in mind examples of each of the areas. Likewise, in the second column they are urged to write the eight areas in which the others might see them as needing to develop to become more effective.

This task is what we might call a "mind wrencher." It is meant to be difficult and usually takes anywhere from thirty to forty minutes for individuals to complete. There is usually some moaning and groaning about the task, which the facilitator should handle by providing some levity and, while taking the task seriously, trying to take the edge off its being a "heavy" emotional task. At this point, one of the participants is asked to volunteer to work with the group. Before starting this new activity, the facilitator announces that following the first volunteer other individuals will be drawn at random from a hat in order to equalize the chance at being selected. The other participants are asked to consider this first person's greatest stengths, as well as areas of needed growth and development. Each individual is asked to develop a list of eight to ten of this person's greatest strengths, as well as eight to ten areas of needed growth. Again, it is suggested that those characteristics could be in areas of how the individual listens, presents information, organizes, designs meetings, evaluates people, handles conflict, rewards or punishes individuals, uses humor, collaborates, problem solves, makes decisions, or does any of a hundred things that influence the lives of others. This process usually takes less than five minutes.

Now, the volunteer is asked to stand in front of the room next to a large easel with newsprint. The participant is asked to compile a list that the group generates first in terms of identified strengths. The group is asked for one strength, the individual writes it on the newsprint, and members provide confirmation by giving examples of how they see that strength being used. It is crucial that specific examples are given to support each of the items that are written in the strength column. Rarely does such a listing generate less than fifteen items. The group is encouraged to indicate specifically when it agrees with a strength identified by another member. The individual writing the list is encouraged to make certain that he or she understands exactly what the strength represents and if necessary to ask for clarification. When the list has been compiled, the individual is then asked to place his or her own list beside the one generated by the group and to speak directly to each of the eight or ten items he or she has identified, being sure to give examples. Once finished with his or her own list, the individual is asked to talk briefly about how he or she would be viewed by others. At this point, the facilitator asks the group and the individual to identify possible discrepancies between how the group saw the individual, how the individual saw himself or herself, and how the person thought others would in fact see him or her. Usually the tendency is for a high degree of agreement, with disagreement perhaps among 25 percent of the items the group has identified. This information is what becomes important and what should be examined by the group. Similarly, there may be areas that the group did not identify, which the individual believes represent real strengths. Again, this discrepancy provides the opportunity for shared discussion to determine whether the group simply takes the strength for granted or in fact does not see the area as a strength and, as sometimes occurs, may even see it as a liability.

The role of the facilitator is to support and clarify and, when necessary, to supply examples from his or her own observations to bring the "feedback" into the "here and now." The facilitator should encourage participants to talk directly to each other and not to intellectualize the process by speaking as if the person were not there. While the design encourages and deals with "lists" of behavior, the feedback session should be anything but a simple listing. By providing specific behaviors and confirming those behaviors with other members, an opportunity for discussion and plenty of examples is created. Eventually, a clear pattern of certain kinds of behavior (such as supporting, confronting, taking charge) that are important to identify will emerge. This is particularly true since so often people "overuse" their strengths, which gets them into as much trouble as anything they do. This part of the activity usually takes at least thirty minutes and is highly stimulating. However, since it is quite difficult for individuals to listen attentively to positive information about themselves, it is imperative that the facilitator make certain that the strengths are not run over lightly and that examples are encouraged. It is often helpful to have individuals summarize as many strengths as possible without looking. Hearing their own words can reinforce the entire process.

Dropping the other shoe or asking for a list of areas that need improvement or growth is often easier for the individual receiving feedback to take than is listening to his or her strengths. Obviously, for the activity to be successful, the participants must be willing to risk being direct and candid and to provide specific examples. Generally this awareness and growth almost always occur, and as the process develops, the specificity of feedback increases and becomes even richer and supported by better examples. In some ways this activity is similar to an initiation rite in that individuals in the group see themselves as vulnerable and thus are very careful to be fair and even-handed with one another by providing helpful and not punitive examples. There is a tendency for the group to cohere as the process continues, and the shared tension—and sometimes relief when it's over—provides an important foundation on which trust is built.

What we are looking at here is a powerful and constructive design that virtually never becomes negative. This is where the "I gotcha" comes into play. In this instance "I gotcha" refers to the facilitator's being able to place the group in a position where because of the nature of the design the participants have to be honest and supportive. It becomes apparent from the beginning when individuals are asked to write the list of their own strengths and areas of needed growth, that they do not want their own list to differ radically from the list of what they believe others will see. Furthermore, since they realize there will be a "reality test" when their own lists and perceptions are compared with the actual perceptions of the group, they know to not be honest would only make them appear "out of touch" in the eyes of their peers. Thus, individuals are particularly "hard" on themselves and very candid in terms of their own strengths and limitations. The reward for their own trust is the enormous amount of agreement between their list and that of the group. Thus, if members of the group come up with an area they believe could be improved upon and if it is also on the individual's list, then it is very difficult for the person to be defensive about a point with which he or she already agrees. It becomes much easier to consider "change" when there is mutual agreement over the areas that need improvement. Thus, the lack of discrepancies is what usually creates the greatest impact. It is not that we do not know our areas of limitation; rather, we tend to deceive ourselves into believing that others do not realize them as well. With agreement by the group, the pressure for an individual to change increases, and in an interesting way this pressure is synonymous with permission—the individual receives "permission" to change, with the full support of the group.

The entire activity for each individual takes at least an hour and a half. The process is tiring and intense and requires at least a ten-minute break between individuals. That the process itself will become boring is simply not a concern since both the participants and the individuals are so highly involved. Whenever possible, however, the process should be broken with periods of recreation or alternative activities to break the intense pace.

At the end of the workshop, at least an hour and a half should be set aside for individuals to propose contracts with the group. Such contracts should focus on two or three areas of change that the individual would like to initiate and that would not only affect the relationship with the members of the group, but also might require some support and help from the members themselves. Often such behaviors as cutting people off, not listening, poor eye contact, and inability to express feelings or ideas can be worked on with the support of the group. Each contract should include the following:

1. A description of the behavior that is to be changed.
2. The help that will be needed—from the group in general—or certain individuals in particular.
3. A plan for measuring the degree of change that will hopefully take place.
4. A time table for completing the contract.
5. Other support that might be necessary to make sure the attempted change has the best chance of occurring.

It is assumed that such groups meet periodically and that time can be set aside to provide later feedback and support as to how people see individuals changing and developing around their areas of needed improvement or development. Again, the experience is highly intense, positive, and is the single best team-building activity that we can recommend. However, it is demanding and requires that a group desire to be a team and have some basic element of trust before beginning.

Case 5: The Old Feedback Reversal Trick

Any kind of personal or organizational change can only begin when the individuals involved will acknowledge the fact that change is necessary. This assumes that a problem has been clearly identified and accepted not only as existing but also as possible to change. Thus, for change, it is relatively easy to develop mechanisms for gathering data. What is much more difficult is helping an individual or client system to hear and internalize the information; personal resistances and defenses can throw up a hundred barriers to the process itself. Many of our colleagues agree with us when we say that finding solutions to problems tends often to be less difficult than accepting the fact that there is a problem and then airing the problem so that it can be solved.

Many people are willing to leave their inherent conflicts unresolved and thus maintain the status quo. For them the present situation of predictable conditions and stress is what they know. The conditions under which stress may be reduced represents an unknown and less predictable situation that raises doubts about the price to be paid and whether true benefits would indeed be reaped over the long run. People usually will be inclined to move with what is known and predictable over that which is not. Therefore, dealing with our own internal resistances to change and toward the resolution of such conflict is often just as difficult as dealing with actively hostile relationships or problems, which are more overt and easily identified. In days gone by, facilitators, counselors, therapists, and consultants were hired with the expectations that they would provide the expertise to move individuals or systems to change and even to help them through the change process. But, often the impact of such expert authority is greatly reduced because the individuals receiving the information may quite simply have not "bought it"—nor have they identified personally with the information. In other situations people often look to the authority for the solutions and are consequently less dedicated or committed to the solutions than had they been more independent and self-sufficient in the problem identification phase of the problem solving.

Background

In the following situation, twenty-five middle managers have been involved in a rather intensive program aimed at providing information about their own leadership behavior and problems with their own areas of responsibility within their organization. After perhaps twenty-five hours of having worked together over a number of weeks and having gathered a considerable amount of data—anonymously contributed by their subordinates—the group is in a position to consider what changes, if any, might be warranted. Up to this point, most of the participants have indicated a tremendous amount of interest and enthusiasm for the process. But, as facilitators well know, the greatest resistances can be anticipated at the very point of change. To reduce these resistances and help the individuals hear and internalize the wide range of data being provided them, the following design has been developed.

The Design

The individuals are divided into groups of three, based on some mutual trust and shared interest. (A simple sociometric has been developed and utilized in this process so that people can only be in clusters because of some shared common interest or by choice.) At this point, the participants are asked to take all the data they have been able to gather from their subordinates and peers (which have been summarized for them), as well as information from the preceding workshops in which they have participated in a variety of simulation experiences, and over the next hour integrate the data into a complete description of their strengths and limitations as leaders and individuals. They are to ask themselves why they tend to over- or underutilize certain skills or behaviors, what problems seem to exist in their own departments that are at least partly created as a result of their own behavior, and which problems seem to be independent of them. They are also to determine what areas of their performance seem to require immediate attention and which demand some long-range consideration. In painting this picture, they are all to act as if they are consultants to themselves—as if they are going to report all of the critical information back to themselves so they can understand and "hear it." Thus, they need to be specific, data based, and able to deal with those conditions that indeed could be changed or that warrant attention.

At the end of an hour, the individuals reconvene in their groups of three, and then one at a time each person is allowed fifteen to thirty minutes to report findings to the "client." In this situation, the other two members of the group act as if they are the individual who is actually feeding back the data. In other words, they listen to the data—to the self-portrait being drawn by the "consultant" as if they are in fact the person. Thus, the individual acts as his or her own consultant, and "he" or "she" is played by the two other members of the group. The individual is forced into a position of objectivity; the two individuals who are playing "him" or "her" are given an opportunity to ask clarification questions in order to increase self-understanding and personal insight. A dialogue is thus created, which forces the "consultant" to expand his or her own self-portrait.

Acting as a consultant to yourself makes it quite difficult to become defensive or resistant. Certain psychological pressures are created, which encourage the consultant to be extremely knowledgeable and sensitive to the client who, again, is herself or himself. As strange as this may all sound, it inevitably works after perhaps a few initial moments of discomfort. The fact is that the "consultant" does know herself or himself better than anyone and tends to be incredibly candid and personal when expected to reveal personal data. As one's own consultant, the individual does not find the need to justify information as he or she might if it were being presented by some outside authority or peers.

The painting of the picture by the consultant and the interchange that develops usually take a total of anywhere from thirty to forty-five minutes. The total activity for all three participants, including the one-hour preparation time, may take up to three and a half hours.

Logically, this design of integration and self-exploration can be followed nicely with problem-solving activities, which again would allow the three-person group to work together developing strategies for the resolution of a number of issues raised by the members during the time they spent "painting" their own pictures. It would be a shame not to utilize the understandings and the insights gained from this feedback design in a hard-nosed yet sensitive problem-solving design. By simply reversing roles and having ourselves look at ourselves—being objective consultants to ourselves—we can in this design gain distance from our own problems and integrate what data we have been able to receive along with other data we already know about ourselves. This design provides a rare opportunity to explore specific areas that need attention in our lives and to place them in a rational perspective around data rather than simple intuition and feelings.

Case 6: Reducing Adult-Student Antipathy by Merely Changing the Rules of the Game

A tremendous amount of the conflict generated in groups is based on previously borne antipathies toward that group and the expectations we have of the group's behavior. In one sense we lie in waiting for the group to fulfill our expectations or predictions and then having done so respond in a predictable fashion—no doubt leading to a further polarization of the situation. The problem is somewhat akin to the self-fulfilling prophecy that we all know so well in which our anticipation of a problem actually helps to make the problem occur because of our own defensiveness or attitudes that we bring to the situation. In some ways the facilitator needs to be a mind reader to understand the kinds of antipathies and antagonisms that prevail in a group at any one time among the subgroups or cliques that exist.

One goal of the facilitator is to make sure that the preconceived notions and biases of the various members of the group are not allowed to misdirect the group from a particular task. For example, just because there are prejudices and antagonisms within a group does not mean that the issues underlying these all have to be "dealt with." Often the need to "deal" on the part of the facilitator is, in fact, the facilitator's need and not the need of the group. More important in many cases is the facilitator's role as an intermediary and helper—to get the job done without having to deal with all the underlying currents of tension and conflict. Nor does one have to "like" everybody in order to work effectively. Many times personal issues may remain even after the task is successfully completed. Ideally, the experience itself will prove positive and lead to greater personal harmony. The following example is a good illustration of this point.

Background

The nine school board members sit stiffly—the image of respectability—awaiting the onslaught. They had desired to gain a better understanding of the human relation problems that existed within their school district across ages and grades, between faculty and students, and in a variety of other situations. In a weaker moment they had agreed to meet with an equal number of high school students who had been selected because they—in the words of the principal—"are a representative group who have their hand on the pulse of the system." The session is to begin at eight o'clock; it is now two minutes to eight and still no students are to be seen. Several "knowing" glances are passed around the table about the "unreliable" adolescents. Word trickles in that a number of students are outside waiting for the meeting to begin.

At one minute after eight, the door bursts open and all nine of the students appear out of nowhere, talking noisily and dressed in the usual array of adolescent rags and riches paraphernalia. Their discourteous and rather raucous entrance only confirms the expectations of many of the board members, who can almost be seen checking the individuals off as to degree of belligerency, neatness, and politeness. Of course, one can also imagine the students' picture of the school board. There they all are, enthroned in an aura of power and arrogance, not really wanting to listen to kids and easily reading the expressions of doubt and suspicion on their young faces. Thus, the stage is set for a classic confrontation between people of different values, generations, and expectations.

The Design

There is no complex design, no creative set of strategies to bring the two groups together—only the following set of simple instructions:

The young men and women who have come here tonight at your request are expert consultants in an area in which you have limited information because you do not live as they live in their system. As consultants their task is to provide you with clear and specific information that can broaden your view of their system so that you can be more sensitive to the needs and problems that exist. Clearly, your role as board members in this session this evening is to probe and utilize the resources available both in terms of what exists and what could exist in order to make this a more productive school system.

Our approach will be rather simple. Our purpose this evening is not for our consultants to agree with the board, nor is it to resolve any differences that may exist. Rather, it is to make quite sure that these young adults are heard and are able to provide you with the kinds of information you need to do your job as effectively as possible. My job is to make sure that lines of communication—and thus information—remain open during the course of this evening. During the first thirty minutes we will have three board members interview three students using, among others, the questions on the card you were each given as you entered tonight. At the end of this thirty-minute period, the groups of three will be switched, and you will interview another group of three students. We will then have a break followed by an opportunity to brainstorm some solutions to several of the more salient issues raised during the interviews. This will be a session for idea building—again, not for criticism or debate.

What follows is an amazing change of events. The students, given permission to be adults, start to act like adults. Once labeled as "expert resources," they can afford to give away some of the affectations of the adolescent and replace them with the maturity of the adults. Similarly, the board members have received permission to avoid looking critically at the ideas of students, and instead to listen carefully to them as resources of the system in which they have been voted responsibility. The interviews are candid and extremely informative for the board.

In the following brainstorming session, students and board, working collaboratively with each other, are both surprised at the insight, creativity, and originality of the other group. By focusing clearly on the task of the evening rather than on the typical differences in values and beliefs found in the two groups, a successful program has occurred. By merely shifting the expectations and providing a few simple basic permissions, the climate of the problem-solving group has changed from one that predictably would have been a failure to one that has resulted in a positive and constructive experience.

Case 7: Changing Attitudes: The Key to Conflict Resolution

It has often been said by management that unions breed antagonism and initiate adversarial relationships where none previously existed. The fact is that once unions appear, there tends to be increasing mistrust between them and management—a mistrust built upon a foundation of misunderstanding and inadequate communication. Upper management is often so distant from labor that it only hears what is happening when it concerns negotiating, bargaining, or perhaps grievances. Over the years, the union becomes cast in the shadow of an aggressive, power seeking, antagonistic body, and management is cast in the cloak of insensitive exploiters who care much more about dollar profits than the quality of life of the workers. The collective bargaining process intensifies the adversarial nature of these relationships with the agreed-upon game being one of exaggeration, threats, and intimidation, and with collaboration being seen as "selling out."

One result of all this is that management reacts negatively to the predictable gyrations of the bargaining table and, in between contracts, may tend to take a hard-nosed, contract-guided, authoritarian approach to the management process itself. The "you made your bed, now sleep in it" attitude can be laced with hostility and may act to further drive the two groups apart. It is also assumed that if labor and management come to the bargaining table in an antagonistic frame of mind, the negotiations will tend to go in the same manner. Increasingly, we are learning that if management treats labor with respect and consideration between contracts and attempts to draw them into the collaborative process, the problems that affect their lives and the environment of the negotiations may change, and an attitude of increasing trust between the two groups may develop over time.

To bring this about clearly takes more than a single design. However, we feel it important to share at this time a design of ours that seemed to catalyze management into a different approach and attitude toward labor, and which over time seemed to result in major benefits for both management and labor.

Background

The group of twenty-five upper-, middle-, and top-level executives has been meeting in two-day training workshops every few months for a period of ten months. During these programs, they have experienced a variety of activities that are intended to increase their awareness of the benefits of alternative management styles and lead the organization from a rather aggressive top-down autocratic approach to management to one of greater moderation and collaboration among various levels of supervision down to the line of laborers. Although the participants have involved themselves with enthusiasm, there is a continual thread of skepticism, based on deeply ingrained beliefs that labor is basically antagonistic — if you give them an inch, they'll take a mile. Further, the beliefs exist that labor doesn't care about the organization, only themselves, and that you have to watch them every minute or they will rip you off. So it is, that in spite of what appears to be a rather effective workshop program, very little change is being perceived within the organization, and the attitudes that management carries toward labor seem to be maintaining themselves. At this point in time the facilitators believe that unless management can begin to see labor in a different light and somehow alter its belief systems, it will never even have a choice of altering its own management approach or begin to utilize some of the skills learned in the workshops. The facilitators thus initiated the following design.

The Design

Each of the participants receives the names of eight line workers and two supervisors. The task between the end of the workshop and the next two-day training program (six weeks later) is to conduct ten, thirty-minute interviews of the people on the list, based on a series of questions the group itself has developed to help the members understand the attitudes and problems of the line workers and the supervisors. Once the interviews are completed (a total of five hours), the participants are asked to organize their data around each question and make a series of statements that represent some kind of truth or at least trend that was substantiated throughout their interviews. It is understood that although they might not come up with any truths or even trends, there just could be some, and these should be noted as specifically and clearly as possible.

The next workshop's first order of business is to assemble groups of five participants and have each group integrate members' data across the eight questions that had been asked. Thus, each group of five is to derive a series of statements representing "truths" or trends that all five members of the group can agree on. In addition, the groups are asked to discuss the most significant thing they discovered from the interviews, either about themselves or about the people that they interviewed. One member of each group then becomes part of a task force whose job is to integrate all the statements across the groups and to come up with a series of final statements of truth and trends that seem representative of the organization as a whole.

Based on these final statements, the president of the organization and two top aides are to develop a "white paper" that will contain a philosophy of management consistent with the management practices so well received in the workshop and the data generated from the workers. Whenever conflicts crop up between management theory and these viewpoints, an attempt is to be made to clarify and reduce the differences. The white paper is then taken to the entire group of participants; they are asked to critique and make suggestions since the white paper itself will be the basis for a coherent system of management practices that evolved from the workshops.

The white paper is then sent out to all 700 employees of the organization. The employees are asked to convey their insights to representatives, who will in turn convey them to management. In theory, the final product will reflect both the views of management and labor and will provide the basis for a continued dialogue that will examine any differences that still exist between theory and practice.

Summary

This design is a precedent-setting venture into the ranks that in the case just described eventually resulted in movement toward utilization of "quality circles" and other collaborative programs between management and labor. What made this design so powerful was that management found in its interviews with labor that the employees were "human" and not particularly antagonistic. What they desired most was to be heard, to have their ideas solicited, and to be given the opportunity to utilize themselves as fully as possible. Furthermore, antagonisms created around the bargaining table were certainly not found to be central to the issues raised by the typical wage earner. Most of the managers had been so dissociated from labor that they had only fantasies and the reports from the tensions of the bargaining table around which to build their own stereotypes and attitudes. This design managed to break the stereotypes and open management's eyes to the positive possibilities of a more collaborative and involving approach to management. By working with labor between negotiations in a developmental and positive manner, the number of grievances decreased, as did work stoppages and strikes. While such outcomes are becoming rather commonplace in the literature today, the issue to be made here is that a rather simple design that placed management in the position of having to "listen" to labor provided the catalyst for significant change within this particular organization.

Case 8: The Paradoxical Clinic—or How to Take Responsibility for Altering Interpersonal Conflicts

The most common source of tension and conflict in most of our lives has to do with the day-to-day interrelationships we have with other people. Let's face it, people are just plain difficult to live with. How many times have we or other people said "so and so is just impossible to deal with—he is so set in his ways." Or, "I'm simply at my wit's end, every time we get into this situation the same thing occurs—it's driving me crazy." If we could get rid of even half of the interpersonal conflicts in our lives, day-to-day living would probably be much more enjoyable. Several years ago we adapted some of the new ideas being generated out of family therapy, especially the utilization of paradoxical problem solving, in developing a design for helping individuals manage conflict and the resulting stress more effectively in their daily lives. The design is uncomplicated to say the least and in a workshop that is geared toward problem solving has been found to offer a wonderfully humorous yet meaningful interlude. Furthermore, it provides participants with many new ways of thinking about problem solving and conflict as well as some very interesting alternatives to their own peculiar situations.

The design itself can be adapted easily within a period of anywhere from thirty minutes to two hours. It is aimed at helping the participants feel more potent when dealing with other people and to increase their ability to influence their own lives—to reduce the belief of many that they are the "victims" of other people's behavior. Our focus is on those specific interactions that occur between two people and that are predictable and aggravating. The aim is to seek direct sources of action or "intervention" into the predictable pattern of behavior in order to change the outcome to one that is more positive or constructive. The fact is that many of the interpersonal problems we have with other people form part of a predictable pattern of response to a particular type of situation. We tend to look at the problem as being the other person's, but if we look hard at the pattern, we will often begin to see how our own responses to the person's behavior are just as predictable and that we are insidiously colluding with the individual and allowing—even reinforcing—the behavior to occur. For example, if Susy uses anger as a means of getting her way and we predictably back off each time because we see no sense in making a "big thing out of nothing," we are colluding; each time we back off we are reinforcing Susy's view that anger is the most sensible course of action for getting her way—because it works.

We must look for keys to change the pattern. Sometimes even small changes can bring a disorientation to the situation so that change can occur. Our problem often is that we are so rooted in predictable patterns that we feel helpless and hopeless and often lose our sense of creativity and humor. Without these, we will surely remain victims. Similarly, if we question the benefits of not changing a predictable pattern, we will find some interesting answers. Thus, by folding our tent and acquiescing in a predictable manner each time an individual gets angry, we simply do not have to "deal" with the anger or perhaps with a loss of the individual's friendship. These are clear benefits to us and help us maintain a negative pattern.

The paradoxical clinic focuses on individuals' predictable patterns of behavior to which we in turn respond predictably. We are looking for ways of altering one-half of the equation—our predictable behavior—so that the situation itself changes. Again, it is necessary to realize that our usual attempts to solve the problem may in fact be reinforcing it. Thus, the depressed person whom everyone tries to cheer up may only feel more out of step, more inadequate, or more misunderstood. The "cheering-up therapy" may reinforce the very depression we would like to alleviate. Or take the example of the child who continually throws tantrums; the parents respond by walking on eggshells and doing nothing to "disturb" their sensitive child. Placating the child spoils the youngster and results in more tantrums. Thus, again, the pattern has to be broken and the predictable response prevented from following the predictable behavior. We are attempting to shift the influence of the situation from the perpetrator to the victim. Put another way, anything a person can do to make a situation more positive should be tried—doing what we can do is the underlying premise. We are not trying to alter the total relationship or to change an individual's personality. We are simply attempting to alter a situation and a predictable set of responses. This is an ultimately rational and objective approach.

The Design

Participants are divided into groups of three or four. They are asked individually to consider a predictable problem they have with another individual. This is a problem that makes them feel impotent and frustrated; they wish they could change the situation, but the problem seems to be in control of the other person. The participants are asked individually to answer the following set of questions about the situation they have identified:

1. What is it that regularly occurs? What does the individual do? What is your response?
2. What is the outcome that is not helpful? How do you feel?
3. What specifically needs changing?
4. What are you doing specifically in response to the predictable behavior that is also predictable and that may be reinforcing the problem?

The facilitators next seek a volunteer to share a problem or conflict situation with the group. At this point the facilitators ask the groups of three and four participants to generate at least two or three paradoxical solutions to the problem. They have five minutes to complete their task. They are told to be both serious and humorous in their approach to the situation and not to be at all limited by *shoulds* and *should not's*. At the end of five minutes various groups share some of their responses—usually seven or eight in a five- to ten-minute period. The job of the facilitators is not to do a heavy critique of any particular solution but to provide the individual who has volunteered the conflict situation with a wide range of new alternatives or ways of looking at the problem. Inevitably, several unique and interesting solutions are suggested.

For example, in one situation a happily married woman who had a nine-to-five job admitted she enjoyed cooking meals and playing the role of the traditional housewife in the family. Obviously, the husband had the best of both worlds and found little to complain about. The wife's only resentment was that on Saturday, her only day for shopping, the husband would usually sit and watch television or play tennis or golf. The wife would end up walking up and down the supermarket aisles seething. She at least wanted him to share and perhaps even take responsibility for this task. Her response to him would be occasional sarcasm but never a confrontation, and predictably there was little reason for the husband to change since he could continue to do exactly what he wanted anyway. Thus, by continuing to shop and by not changing the pattern, the woman was reinforcing the problem of the husband's lack of responsibility and involvement.

One of the solutions generated in the group was to have the woman buy a wide range of diet food such as lettuce, yogurt, and soups—to which she was accustomed in the past from dieting—and to store up for several weeks. When it came time to shop, she would be simply too busy or need to relax. She did this without hostility or malice. She simply did not shop. As with every paradoxical problem-solving approach, the individual creating the change must be willing to be consistent over a relatively long period of time or the pattern will simply reverse and return to its previous state. In this particular situation, it took only two weeks for the husband to get the message, but it took six weeks for the pattern to really change.

Armed with such an example, the participants find themselves incredibly creative as they are given permission to look beyond the boundaries of typical solutions. The humor that is generated is marvelous and the concrete ideas many.

Conclusions

This chapter is in no way intended to be a panacea for all conflict situations. Our goal has been to provide a wide variety of designs directed toward helping individuals solve conflicts in a more creative and productive fashion. The value of the chapter lies in the individual designs and the different ways of thinking about conflict. Most important is the knowledge that we can alter conflict situations dramatically if we choose.

7 Evaluation

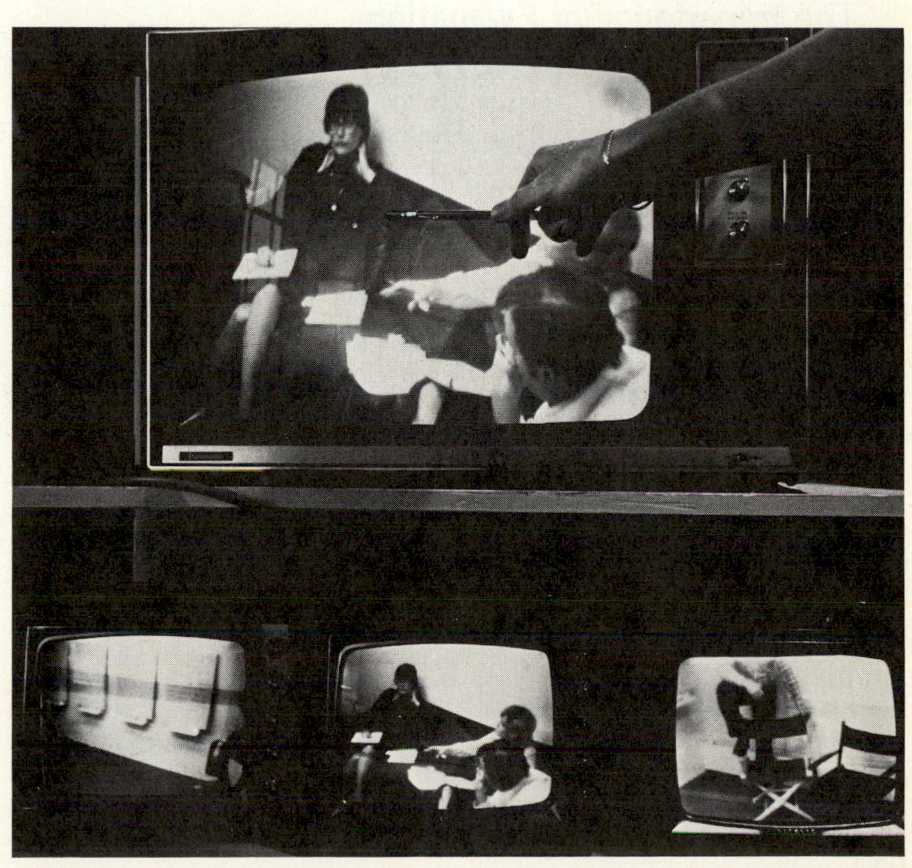

Because this book is being written for trainers working in a variety of situations, a simple answer on how to evaluate is not easy. Obviously, evaluating a half-day workshop is very different from evaluating a three-year organization development program. One way out of the dilemma is to think of evaluation at three levels: (1) low-level, ongoing evaluations; (2) middle-level, concluding evaluations; and (3) long-range process evaluations.

At the first two levels, this chapter will emphasize rather typical evaluations for workshops and programs. At the third level, we will emphasize a very different view of evaluation in the process evaluation—one that we think incorporates evaluation into the entire training process and one that emphasizes evaluation as a process that does not have predictable content outcomes and that includes ongoing data collection to modify learning objectives and outcomes. In addition, to come to full circle, we will invite discussion on how evaluation is used to generate change. Evaluation is used beyond a report and a retrospective but for generating involvement and use of the findings.

The Importance of Evaluation

Trainers cringe at the concept of evaluation. It feels so technical, with a need for precision in defining learning objectives and specifying exact outcomes. Then there are all of these statistical analyses to wade through. There is also the difficulty of being sure what the outcomes will be in advance and trying to express them to the person assigned to help you do the evaluation. There are other fears—that the numbers won't come out right, that your project will somehow be deemed a failure, or that you will be required to demonstrate statistically that there are changes in the participants at their work as a result of the training when all kinds of environmental factors at work can mitigate against the use of the training. And, of course, there is the ultimate fear of a bad evaluation, for your ego as well as your reputation.

Burying your head in the sand like an ostrich won't make evaluation go away. One of the reasons organizations, as well as individuals, are less interested in training today than they were a decade ago when "training was hot" is the lack of demonstrable results to justify the enormous expenditures of money that were poured into training programs. Part of the fault lies with poorly designed evaluations and part lies in nonchalance over the lack of evaluations—happy looks on the faces of participants were too often viewed as sufficient evidence of effectiveness.

Today the evaluation component is absolutely essential. In judging the success of an activity, the trainer attempts to answer the question, "How did I do?" How a trainer did in meeting the learning objectives, which can be both task and process objectives, and how a trainer did in terms of participants' reactions to the content of the workshop have to be of high value for practitioners. For them, evaluation is the only means of proving the success or failure of their work.

Ongoing Evaluations

The final element in training design is evaluation. That does not mean waiting until the end to find out how the program went, but getting feedback throughout the program on how things are going. It is important to establish periodic evaluations while the program is still in progress to get an appraisal of the day's activities or some portion of them. These evaluations allow you, the trainer, to make changes or "midcourse corrections." They are geared to taking the pulse of the group and finding out if it is going as you would like. Through these evaluations you can determine whether participants are learning from the program and also how they are feeling about what is happening. Are they enjoying the experience or is it slow, boring, and repetitious? The data from participants can be the basis for immediate revisions ("We need more time to discuss the conflict of this morning") or it can be the basis for a staff discussion that evening and for making changes in the next day's training design.

In addition to helping the trainer make corrections, there are two other significant advantages of ongoing evaluations. One is that evaluations involve adult learners in their learning process. People do not want to be passive; they want to be heard, and they want to be involved. Too frequently communication is from the "top down," and the people are recipients of the program rather than real participants. People want to be heard, and it is our responsibility to give them opportunities to express what they think and feel about the program. Allowing such expression encourages one of the basic norms of a collaborative process of the trainer with the participants.

Yet another benefit of evaluation is that it encourages participants to get in touch with their feelings and express them. Too often people believe that because feelings are personal, they should remain private—that an expression of feelings will be harmful, dangerous, or inappropriate in a work setting. The expression of feelings is somehow equated with getting out of control or revealing a personal inadequacy. Even expressing feelings in the safety of the workshop is discounted because participants are afraid "it won't change anything" or "who would be interested in how I feel." By asking for feelings, trainers can help participants learn that feelings are appropriate in the present, they can be asked for, and they are helpful in revising a program and making the experience a better one. Often participants find that their feelings are shared and that if no one had expressed them, the possibilities for learning would have been reduced.

And there is more. Participants giving feedback become aware of what they are feeling and are often themselves surprised by what they say. Hearing themselves encourages them to act in response to what they heard themselves say. For example, one man heard himself say the he pays attention when the leader speaks but thinks that when group members speak, it is a waste of time; they don't know any more than he does—they're not experts. After he said it, he thought about what he had said and recognized the implications of his statement for him as a team member or as a staff participant. It was as if his saying it and hearing himself created a "click"—a new insight—and because he had said it, he now had "permission" to think about it and to change.

Giving feedback also provides an integration for some people of what was learned during the day. In response to the question, "What did you get out of today?" they begin to think and mentally review the day. They tick off what they heard and begin focusing on what they learned—"How would I use that at work?" "How would that get me out of the bad situation that I find myself in frequently." The events of the day become integrated with personal learning experiences.

Ongoing evaluations can be done very simply. The following suggestions for ongoing evaluations are provided for your use; feel free to adapt and modify them.

- At breaks or at lunch casually ask participants how things are going.
- Set up evening rap sessions when people are relaxed; then ask about gripes and satisfactions.
- Set up a planning group made up of participants. Each session of the planning group begins by having members report how they "saw things" since their last meeting.
- Have a different representative from each group (team, department) in the training take turns at meeting with the trainer daily to feed back impressions of the day.
- Ask the planning group to interview a number of participants each day, and then at the planning sessions to report on their interviews.
- At a given time, ask participants for a one-word description of how they are feeling at the moment. (You can get the feeling tone of the group—how are people feeling at the moment.)
- Ask participants to name one adjective that would describe the workshop so far. (You will find out how things are going—if the response is negative, plan for redesign.)
- Ask participants to rate the workshop on a scale of 1 to 10, with 1 being a waste of time and 10 being very worthwhile. Or 1 might be defined as boring and 10 as very stimulating. (You will find out how the workshop is being received and how meaningful it has been up to the present.)
- Ask participants what has been most helpful or most useful. (You will get an idea of what to include more of in the design.)
- Go around at the end of the day and ask participants, "How are you feeling at the end of the day?" or "What will you remember from today?" or "What was most meaningful to you today?" (Participants can integrate what they learned, and a bond of new communication will be created among members. Also, you will find out if someone was potentially harmed by the day's experience.)

Although ongoing evaluations can be verbal or written, both should be used. For example, the last evaluation suggestion mentioned is most effective when done verbally. You can initiate this closure experience about half an hour before the end of the program. You begin by asking each person to express "where they are" in response to the question, "How are you feeling at the end of the day?" Explain that it will be helpful to know where people are at the end of the day. Acknowledge that you realize there may be some people who are reluctant to express how they are feeling; they can say, "I pass," and the next person will continue. You begin the process by asking, "Who will start?" and then you can ask the group whether the members wish to continue to the right or to the left from the first person and then around the group.

Some trainers are reluctant to do this, saying that the responses are too structured or too formal. Our experience has been that it works well. Since it begins with someone who volunteers, that person's anxiety may be reduced by being first and "getting it over with." The next person also has a choice in terms of whether the discussion will go around to the left or right. That seems enough to get people comfortable with the idea. You encourage the norm that you want to hear from everyone and each person is important. You also establish the expectation that expressing what a person feels is safe and appropriate. People who are generally reluctant to express their feelings often do so in this format. When it is done frequently (a similar question asked at the end of each day), there is an acceptance and a building of skills in expressing what participants feel.

Another method of evaluation is to ask at the beginning of the day, "Did anything happen to you as a result of yesterday's experience?" (or if the program is weekly, as a result of last week's program). Again, begin by asking, "Who will go first?" and select the volunteer (sometimes there is a pause and you have to wait; sometimes three or four hands instantly shoot up). Then go around as in the previous example. In both exercises you, as the trainer, may also go, either in turn or last. This second method of evaluation allows participants to raise disturbing aspects of the training that they thought about overnight or to report how they tried what they learned, whether the experience was successful or failed.

Yet another method of evaluation is to set up a session about halfway through the program, in which you ask participants to respond to a series of questions on the content, staff, materials, format of the day, activities, and so forth. This sort of evaluation can be done with paper and pencil, or it can be a process in which participants work in groups to respond to the questions. Then the data are analyzed by the participants, and the entire group is invited to make recommendations for revisions.

During any of these methods of evaluation, you should be noting nonverbal behaviors, and based on those clues you should ask about what you see. In fact, you might be involved in any number of these not-so-formal ongoing evaluations during the course of a day. When you want to know how participants are responding to a particular experience, for example, stop and find out. You might ask some of the following questions:

- Are we [the trainers] spending enough time on this segment?
- Are you [the participants] having difficulty with this concept or exercise?
- Are you ready to move on?
- Do you want us to present an example or a demonstration?

Post-meeting reaction (PMR) sheets can be used at the end of the day for still another method of evaluation. Usually four to six questions are asked; participants respond anonymously and then turn the sheets in. The responses may be summarized by the participants and then fed back to the group for changes in their own structure. Or the sheets may be kept by the training staff to be used for possible design revisions. (For an example of PMR's, see Appendix A.) Sometimes at the end of the day, groups who have worked together are asked to create a slogan or a motto of how they are feeling. A "cheer" or a four-line poem serves the same purpose—that is, to end the day on a different tack by using the last of the group's energy to have fun, by letting participants tease each other at end of day, and by introducing that valuable ingredient "humor."

Ongoing evaluations allow you as trainer to find out how things are going and to make any necessary revisions. They also allow you to spark the program—to encourage process evaluation and to focus on how people feel in addition to content objectives. It also prevents both you and the participants from being unpleasantly surprised or disappointed at the end of the workshop when their expectations are not met or their hoped-for outcomes are not the real outcomes.

Ongoing evaluations allow you to assess where and when to make changes as indicated by the data, increasing the likelihood that the final evaluation will be positive.

Concluding Evaluations

What we are calling middle-level evaluations are evaluations at the end of a program that put the picture together more formally by describing the program as a whole and the way it turned out. It is essential to evaluate a workshop at the end to determine whether it satisfied the objectives it was designed to meet. Where are participants at the end of the experience? Do they have new skills? Are they more competent? How, at the end, are they feeling about their experience? Do they believe they wasted their time—that they were scapegoated and as a result are reluctant to be in a training program in the future? Or do they believe they were valued and thus have a good feeling about their organization. The concluding evaluation gives trainers a sense of the whole program as well as a sense of the various parts; it allows them to think in terms of future training objectives, or how the present design needs to be changed to increase its effectiveness with a new group of participants. It further allows participants to reflect on their experience and give feedback to the trainers as well as each other on what their experience has been. The process of a concluding evaluation creates a sense of closure. Finally, the evaluation process can build a new level of understanding among staff members and more effective methods for dealing with boring meetings or futile interactions.

It is important to remember that concluding evaluations are related to the learning objectives. Unless the objectives are well formulated, and even revised during the training, the outcomes will be less than helpful. Concluding evaluations can take a number of forms. Several of these are discussed in the following sections.

Interviews

Participants can be interviewed to see if their attitudes have changed, if they have acquired new skills, and if they feel the training was worthwhile. The advantage of interviews is that people tend to respond more fully than they might respond to a questionnaire. However, interviewing a large number of participants, both in terms of money for interviewers and in the amount of time required, is difficult.

Observers

Outcomes can be measured by having trained observers watch the actual behavior of workshop participants. They can note whether participants perform a task effectively at the workshop or they can observe participants at work to see if they are utilizing what they learned. The difficulties are obvious; skill in the workshop does not prove the skill is transferable to the real work situation, and observing the workshop participants at work may be difficult. Further, the reason participants do not implement the training may not be because of the poor training but rather because inhibiting factors in the work environment make it dangerous to try those new behaviors. Sometimes observers can ask colleagues and supervisors about the trainees' behavior prior to the training and then ask them for ratings on the same measures after the training.

Tests

Outcomes are often measured by tests. If what is to be used can be measured by tests (for example, improvement of written staff memos), then tests are an appropriate measure. However, if what is to be learned needs to be expressed in behavior, a test is an inadequate measure—that is, giving the "right answer" on paper is different from being able to do what is needed.

Although evaluation using tests can take many forms, the evaluation should be a test that simulates or approximates the way the behavior will be used in real life. For example, a training program may have focused on teaching the Hersey-Blanchard Situational Leadership[1] approach to managers. In that model, how a manager supervises is related to the "maturity" of the workers. Prior to the training, a test will be administered listing situations and alternatives the manager might decide are the "right" ones or most effective ones. The participants are then taught the theory and will practice how to determine the maturity level of the subordinates so that they know which managerial style will be most effective. At the end of the training, a test similar to the first one will be administered to determine if they have learned how to be effective leaders utilizing the model. It is the standard adaptation of a pretest-posttest format.

More often evaluations can take the form of case studies, role plays, simulations or other activities. Conducting this kind of an evaluation with a large group is difficult, but to the extent such evaluations can be designed (evaluations are as much an area of design as the program), the outcomes of the workshop will be known.

Paper and Pencil Evaluations

Because of their ease in administration, paper and pencil evaluations are the most frequently used. These are not measures of behavior but rather methods of allowing participants to describe changes that have occurred, what they have learned, and how they feel about the training program. Paper and pencil evaluations can take any of the following forms.

Open-Ended Questions. A series of questions are devised to allow participants to express how they felt during the course of the workshop or program. Questions might take the following form:

- What I liked best was ______________________________.
- What will be most helpful to me in my work was ______________.
- This workshop did not help me in solving my problem with ______.
- I am disappointed by ______________________________.
- Next time I would like ______________________________.
- The staff was ______________________________.

The questions allow participants to record their feelings and opinions without being bound by a structure; they are a good way of getting a broad base of information. The difficulty, however, is that summarizing the results is very time-consuming, especially with a large group. Often there is a feeling of adding apples and oranges—how people respond to the various questions may be so disparate as to preclude an organization of the data in a meaningful, objective way. Further, the results do not directly relate reported experiences to learning objectives. Although questions can be asked that relate to learning objectives, obtaining specific replies to an open-ended question is difficult.

---

1. Paul Hersey and Ken Blanchard, *Management of Organizational Behavior,* 4th Edition (Englewood Cliffs, N.J.: Prentice Hall, 1982).

Questionnaires. Post-meeting reaction sheets are frequently used to evaluate a training program. A series of questions relate to all parts of the workshop from the types of presentations to the hours of the program to the learning objectives. Participants fill the sheets in anonymously and generally hand them in as the program ends.

Any evaluation measure, including questionnaires, needs to be geared to the specific workshop, and the more specific the questions the better. The following questionnaire is typical and lends itself to adaptation.

How would you rate this program (workshop)?

1	2	3	4	5
a disaster	some parts helpful	moderately helpful	excellent	outstanding

---

Another example of a "two-tailed" rating to the same question is:

1	2	3	4	5
very dissatisfied	somewhat dissatisfied	neither satisfied nor dissatisfied	quite satisfied	very satisfied

---

Other questions:

What were the three most helpful parts of the workshop?

1. ______________________________
2. ______________________________
3. ______________________________

Could you explain why these parts were helpful?

What were the least helpful parts of the workshop?

1. ______________________________
2. ______________________________
3. ______________________________

Could you explain why these were least helpful?

What have you learned that you can use Monday morning?

What have you learned that will take you more time to integrate?

What are some skills, understandings, ideas you now have that you did not have when this program was started?

From your point of view how could this program have been improved?

Are there any comments you would like to make?

Although such questionnaires are easy to administer, their validity is based on how the questions relate to the learning objectives. Such evaluations are sometimes a guise for going through the "motions" of evaluation—to be briefly glanced at and tossed into the trash can. Sometimes they are used to buttress a continued need for training because there is a euphoric moment at the end of a workshop when participants are feeling good (at least that it is over) and thus tend to be "too polite" in their evaluations. However, evaluations should be used to see how participants have changed in relation to the learning objective, to revise the training program, or to implement recommendations. In other words, for questionnaires to be effective, they need to be taken seriously.

Ratings. Sometimes for ease of scoring, ratings are used as a method of evaluation. Often, there will be a bipolar scale in which participants are asked to record using a check or an X how they rate a particular area. Or there may be a dimension, and participants are asked to rate their program by questions along that dimension. Figure 7.1 is an example from a team-building program.

Group ID ____________________

Individual ID ____________________

Group Rating Questionnaire

This questionnaire asks you to consider several common dimensions in groups and to rate your group with respect to these dimensions. Check the place on the scale that fits your view.

1. **Productivity:** Given the time the group has been together, given the nature of the task it is supposed to be working on, do you believe that your group has been

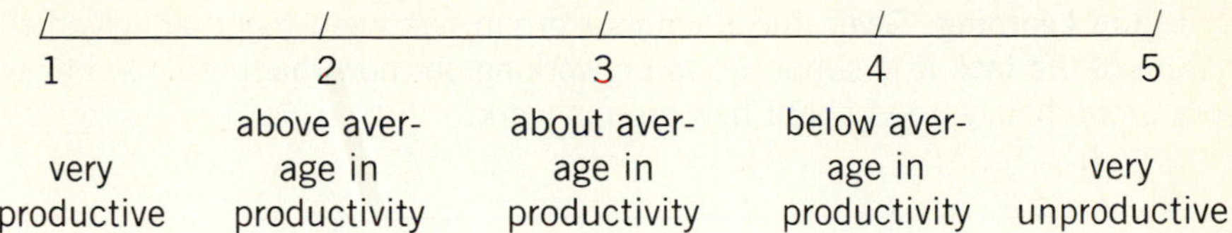

1	2	3	4	5
very productive	above average in productivity	about average in productivity	below average in productivity	very unproductive

2. **Cohesiveness:** Cohesiveness refers to the degree of solidarity and "togetherness" that is present in a group. Given the time the group has been together, given the nature of the task it is supposed to be working on, do you believe that your group has been

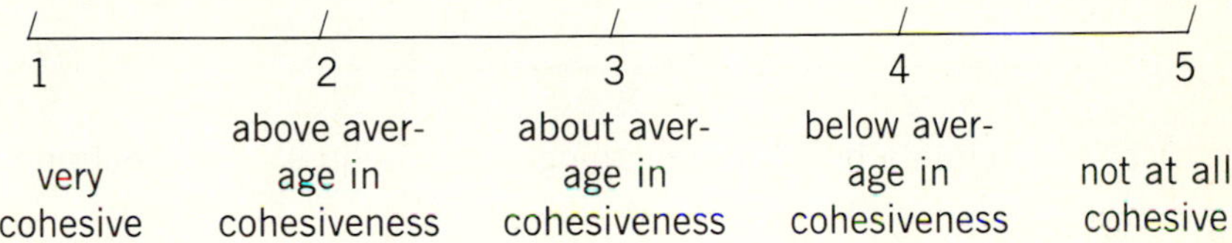

1	2	3	4	5
very cohesive	above average in cohesiveness	about average in cohesiveness	below average in cohesiveness	not at all cohesive

3. **Emotional Climate:** Given the time your group has been together, given the nature of the task it is supposed to be working on, do you believe your group has been emotionally

1	2	3	4	5
very tense	above average in emotional tension	about average in emotional tension	below average in emotional tension	not tense at all

4. **Task vs. Group Solidarity:** As a group do you believe your group has been

1	2	3	4	5
primarily interested in accomplishing the task	more interested in accomplishing the task than in maintaining solidarity	about equally concerned with accomplishing the task and maintaining solidarity	more interested in maintaining solidarity than in accomplishing the task	primarily interested in maintaining solidarity

5. **Personal Satisfaction:** How satisfied are you with your experience in this group?

1	2	3	4	5
very satisfied	satisfied	somewhat satisfied	dissatisfied	very dissatisfied

6. **Group Learning:** Given the time your group has been together, given the nature of the task it is supposed to be working on, how much do you believe your *group* has learned about how groups work?

1	2	3	4	5
a lot	quite a bit	something	a little	nothing

7. **Personal Learning:** How much to you believe *you* have learned about how groups work?

1	2	3	4	5
a lot	quite a bit	something	a little	nothing

FIGURE 7.1. Example of Rating as a Method of Evaluation

Ratings are easy to administer and to score. Further, summarizations are simple, especially since each point on the scale is given a number for ease in statistical analysis. However, the "why" underlying the check is missing, and unless some open-ended questions accompany the rating, or the ratings are used as a basis for further interviews, the data derived are very limited in terms of future planning.

It is not unusual to combine a rating, a questionnaire, and open-ended questions. Figure 7.2 is an example of such a combination; it is an evaluation of a training program for community leaders.

Course Questionnaire

1. Below is a list of potential training techniques. Please give your opinion as to whether you would recommend more or less emphasis on each device for this course.

	Much Greater Emphasis	*Slightly More Emphasis*	*No Change*	*Somewhat Less Emphasis*	*Much Less Emphasis*
a. Lecture—discussions	1	2	3	4	5
b. Role playing	1	2	3	4	5
c. Individual testing	1	2	3	4	5

d. Group observation	1	2	3	4	5
e. Problem analysis	1	2	3	4	5
f. Group presentations	1	2	3	4	5
g. Readings	1	2	3	4	5
h. Other: specify _____	1	2	3	4	5
i. Other: specify _____	1	2	3	4	5

2. How has this course benefited you, if at all?

3. How would you have liked this course to have benefited you?

4. Would you recommend this course to other members of Young Leadership? Why or why not?

5. At what time in the leadership development process do you think this course would be most effective?

6. Which was the most effective class session? Why?

7. Which was the least effective class session? Why?

8. How would you change this course to make it more effective?

9. Did your interest and enthusiasm toward this course increase or decrease as the course progressed? Explain.

10. Use this space to make any other comments about your reactions to the course.

FIGURE 7.2. Concluding Evaluation of a Program to Train Community Leaders.

Impact Evaluations

Sometimes a simple evaluation is done at the conclusion of the workshop, but the real evaluation is measured by the workshop's impact on participant behavior back on the job and its impact on the organization itself. A selected behavior is first measured prior to the workshop, and a prediction is made of what the workshop might change. Other variables are monitored for their potential impact, and the selected behavior is again measured after the workshop using some measurement tool. Although this approach attempts to measure the effectiveness of the workshop in terms of impact on the organization, numerous difficulties stemming from the very different environment of the organization versus the workshop may preclude the use of the new skills. For example, some members of the staff may have attended the workshops, and others who have not been to the training are resentful and unreceptive toward new behaviors. Thus, direct measures of transferability may not measure the effectiveness of the workshop.

Follow-Ups

Used increasingly as a method of evalution in addition to the concluding evaluation is to have participants return some time after the training to report on the effectiveness of the training. How did they use the training? How did what they learned help? Having tried their new skills, what questions do they now have? Follow-ups may not be a part of the original contract and so may be difficult to arrange at a later time; it is in our opinion, however, imperative that each training program, even a half-day workshop, include a follow-up. In addition to allowing the trainer and the staff to determine how valuable the training was, follow-ups provide an opportunity to help participants deal with problems that did not emerge in the workshop, demonstrate how certain conflicts can be resolved, build new skills, and perhaps even create an understanding of nuances previously missed. Follow-ups especially ensure that new skills will be used rather than relegated to a back-to-work mentality, business-as-usual style, with the concomitant attrition of whatever learning was acquired.

Follow-up programs, evaluations, and revisions are one of the major changes in recent years. They ensure that training and the objectives sought are not fleeting and related to the training program.

Process Evaluation: Program Development and Organizational Applications

Real evaluation is not in the ongoing evaluations, the concluding evaluation, or even in follow-ups; rather, the most effective evaluation occurs when trainers consider the entire process of evaluation as being a part of the organizational diagnosis, as being content and process, and being an integral part of every aspect of the training.

If there is anything we have learned in our more than fifteen years of consultation, it is that long-range evaluation is essential in the development of programs and in the effects of the training on the organization. Where to begin, with whom, at what level there are difficulties, developing stages in the program, how to proceed, where to make major revisions, how to build credibility—all these factors evolve through a way of working we call process evaluation.

The "Process" Versus "Product" Mentality in Evaluation*

The majority of the evaluations conducted today follow a classic laboratory research design, in which outcomes are hypothesized, an independent variable, such as a new skill or a new teaching method, is introduced to an experimental population, control groups are identified, and pre- and postdata are gathered on both the experimental and control populations. The task of the evaluator is to make sure the objectives are clear and measurable, to develop the appropriate instruments, and to report the results in a systematic manner, in terms of which hypotheses have been supported and which should be rejected. The evaluator's goal is to follow the research design exactly, keeping the extraneous or nonmeasurable variables to a minimum.

The futility of attempting to apply classic research designs in evaluation situations was widely recognized by the late 1960s, and development of a new evaluation methodology was begun. Thus, process evaluation became a vital component of the set of procedures now defined as evaluation, because it attended to untouched concerns and unanswered questions in the classical experimental approach. The problem with the classical, or product, approach was that when a project failed or when the results were not as predicted, no one was quite certain why. Statistically significant data did not provide enough of a basis for critical decision making.

Outcomes are important, but the reason or reasons for a project's success or failure may lie in its design, in the charisma of the director, in community support or resistance, in the overall administrative efficiency, or in the nature of the selected population. Thus, the decision to extend, maintain, or drop a program depends on a wide range of carefully gathered and analyzed data, some of which are historical in nature (antecedent) and some of which are based on results (product or content evaluation).[2]

For example, a program was initiated in an attempt to improve students' reading levels. A special reading program was developed, which involved parents in a variety of activities both within and outside the school. After two years, postmeasures of reading ability were taken, and it was discovered that there were no significant improvements as a result of using the new method. Thus, the program was abandoned without warning since no further funds were

*Pages 223–242 are reprinted with adaptations from John L. Hayman, Jr., and Rodney Napier, *Evaluation in the Schools: A Human Process for Renewal* (Belmont, Calif.: Wadsworth, 1975), pp. 58–79. Used by permission.

[2]Other words used in the literature to describe what is here labeled "process" evaluation are: formative, dynamic, transaction, operations, evaluative, and clinical evaluation.

forthcoming. The school community was appalled, and an informal survey revealed that many teachers and community members believed the program was the most successful supplementary program ever developed for the school.

Of course, the teachers' and the community members' criteria for success was quite different from those established prior to the study by the evaluation team assigned to the program. The teachers recognized that the children were completing more homework and that there seemed to be less absenteeism and more interest in classwork. They also perceived increased parent interest in the children's education; the parents took an interest in "their" children. By drawing parents more actively into participation with the children, the program seemed to improve the entire climate of the school. But, since almost none of these outcomes had been measured in the formal study and since the reading program apparently did little to improve the overall reading performance in the school, there was only informal opinion in support of continuing the project. Even other benefits appeared to matter little as far as maintaining the program was concerned. For example, the project established a more accepting attitude on the part of the parents toward the schoolteachers and toward the development of other possible experimental programs. Teacher attitudes seemed also to change in a positive way in relation to in-service training and community participation in decision making.

Thus, when the program procedures are narrowly defined and the accompanying evaluation is inflexible, one assumes that the resulting product will reflect only the narrowest view of what really occurred. It seems to follow, then, that, as a project becomes operational, the evaluation must remain fluid and sensitive enough to capture the process as it evolves—the changes and adaptations that occur—as well as the impact of these changes.

This section focuses on the nature of process evaluation, its historical development, and its functional use as an aid to organizational decision making.

Some Basic Distinctions. When conducting a process evaluation, the evaluator collects data that might explain why certain events occur and why certain attitudes exist. The information gathered tends to be oriented in the here and now, and there is an attempt to use it as a means of explaining why present conditions exist and what the underlying factors behind success or failure are. Some distinctions between the more traditional product evaluations and evaluations with a process orientation are as follows:

Traditional Product Evaluation	*Process Evaluation*
The evaluation is clearly defined in a specific framework of time.	The evaluation is continuous and intentionally flexible.
The evaluation is a planned program of deliberate interventions.	The program is nonmanipulative and developmental rather than fixed.
The focus is on prediction.	The findings are conditional.
Goals are predesignated, with assumed values.	The focus is on the here and now—on what is happening and why.

Measurement is in terms of the degree to which the projected outcomes are met.

Findings are used in decision making but are also often valued for their own sake—that is, their role in esoteric research.

Tests of hypotheses are common and deterministic.

One aim of the evaluation is to clarify objectives and to note any deviation from the way they are specified.

Information is used in decision making and for internal improvement of the project.

Most data are descriptive and nondeterministic.

The program is often seen as a part of ongoing diagnostic processes in which feedback is an integral aspect.

Total process evaluation can provide a developmental history of the program being measured.

Thus, process evaluations provide data to determine why certain events are happening and how the events can be either maintained or altered (whichever is appropriate). The product evaluation is only one important ingredient in the overall appraisal of what has occurred and what implications these occurrences may have for further decision making.

A Historical Perspective. In addition to an awakening of interest and concern for educational innovation, the two decades following World War II witnessed the rapid expansion of group dynamics, an area of social psychology, which had important implications for educational measurement methods. The study of group dynamics, which implies a view of both task content and process dimensions, provided many of the research methodologies demanded by the current systems approaches to educational, community, and organizational decision making and by the increasing needs of process evaluation. Thus, as the theoretical construct of the group and of the organization was explored, theorists and experimentalists became interested in much deeper levels of process evaluation than simply outcomes of group activity. Analytically oriented social psychologists (Redl, 1942; Bion, 1964; Bennis & Shepherd, 1956), field theorists (Lewin, 1951), sociometrists (Moreno, 1960), and many others (Bales, 1950; Homans, 1950) explored the process of group life from their unique theoretical positions. As these theorists and experimentalists found that consistent behavioral patterns existed under various conditions, they became increasingly adept at predicting future events. Their new approach focused on methods both to prevent obstacles from developing and to maintain effective group activity. Once the importance of understanding the process was firmly grasped, tools with which to observe and comprehend this process were developed. Thus, in the short span of twenty years, between 1950 and 1970, no fewer than seventy different observational systems were developed as a means of ensuring greater objectivity and reliability in the understanding of group behavior (Simon & Boyer, 1967).

It became increasingly apparent that to predict outcomes without understanding the causal factors was of little value and that only by studying the factors emanating from the process itself could behavioral alternatives be developed for facilitating the group or organization in its operation. But, for the evaluator, focusing on process variables was like opening Pandora's box. By asking the process-type question, he or she had to discard the compulsion for the tight research design of this period. The art of prediction in the true scientific sense was being replaced by the often speculative and occasionally inaccurate approach of looking at internal processes. Suddenly such intangibles as group pressure, feedback, trust, resistance, and attitudes had to be drawn into the research equation.

Process evaluations are not by nature haphazard or unscientific. There can, of course, be problems of definition, overzealous interpretation of information, unreliable data-gathering methods, and poorly defined theoretical rationale upon which conclusions are based. Thus, each factor must be carefully weighed when using process evaluation. Yet too often the myth of objectivity has been used as an excuse for not exploring the foundation of a program, in which the noncontrolled and ill-defined factors often can spell success or failure. There has always been a large problem of subjectivity in any research-evaluation design because the evaluator develops the questions to be asked, the population to be studied, the instruments to be used, the framework of time in which the data are gathered, the methods of analysis, and, finally, the crucial interpretation of the data in relation to selected theoretical assumptions. This subjectivity factor merely suggests that good product or process evaluations are a risky business that requires consummate skill. This requirement should keep the evaluator in a position of some vulnerability and, hopefully, create some sense of humility.

Organizational Assumptions in Process Evaluation

In many respects, process evaluation is a way of thinking about an organization, a group, or a project. The evaluation explores the reasons why events occur in a particular manner at a particular time. One can develop a "process mentality" for looking at what happens at all levels of an organization—the impact of a meeting, the organizational "climate," or the evaluation of an executive program. The following assumptions should be understood by the trainer or organization development consultant who wishes to be involved in the process evaluation:

1. Process evaluation is collaborative at all stages of program development, from the initiation of the original idea to its final adoption and dissemination.

2. Process evaluation is a trouble-shooting approach to uncovering problems; it looks for discrepancies among methods, goals, and outcomes.
3. When problems are discovered, they will be reported in full, and attempts will be made, whenever feasible, to resolve them.
4. Process evaluation involves a flexible approach to the formation of program objectives, and it is implied that short- and long-run objectives may be altered as the program develops and as various problems are encountered and solved.
5. Both task and emotional or maintenance problems arise as a program develops. Task problems are issues that surround the structural and operational methods used in an effort to accomplish the program goals. Maintenance or emotional issues relate to how people feel about what is happening to them and others as the program evolves and how these attitudes and feelings influence program outcomes.
6. Process evaluation looks at all the consequences of behavior—both anticipated and unanticipated, positive and negative.
7. Communication is open, and information is shared as much as possible with all those involved in the evaluation process.
8. The entire evaluation process is based on an interventionist perspective—one that assumes action, a questioning of the status quo, and an implementation of change strategies at any point that is appropriate.

Organizational Resistances to Process Evaluation

The danger of using a process approach to evaluation is that it builds expectations of a provisional and developmental approach to growth in the minds of those participating. If the flexibility and openness that is implied in this seeking out of information and alternative procedures are not validated by collaborative inquiry and eventual action, then there will be frustration and discontent; that is, the person who looks for problems is likely to find them and had better be ready to do something about them. Such a dynamic approach to organizational development also implies that there will almost never be "no problem," since change assumes that at least some dislocation or adjustment will be necessary. The goal, of course, is an effective operation with assurance of meeting the established objectives of the program. Too often it is revealed that good intentions and effective methods of gathering process data do not ensure effective decision making. In too many cases, decisions are based on what is expedient; all available data are not shared, because the implications of the information run counter to the ideas or expectations of various individuals. In still other situations, data may reveal such things as inefficient operations or ineffective management, which, if disclosed, may jeopardize the evaluator's job or future attempts to gather data.

Beyond the idiosyncratic fears of administrators, evaluators, or participants of the results of process evaluation, there are the general resistances that are predictable within any large, hierarchical organization—for example, the tendency for many organizations to be static, with limited capacity (or interest) to be responsive to here-and-now problems. It is this inability of the organizational hierarchy to respond quickly when problems occur that leads to an increase in internal tensions. Only when some kind of crisis is precipitated will immediate action be taken and time-consuming "normal channels" be bypassed to meet the needs of the current situation.

The nature of process evaluation assures a responsiveness to present needs and the establishment of an appropriate strategy for whatever eventualities occur. These assurances strike at the heart of the crisis-oriented administration; that is, they strike at the system in which accountability is unclear, objectives are hazy, and judgments of success are compiled months after a program has been completed and then are placed out of sight on a library shelf.

The Discrepancy Model—The Key to Process Evaluation

Process evaluation can provide three kinds of useful information. First, it can provide a framework for observing the development or the growth of a program toward specific goals. Second, it can reveal points of tension or program dysfunction that exist as the result of either task (structural-organizational) or emotional (human-interpersonal) issues. Finally, it can pinpoint, with considerable accuracy, discrepancies that exist between the terminal, enabling, and facilitating objectives and the activities that are actually occurring at a particular time. This information generated by process evaluation and the interdependence of these three procedures hold the key to understanding the basic value of process evaluation. The discrepancy between the actual and the planned or the ideal and the real provides the focus for ongoing adjustment and change.

The Question. One certain way to generate tension in people is to have them commit themselves to clearly stated goals that must be achieved within an agreed-upon framework of time and that will be measured with specific criteria (Provus, 1969). The implicit accountability, rather than the goal itself, is the tension source. Rare is the meeting, project, or organization that subjects itself to the pressures created by clear, operational, and measurable goals. For a discrepancy model (generating operational and behavioral discrepancies from reliable data-gathering methods) to be effective, the clarity of such procedural outcomes is absolutely essential. Also, gross macro-goals such as building a dam, completing a project, or constructing an educational unit must be broken down into meaningful and obtainable subparts. These specific goals and the criteria for measuring their successful completion provide the basis for many of the most important process-evaluation activities. The effectiveness of evaluators in asking penetrating questions at various points in the program development and their success in answering these questions will determine their ability to reveal any discrepancies that exist and the reasons for their existence.

The Information. Once programs begin, once behaviors are routinized, and once individual needs are tied into a previously intellectualized task, it becomes increasingly difficult to alter the pattern of events that begins to evolve. The tension created by having to establish concrete, operational goals is minimal compared with the tension produced when an individual or a group is confronted with not having fulfilled the commitment. Thus, a critical part of the discrepancy model is the gathering and the presentation of information relating to what has actually transpired as people have attempted to reach their agreed-upon goals. The awareness of the discrepancy between reality and expectations can produce a line of tension that can provide an important source of energy for moving toward another level of involvement or into new modes of behavior. In one sense, the information that has been generated creates a small internal crisis within the system. An ideal time for developing alternative operating strategies, changing roles, and reassessing objectives is during this crisis (a time of uncertainty). It is essential to this development process that the data generated must be owned (desired and accepted) by those involved. With this attitude there is little chance that the "crisis" will result in a defensive entrenchment into old and unproductive behaviors. The energy is directed into positive new directions. Field theorists (Lewin, 1951) believe that there is a disconfirmation of old positions and an unfreezing of past behaviors. The internal dissonance created by looking at the existing contradictions pushes individuals toward exploring new methods for reaching their previous or to-be-revised goals.

The Decision. The questioning and information-sharing process, undertaken in an environment that supports self-examination and feedback, should set the stage for new decisions. The period of appraisal should lead to a clear discrimination among alternatives that exist (and were not clear at the outset of the project) and a differentiation according to the new needs that have been diagnosed. Most important is the belief on the part of those participating in the process that it is a shared venture, and, although certain individuals are accountable for various aspects of the program, it is essentially collaborative.

A Specific Methodology for Supporting Program Development Through Process Evaluation. In this section, we will describe an eight-stage program for systematically organizing a reasonable view of process evaluation. This methodology integrates the views of many practitioners and theorists[3] and thus presents a clear, if somewhat ideal, picture of what is possible.

[3]The ideas of Cochran (1969), Friedlander (1968), Grobman (1968), Provus (1971), Schein and Bennis (1965), Scriven (1967), Stake (1967), Stufflebeam (1966), and Suchman (1969) have been freely adapted in this developmental approach to process evaluation.

General Sequence of Development *Stage I*	Evaluative Activity *General Inquiry*
Developing an awareness of the problem.	
Confirming the "awareness" of a problem by means of a more systematic diagnosis.	Individual initiative—sharpening the focus of a perceived problem through a variety of methods that differ according to the nature of the organization, its readiness, the information available, and the communication processes that exist.
Reviewing the literature and related research to determine which areas have been covered and which areas still need to be explored.	
Exploring and developing general goals and methods.	
Testing ideas on staff, students, and interested professionals.	Building of internal support.
Determining general feasibility and support for the project.	Use of internal and external sources.

This general-inquiry stage is characterized by the informal investigation of needs by interested individuals, the ascertaining of whether or not a program is feasible, and the initiation of an internal support group that favors the idea of the program as it is evolving.

General Sequence of Development *Stage II*	Evaluative Activity *Program Formulation*
Formulating specific long-term or "terminal" program objectives.	Involvement of total or representative group at this time.
Establishing "enabling" objectives for various stages of the program's development. This process involves identifying methodological inputs for reaching interim and terminal goals.	Acceptance of the evaluator (or team) as an integral part of the planning and design phases.
Building clearly defined criteria for measuring the degree to which the "enabling" objectives (and thus interim goals) and the terminal goals are met.	Understanding of the discrepancy model and of the concept of process evaluation.
Developing a realistic time frame, with explicit target dates, points for major reviews of goals and procedures, and alternative strategies.	Agreement by internal staff and evaluator on all objectives, measurement criteria, and process-evaluation sessions.

Establishing necessary facilitating objectives in light of both terminal and enabling objectives.

During this stage, specifics of the project are worked out both in terms of objectives (criteria for measuring levels of success at any given point) and in terms of the relationship these specifics have to participant commitment. Extensive workshop time will be essential to involve the staff in this process and to ensure their understanding of the developmental nature of the program and the critical role of process evaluation at every stage of its growth. This is the time when open communication must be established, including feedback among the participant staff and a position of flexibility by the project leadership.

General Sequence of Development	**Evaluative Activity**
Stage III	*Program Preparation*
Defining administrative roles and responsibilities.	Clear communication among all involved.
Identifying material needs in reference to the time frame.	
Testing the necessary measurement instruments and carrying out pilot studies if required.	Definition of evaluator responsibility.
Training staff and necessary support personnel, with a focus both on task and maintenance issues, and developing necessary skills to ensure meeting the enabling objectives, which mediate between present action and eventual outcomes. These skills and accompanying structural or organizational requirements are classified as facilitating objectives.	Evaluation of training program in relation to interim objectives (training objectives), both facilitating and enabling. Appraisal of objectives and time frame in terms of training and present staff needs (*open critique*).

This stage focuses on providing the essential materials and skills to ensure that the interim goals of the program are reached on schedule. If the materials and skills are not available, alternatives should be considered. If, for example, the training program is not effective in providing the staff with enough practice to ensure the level of competence established in Stage II, then additional steps must be identified and taken. It is one role of the process evaluator to help gather the data necessary to determine whether administrative or staff training has been sufficient for the program to move into the next stage of development, which involves implementation of program activities. Similarly, the evaluator should be sensitive to maintenance-type issues that tend to arise in any new program; the evaluator should help participants become aware of these issues in a constructive manner by sharing the process data. Thus, if individuals feel that their ideas concerning project development are not being given proper consideration by staff planners, sharing the process data might help reduce the possibility that these tensions will carry over into the daily operation of the project.

General Sequence of Development	**Evaluative Activity**
Stage IV	*Program Installation*
Beginning the innovative program with expected tensions, mistakes, and unanticipated consequences.	Use a variety of process instruments. The evaluator attempts to gain a description of the initial impact the innovation(s) is having.
	Awareness of problems of logistics and communcation as well as of strengths and limitations revealed in staff performance. (Use of questionnaires, interviews, and observational data may be helpful.)
Making decisions (based on data analysis and new information) to maintain, delete, or alter goals or innovative strategies. If more training is needed, for example, arrangements are made to provide it. Particular emphasis is placed on how those involved are adjusting to the new program.	Comparison of data with interim objectives established for this stage during Stage II and determination of discrepancies. Both enabling and facilitating objectives are scrutinized.
	Appraisals of objectives in terms of discrepancy data and perceptions of staff (open critique.)

During the installation phase, the evaluator must be sensitive to the range of program factors that are facilitating or hindering both short- and long-term program objectives and general program goals. It is the evaluator's role to understand what is happening and to provide necessary data for administration and staff assessment. Such an assessment early in the development process should provide the opportunity to alter certain conditions that might pose more serious problems at a later time. In the same manner, it is from the descriptive data generated during this phase that additional training may be recommended, consultant services added, or supplementary programs written into the program. Thus, Stage IV is still very much a time of change, adjustment, and even experimentation.

General Sequence of Development	Evaluative Activity
Stage V	*Evaluation of Enabling Objectives*
Working out problems of installation and implementing initial adjustments.	Determination of the degree to which the methods being used to reach the terminal objectives of the program are working.
Becoming familiar with and thus gaining control over the treatment conditions (a period of general stability).	Focus on the usefulness of methods rather than on logistics, problems of preparedness, or general issues common to any new program.
Responding to discrepancies between the enabling objectives in Stage II and the results at this point in the process. New strategies are developed to bring enabling objectives and performance of staff and participants into greater agreement.	Study of data from different sources to determine whether any adjustments are necessary to ensure the meeting of the previously agreed-upon enabling objectives.
Creating new enabling objectives based on performance to this point and, when necessary, adapting the criteria of success to correspond more closely to reality.	Decision-making based on these data.

Stage V is a period during which data relating to program operations have been gathered so that a hard look can be taken at "performance" in relation to previously established criteria. The key is to discover how effective the methods designed to move participants toward long-term program goals are. Thus, this period is performance oriented, with an emphasis on helping the staff gain a firm control over the "treatment" variables. Again, a wide variety of data are used, including observational data, questionnaires, and information of a product variety. It is essential to note that, as in the previous stage, important data relating to staff relationships are also gathered and shared, with the objective of keeping lines of communication open and reducing the possibility of interpersonal problems developing at any level of operation.

General Sequence of Development	Evaluative Activity
Stage VI	*Period of Stabilization*
Maintaining a period of relatively few changes after the adjustments dur-	Awareness of unforeseen problems that may arise. It is unlikely that

ing installation and the recommendations resulting from the evaluations of enabling objectives. The newness of the program has theoretically worn off and problems have been ironed out; the program should function smoothly with few internal problems.

serious problems will arise if the previous steps have been followed.

It is during this period, that, for the first time, the program is expected to run smoothly, with few technical or interpersonal problems. If problems do arise, they will be dealt with quickly and effectively, since methods for problem identification and communication should have been clearly established and operationalized during previous stages.

General Sequence of Development

Stage VII

Conducting traditional "product" or terminal evaluations as a result of the period of program stabilization, including adjustments in enabling objectives and procedures.

Reviewing terminal objectives, since it is almost certain that a variety of changes will have transpired since the terminal objectives of Stage II were established.

Developing an appropriate time frame for product evaluation.

Evaluative Ability

Evaluation of Terminal Objectives

Designing of studies that measure participant performance in relation to before-and-after results. It is assumed that unanticipated consequences will be minimized by this time so that a true measure of the program will be gained.

Establishment of control groups. Process data should still be gathered during this period to account for unanticipated consequences.

The well-tested and, by now, thoroughly familiar program is ready for a traditional evaluation. The aim of this evaluation is to establish whether or not the new procedures and methods are more effective in the attainment of specific educational goals than other procedures and methods based on specific predetermined criteria. Until this period of proven program stabilization, staff members and participants have been too much in flux to produce meaningful data (although it is not unlikely that "significant" data have been generated). The evaluator's goal is to determine as carefully as possible the impact of the new program. The first six stages help to ensure that such a terminal, or product, evaluation could be understood developmentally and that success or failure would have meaning to those decision makers reviewing the total process.

General Sequence of Development	Evaluative Activity
Stage VIII	*Program Analysis*
Determining whether the program under evaluation should be adopted, altered, or rejected. The program analysis facilitating this decision might include the following. 1. Analysis of data from terminal and enabling evalutions as well as analysis of process data gathered throughout the program. 2. Discussion of the data by various participants, staff members, and administrators. 3. Recommendations drawn from these various groups. 4. Development of time-cost analyses to supplement other evaluation data. 5. Determination (by the appropriate body) of the program's future. 6. Establishment of strategies for dissemination and follow-up if the program is to be continued.	Presentation to the appropriate administrative staff personnel of data and tentative conclusions of the terminal, or product, study plus a summary of findings of the entire longitudinal process evaluation (across eight stages). Development of a number of formal presentations during which data are interpreted and implications drawn. Development and presentation of conclusions and recommendations. The evaluator should be an integral part of the decision-making process through this point.

After an eight-stage developmental process, it is difficult to imagine that the completed program would not result in some "real" and measured benefits. The constant process of adaptation and change and the potential rejections at each stage of the process ensure an ultimately functional approach to program building—one that reaches far beyond the narrow possibilities allowed by the traditional pre/post approach to evaluation. But, of course, one pays a heavy price in both time and money for the "luxury" of such a comprehensive approach to program evaluation. Such an approach cannot be squeezed into a six-month or one-year timetable. Each program requires its own unique and flexible time frame since, for example, program stability cannot be accurately determined in advance and since it is difficult to determine exactly when the introduction of a terminal evaluation will be appropriate. The total evaluation program assumes that a collaborative process of problem solving and decision making should exist—one that is responsive to current conditions and to new and appropriate program alternatives.

A Case in Point—Good Intent, Poor Evaluation

The situation was classic. An innovative education project supported by Title I funds included a required evaluation component. Project funds were renewable after one year with evidence that the program goals were being met. Funds for the evaluation itself were severely limited (less than 3 percent of the project budget), as were time and available resource personnel. The evaluator was a young university professor, with no experience in the public schools, who saw the project as a means of gaining needed experience. He also hoped to be a useful resource person in what appeared to be an interesting experimental project. His major assumption was that the program, even with its obvious limitations for evaluation, had to be evaluated so he might as well try to create the most meaningful study possible. As with many innovative programs, the basis for funding rested as much with the reputation and charisma of the program innovator as with the program design. In fact, the proposal was loosely defined and based on a still-evolving theoretical foundation.

The result of the evaluation (one year later) was a 350-page report with graphs, diagrams, and statistical tables. There were enough "statistically significant" findings to please the aesthetic tastes of the most statistical game player. And, of course, the report fulfilled the evaluation requirement of the project, which in this case (and many other cases) was viewed as an end in itself. However, the evaluation had no impact on the program in relation to its day-to-day functioning, staff practices, or long-term goals. It also had no impact on decision making at any level, during any stage of the program's development. It could be classified most satisfactorily as "futile" and filed next to the hundreds of other valueless reports that are representative of the evaluation exercise. However, it does provide a clear avenue for understanding the benefits that may accrue from viewing program evaluations from a process perspective and in relation to the eight stages previously outlined.

The Program. The project was designed to introduce the concept of open-classroom education into elementary schools of a large inner-city area. The proposal established specially furnished mathematics laboratories in nine representative schools so that students from the first three grades had the opportunity to freely explore an open-learning environment for one or two hours a week. Specially trained laboratory teachers guided students by answering their questions, involving them in a wide variety of activities, and, in general, stimulating them by organizing a range of possible experiences. Teachers voluntarily sent their students to the lab (half a class at one time) and accompanied them whenever possible. The teachers were also offered the opportunity to attend special seminars held after school to explain the open-classroom concept from both a conceptual and an applied point of view. Thus, the major thrust of the program was aimed at teacher education and curriculum development, with the mathematics laboratory providing an important vehicle for the reeducation of the classroom teacher. The program goals were to provide teachers with new approaches to teaching in a nondirective and noncoercive manner; to change attitudes toward the teaching-learning process, and, at the same time, to introduce children to a self-stimulating and self-motivating approach to learning that might favorably influence their attitudes toward school as well as their learning progress.

More specifically, the terminal objectives of the project were directed toward the following goals:

1. Improving the attitudes of laboratory teachers and participating classroom teachers toward school and their students;
2. Developing a more indirect pattern of teaching among laboratory and participating teachers than that which would be found among a control group of leaders;
3. Establishing a higher level of questioning among laboratory and participating teachers than would be found among a control group of teachers;
4. Improving true gain scores among children participating in the laboratory program in such areas as attitudes toward school, attitudes toward teachers, attitudes toward learning, self-image, self-confidence, speaking vocabulary, and language fluency.

Problems Created by a Traditional Approach to Evaluation. By viewing the evaluation as product oriented, the evaluator and his assistant directed their energies almost totally toward outcomes. However, such an approach was premature and totally inappropriate considering the stage of the project's development at that particular time. A discussion of problems and issues that explain why this evaluation was meaningless and why innumerable other evaluations are ineffective follows:

Time as a Critical Factor. The factor of time worked against the project and its effective evaluation in the following ways:

1. The idea of the project was originated more than two years prior to its installation in the nine schools. The evaluator entered the project three weeks before its installation in six of the nine participating schools. He had no opportunity to explore the long-range or interim goals with the program developers, and, from the beginning, he was seen as peripheral to the major thrust of the project.

2. The lack of preparation time ruled out the development of new instruments and limited the feasibility of an intensive investigation of theoretical and empirical literature relating to the area being explored.

3. From the beginning it was clear that a one-year study would drastically limit the value of any report outcomes. First, the nine participating schools were by no means at the same level of preparedness in terms of either their physical facilities or the laboratory

teachers' readiness. Second, even in the programs that were "ready" from the first day, an enormous number of changes could be predicted before schedules and various other problems of logistics were resolved.

4. Finally, the one or two contact hours a week for participating students and teachers did not warrant the kinds of pre/post hypotheses that were developed for the program. Common sense suggested this conclusion, but the constraints of the traditional view of a good evaluation (to reveal significant change) led to the building of many unrealistic program and evaluation hypotheses.

Unclear Goals. While it was clear that the program was designed to alter student and teacher attitudes and student-achievement patterns, these goals were premature in relation to the development of the program itself. As the program progressed, it became apparent that the laboratory teachers were learning an enormous amount about the open classroom and how to use the limited one-hour meeting time most effectively. Thus the first six months of the program were focused on the following areas:

1. Developing innovative curriculum methodologies for the mathematics open classroom;
2. Helping the teachers in the labs to use the new methods effectively;
3. Working out overall educational procedures.

Had the program been working from the perspective of a process evaluation, a variety of clearly defined, short-term objectives (both enabling and facilitating) would have been developed, focusing on the needs of the project as they became apparent in the installation phase. Supplementary training programs for the laboratory teachers would have been implemented. The evaluator would have helped to develop enabling objectives for this phase of the project's development, and he would have attempted to measure them systematically. The lack of effective enabling objectives has been common to many Title I projects in which the program becomes clearly defined only as it develops. Yet, because of unrealistic time expectations and evaluation schedules, the evaluator often intervened with an inappropriate pre/post measure during this tenuous developmental phase.

It also became clear as the program developed that, regardless of guidelines and early plans, the program was going to make its major contribution in the areas of classroom management and curriculum innovation. The stated goals of teacher reeducation and improved student attitudes and achievement became secondary in the minds of almost everyone; yet these were the criterion measures.

It became essential that the project have the flexibility to alter its projected time frame, to create appropriate enabling objectives and procedures for reaching them, and to supplement the program as needed to discover the most appropriate resources to ensure an effective use of staff and participant time and available materials and facilities. None of this flexibility was possible within the narrow view of program development and evaluation that was established.

The Inappropriate Nature of the Pre/Post (Product) Evaluation. The evaluation guidelines stressed the importance of pre/post data and underlined the need for proper control populations. As suggested previously, this is where the majority of evaluator time and energy was directed. However, the pre/post evaluation was inappropriate for the following reasons:

1. The study should have focused on the unique developmental process and problems within each school rather than looking for "achievement of product goals" from the nine schools together.

2. By observing the relatively short-term changes in participating teachers and students, the evaluator assumed that one to two hours a week for a part of one school year is enough time for new behaviors and attitudes to be internalized. However, such a judgment should not be attempted until some semblance of stability is reached in the program and until data are gathered relating to short-term behavioral goals. Only then is it possible to predict long-range outcomes and to develop a design for measuring them.

3. The use of a control group implies that there are specific changes that should occur—for example, in third-grade students. Yet, the nature of the open class was such that prediction was impossible except in terms of student attitudes, which are tremendously difficult to measure effectively (in this project only three or four weeks were allowed to develop instrumentation), or in areas of less direct relationship, such as language usage. Furthermore, the evaluation guidelines put great emphasis on differences in achievement even though the innovative program was basically directed away from traditional achievement goals.

4. In retrospect, observational data of student activity in the mathematical laboratories should have been gathered and viewed in relation to changes over time, intensity of involvement, range of involvements (by class and individuals), and amounts of student-student or student-teacher interaction. In such an evaluation, there is no place for a control group.

5. The attitudes of the participating teachers were hypothesized to change as a result of their acquaintance with the practices used in the laboratories. The participating teachers were intellectually aware of the values espoused by this type of learning. The question was whether or not the intellectualized values were internalized in terms of practice. To ask experimental and control groups questions about values on a paper-and-pencil instrument would be of little value in determining the success of the project. Also, it has been discovered that teachers must have a chance to practice a new method in a nonthreatening

> environment before they are willing to try it in the classroom. Thus, although many new ideas were learned by the experimental group of teachers, few were tried in the classroom in the initial year. These discoveries suggested the need for a training workshop. Only after such training would a control study make sense, since then would values and practices be integrated to any degree among the experimental population.

The Need for Process Evaluation—Focus on Interpersonal Relationships. There are times during the development of any program when it is of great importance to gather information relating to how those working on the project are functioning and how they might operate more effectively together. In this particular project, it was crucial that periodic feedback should be generated from among the laboratory teachers, the participating teachers in the nine schools, and the students involved in the program itself. Although the administrator did her best to keep the lines of communication open and to be sensitive to what was happening, the range of her responsibilities kept her from being as effective as she might. Also, her own interest in and closeness to the project made it difficult for her to be as objective in this process as was necessary. Several examples suggest how important this function of process evaluation is and how it could have helped the success of the overall program.

> 1. It became clear late in the first year of the program (the first year of a five-year program was being evaluated) that the administrator was assuming too many roles and thus hurting her own effectiveness in the project. She was attempting to be a teacher, a supervisor, an innovator, a liaison with the central administration, and a general resource person to the nine laboratory teachers as well as to the participating teachers. As a result of these many roles, tensions increased as she reshaped her working priorities and use of time. But those dependent on her in her previous role maintained their old expectations for her personal attention. They resented the change, and it influenced their work. Process data could easily have uncovered this source of tension early in the program and led to a more equal distribution of administrative responsibilities.
>
> 2. Neither the role of the evaluator nor the ways in which the evaluation could facilitate the working of the program was ever clearly defined. As a result, symptoms of resistance to the evaluation became apparent midway through the year. The staff and participants should have been maximally involved in establishing the parameters of the evaluation and then involved in establishing periodic feedback sessions to determine how successfully the goals were being met.
>
> 3. As programs develop, numerous unanticipated consequences occur that impact the total program and that should be brought to the

awareness of those being affected. In this example, an unanticipated consequence of considerable importance developed, which, if understood at the time, might have been changed from a negative influence to a positive influence. It resulted from the fact that, as the children returned to class from the mathematics laboratory, they often found it difficult to settle into the routine of the more formal classroom setting. The response of the participating teachers varied greatly. Many of the teachers saw the behavior as a result of the students' "fun and games" session and began to resent the laboratory as an imposition on their well-ordered classrooms. They also resented the need to increase restrictions because of the additional discipline problems created by the special class. Still other participating teachers resented the students' obvious enjoyment of the laboratory and felt as if they were constantly being compared with the laboratory teachers. This unanticipated occurrence resulted in a building up of resentment toward the entire program by a large number of the teachers for whom the program was to be a valuable service. However, these feelings of resentment came out only in the final evaluation. An internal diagnosis early in the program would have clearly shown the need for special workshops with the participating teachers to discuss their feelings openly and to develop ways of turning a negative situation into a beneficial one. For example, allowing students to share what they had learned proved useful for one teacher in handling the problem. Other ways of taking what was learned in the lab and directing it toward the entire class might have proved useful. The possibilities for building in a positive way from the situation were great.

Summary

This example reflects the main issues of this section and focuses on the critical nature of process evaluation in any action program. The key factor that seems to underlie the failure of the evaluation discussed and many other evaluations is the lack of a developmental perspective. It is clear that the program only began to reach some sense of stability near the end of the first year. Objectives, methods, and teacher, administrator, and participant roles were in a state of flux during the first four or five months; they then stabilized during the next three. Of course, it was this period of flux that contributed to the effective change of the entire program as new methods were tried and the efforts of all those involved led to slow but meaningful adjustments. A crucial problem was that the evaluation design did not allow for the capturing of these important changes. Lost were the developmental processes of individual classes; the behavioral impact of the program on individual students, lab teachers, or participating teachers; and the influence of the lab program on the school itself. There were no methods prescribed for gathering such information. The thrust was almost totally in the direction of performance criteria, which became less and less relevant as the program developed.

As might be predicted, most of the hypotheses for this project were rejected. The demand for a premature product evaluation resulted in a predictable lack of marked changes in teacher and student performance. According to the data available and to the evaluation guidelines, the program probably should have been canceled. But, because decision-making processes are seldom rational, the program survived even in the face of the results from the inappropriate evaluation. Today, the contributions from this program in the areas of curriculum development and teacher training are proving invaluable as many of the schools of this urban educational system are readying themselves for more extensive use of open-classroom teaching. The program's eventual value had little to do with its original, stated goals. Its value became apparent only several years after it had been developed—when its procedures had stabilized, when there was time to explore its theoretical implications, and when it could provide a model that would enable more appropriate research studies to investigate such a program's real worth to urban education.

Thus, without the skills and the inclination necessary for exploring the process dimension of a program, it is unlikely that program objectives will be satisfied, resources will be used effectively, critical changes to enhance the ongoing program will be made, and a clear understanding of the organizational dynamics of the program will be developed so that future programs will benefit from the variety of experiences that occur throughout the life of a slowly evolving program.

References

Bales, R. F. 1950. *Interaction Process Analysis.* Reading, Mass.: Addison-Wesley.

Bennis, W. G., and Shepherd, H. A. 1956. "A Theory of Group Development." *Human Relations* 9:415–437.

Bion, W. R. 1964. *Experiences in Groups.* New York: Basic Books, 1964.

Cochran, L. 1969. "A Technique in Educational Research." *Journal of Educational Research* 63(1).

Friedlander, F. 1968. "A Comparative Study of Consulting Process and Group Development." *Journal of Applied Behavioral Science* 4:368–398.

Grobman, H. 1968. Evaluation Activities of Curriculum Projects: A Starting Point. *AERA Monograph.* Chicago: Rand McNally.

Homans, G. C. 1950. *The Human Group.* New York: Harcourt Brace.

Lewin, K. 1951. *Field Theory in Social Science.* New York: Harper & Row.

Moreno, J. L. 1960. *The Sociometry Reader.* Glencoe, Ill.: The Free Press.

Provus, M. 1969. "Evaluation of Ongoing Programs in the Public School System." In R. W. Tyler, ed., *Educational Evaluation: New Roles, New Means*. Chicago: University of Chicago Press.

Provus, M. 1971. *Discrepancy Evaluation*. Berkeley, Calif.: McClutchan Pub. Corp.

Redl, F. 1942. "Group Emotions and Leadership." *Psychiatry* 5:537–596.

Schein, E. H., and Bennis, W. 1965. *Personal and Organizational Changes Through Group Methods: The Laboratory Approach*. New York: John Wiley & Sons.

Scriven, M. 1967. "The Methodology of Evaluation." *AERA Monograph Series on Curriculum Evaluation No. 1*. Chicago: Rand McNally & Co., pp. 39–83.

Simon, A., and Boyer, G., eds. 1967. *Mirrors for Behavior: An Anthology of Observational Instruments*. Philadelphia: Research for Better Schools.

Stake, R. E. 1967. "The Countenance of Educational Evaluation." *Teachers College Record* 68 (7):523–540.

Stufflebeam, D. 1966. "A Depth Study of the Evaluation Requirement." *Theory into Practice* 5(3).

Suchman, E. A. 1969. "Evaluating Educational Programs." *The Urban Review* 3(4):18.

Supplementary Readings

Cooper, S., Heenan, C. *Preparing, Designing, Heading Workshops: A Humanistic Approach*. Boston, Mass.: CBI Pub. Co., 1980.

Davis, L. N. *Planning, Conducting, and Evaluating Workshops*. Austin, Tex.: Learning Concepts Inc., 1974.

Egan, G. *The Skilled Helper*. Monterey, Calif.: Brooks Cole, 1975.

———. *Exercises in Helping Skills—A Training Manual for the Skill Helper*. Monterey, Calif.: Brooks Cole, 1975.

Gutherie, E., and Miller, W. S. *Making Change: A Guide to Effectiveness in Groups*. Minneapolis, Interpersonal Communications Program Inc., 1978.

Gutherie, E., Miller, W. S., and Grimberg, W. *Making Change: Trainer's Manual*. Minneapolis, Interpersonal Communications Programs Inc., 1978.

Johnson, D. W., and Johnson, F. P. *Joining Together: Group Theory and Group Skills*. Englewood Cliffs, N.J.: Prentice Hall, 1975.

Kirschenbaum, H., and Glaser, B. *Developing Support Groups: A Manual for Facilitators and Participants*. La Jolla, Calif.: University Assoc., 1978.

Lieberman, M., Borman, L. D., and Assoc. *Self-Help Groups for Coping with Crisis*. San Francisco: Jossey Bass, 1979.

Merritt, R. E., Jr., and Walley, D. D. *The Group Leader's Handbook*. Champaign, Ill.: Research Press Co., 1979.

Miles, M. B. *Learning to Work in Groups*, 2nd ed. New York: Teachers College Press, 1981.

Schein, E., Bennis, W., and Beckhard, R., eds. *Organization Development Series* (6 books). Reading, Mass.: Addison Wesley, 1969.

Schmuck, R. A., Runkel, P. J., Arends, J. H., and Arends, R. I. *The Second Handbook of Organization and Development in Schools*. Palo Alto, Calif.: Mayfield Publishing Co., 1977.

Smith, P. B. *Group Processes and Personal Change*. London: Harper & Row, 1980.

Underwood, Wm. J. *A Collection of Essays for Analysis of Group Participation*. Philadelphia: Temple University, 1969.

Appendices

Appendix A: A Guide for Facilitators*

Table of Contents

---

*Adapted from Rodney W. Napier and Matti K. Gershenfeld, *Groups: Theory and Experience* (Boston: Houghton Mifflin, 1973), pp. 285–304. Used by permission.

No one consciously plans a disaster. On the contrary, facilitators hope that their presentations or interventions will be helpful to their group members. Often, subconsciously, however, the informality of a model facilitator's style is equated with informality in the facilitator's preparation; casualness in manner is construed as a casual approach; and a spontaneous bit of humor is regarded as a spontaneous attitude. Such reasoning invites trouble. The effectiveness of facilitators depends on adequate and frequently extensive preparation that involves careful self-diagnosis and a diagnosis of their role, the group, the group's readiness and expectations, and the situation. Facilitators consider and discard several alternative plans prior to determining which approach will most likely help the group; they may even enter with several other alternatives that could be activated under varying conditions. Their casual manner and informal approach are typically part of the design to elicit a climate more conducive to the learning and sharing of both information and feelings. Their spontaneous humor is a personal plus, as is their ability to shift a portion of a design or appropriately change a program. Effectiveness as a facilitator requires careful diagnosis, planning, knowledge, and, always, consideration of alternatives.

The following pages are meant as a guide for facilitators. While we have written extensively about the leader and design, this appendix is intended as a quick review of some of the most basic elements in design. Our expectation is that trainers are already familiar with most of this material, but we believe a quick review, as a reminder, will be helpful here.

Some Basic Understandings

Let us assume that you are the facilitator planning an intervention for a group. Prior to determining the theory input, the exercise to be used, or the design to be developed, you must first ask some basic questions. They may sound commonplace, but failure to consider them is most frequently the cause of frustration for the facilitator and the group when the intended goals are not attained.

Who Am I? First, there is the question of personal identity in relation to the group being considered. As a facilitator you must seriously and analytically ask yourself who you are with regard to this group. Do you have a legitimate role in the group? What is it? How will it influence your effectiveness? From that vantage point how and what kind of intervention can you make? The answers to these questions determine at what level you begin. For example, if you were a teacher in a typical elementary school classroom, you would legitimately design interventions (an activity, project, special program) for your class. You might set up a role play based on fighting among the children. You might explain the situation and ask for role players to enact the problem. The role play begins, the children enact the fight sequence with a rare opportunity to "fight" in class, and then you stop the role play. Now you are ready to discuss alternative methods for resolving fights with the role players and the other students. The students fidget, or reexamine the floor or ceiling, or become suddenly absorbed in other activities. They know that discussing ideas on fights, or alternative methods of coping with hostility, are "exercises in futility." They know from previous admonitions that "fighting is bad, and people shouldn't hate each other but love each other." They know that the teacher does not really want a discussion of what they feel, but rather a moralistic conclusion that fighting is bad.

If you had previously made known your opinions in certain areas and would like to have the students reconsider the subject themselves, you will need to reexamine your position or indicate some meaningful change before any intervention on your part can be effective. Any teacher who has previously been interested in "facts, no opinions, please," may encounter great difficulty while attempting to encourage students to express their feelings. Frequently there is a norm that only feelings related to school are appropriate in school and that other subjects (sex, dating, relations with family) should be avoided in teacher-student interactions; if this is the norm, a teacher who is planning such a discussion must possess a good measure of self-awareness.

Often the person making the intervention is an outside consultant, a person outside the organization hired to work on a specific project. Outside consultants can be effective because of their special training in working with organizations and because they are able to influence without being involved in the intricacies of the organization's cliques and power groups. However, outside consultants hired to work with a new organization must carefully consider the level of trust that members will have in them initially, and they should design an initial experience that allows the members to test them.

Interventions may also be made by inside consultants (people employed by the organization). Who they are is again the basic consideration. They are not unknown; they come into a group with a reputation developed through the grapevine as to their style and their effectiveness. Consultants who have a reputation of being well-liked and effective have much greater latitude in being able to make interventions they see as needed. It cannot be stated too strongly that who you are greatly influences the manner of your approach—your legitimacy, and, consequently, the degree of potential influence.

Who Is the Group? Consideration of the facilitator's role is not enough. It is equally important to know the makeup of the group. What kind of people are they? What are their ages? How receptive are they to change? Have they been a group for some time, or is this the first time they are meeting? How can they be expected to regard you? (Some groups have immediate distrustful reactions to university professors, or men with beards, or women in facilitator roles.) These questions are important since they relate to the crucial question of whether the group is ready for what is being planned. The plan may be premature or anxiety-producing because it is beyond the experience of most of the members. Meeting the organization's objectives may require work at regular intervals, but the people in the group may not be willing to commit themselves to regular segments of time.

Are My Goals as Facilitator Clear? A third factor is whether or not the facilitator has clear goals. To say, "I want to be helpful," or "this is a good exercise to give them data," or "this worked in a group I was in and will be stimulating here" are insufficiently clear goals. Wanting to be helpful and being helpful is the difference between fantasy and reality. An exercise that focuses on a problem with which the group is unconcerned is frequently viewed as a waste of time or meaningless "game playing," and what was a stimulating exercise in one group may be an inappropriate bore in another. Thus, as a facilitator you must ask, "What are my goals?" and be able to state them explicitly to yourself; frequently it is helpful to state them to the group. At the beginning of the session, you may state simply and directly what your objectives are, how they will be accomplished, and in what time. This serves as both a framework and a guide for achieving goals. You should develop objectives based on an understanding of the first two factors, your own role and the appropriateness of doing what you have planned, plus a third factor—the readiness, composition, and expectations of the group in that situation.

This third factor can rarely be determined by the facilitator alone. It develops through involvement and participation, as the group sets its goals and expectations given the realistic constraints of time, money, and resources. The goals that develop, and then are stated by the facilitator, become the group's goals.

Communication Pitfalls. Although it is said repeatedly, it is not belaboring the point to state again that situations are perceived and words are heard uniquely. Too often it is assumed that your words as a facilitator mean to the group what they mean to you. *It is imperative that both of you have the same understanding of words.* A term used to refer to the person who professionally works with groups is the word "trainer." For many the term conjures up impressions of mechanistic animal trainers or other forms of compulsory training, and they may well generate defenses in the participants. A more acceptable word presently in vogue is "facilitator"—a word that conjures up other images, guiding but nondirective. Obviously almost any word for leader may evoke different meanings, just as behavioral science jargon may also be a source of anxiety and frustration for those involved. Recently, a group was told that there would be an intervention designed for them the next week. This statement meant that time would be set aside for the group to examine its processes of making decisions, since it seemed to have limited skill in this area. Several members, after hearing of an "intervention," became visibly anxious. When asked why, the members said that they interpreted intervention as meaning a confrontation, and they were terrified at the possibility of such an experience.

Many of the words that facilitators take for granted or that have an accepted meaning for people "in the trade" have little or no meaning for lay people unfamiliar with these terms. The facilitator must either explain the meaning of the term or use a term familiar to the group. Asking a group to form into dyads, for example, generally produces raised eyebrows but little movement; however, asking them to form into groups of two or to select a partner produces the desired response. Frequently, the facilitator only learns too late that there was a misinterpretation; the result is a less than optimal learning situation. The facilitator can minimize such misunderstandings by checking facial expressions of members for inadequate comprehension and asking at frequent intervals if there are any questions. Generally, after directions have been given, the facilitator will ask, "Are there any questions before we start?" If understanding is valued, this cannot be asked as a rhetorical question. The question is asked, and there should be a sufficient pause for questions plus time allotted for answers. Obviously, a question period before the session is more productive than discussions of "I thought you meant" afterward. Since questions are often seen as signs of ignorance, they are often difficult to elicit from a group with whom the facilitator is not familiar. By breaking the group into clusters of three or four and asking for a few questions from each at appropriate times, there is a greater assurance of questions that will help the group and the facilitator in their efforts to understand each other.

In summary, to be an effective facilitator, you should begin with some basic understanding of yourself and your role, the group with which you are working, and a clear formulation of your objectives. These are specific considerations that require careful previous study by anyone working with a group—by a facilitator working with a new group, by a staff member or teacher examining a group at regular intervals, and by facilitators and groups working together in each planning session.

Time as a Dynamic Variable

Too often time is perceived as a given rather than a dynamic component in planning. Typically, we think in terms of having a day to present a specific program, or two hours, or a period, and we design in terms of filling up that time space. We diagnose our group, develop a plan, and attempt to "guesstimate" how long it will take to present it. We allow time for an introduction, a theory input, an exercise, and discussion and implications at the end. Then the inevitable occurs—so frequent an occurrence that it should almost be anticipated. That is, the program does not start on time, someone has an announcement, or we run late and are forced to cut out the most important part of the learning experience—the sharing of information and the implications. In reality, we tend to overplan and assume that we will get more in than we actually can. At one level, time should be viewed as the limits within which learning takes place, and it should be allocated so that both the initial as well as the more important concluding aspects are timed within the unit.

Time can also be a facilitator's tool. It can be used as a means to implement the training goals. The facilitator who wishes to increase involvement can shorten the time allotted for a task; the micro aspect compresses action—there is less time for small talk and a greater motivation to accomplish the given task in the given time. This breakdown of the time component for greater involvement and increased productivity can be formulated in many ways. A number of them will be briefly stated and described.

Micro-lab. As the name indicates, a micro-lab is a condensed version of a total laboratory or workshop experience. Because the time is shortened—usually about two hours for the entire experience—the session is intensive. It is designed to give participants a taste of a laboratory experience that involves them immediately, raises issues, and provides diagnostic data for later analysis. It is especially effective because it can be geared and designed toward the goals of that laboratory. And for the participants it provides experiential data from a number of different approaches to a subject which then allows them to personalize implications. Out of the time pressure, out of the many senses and feelings generated in the micro-lab, people internalize more than they would in a typical introductory program or initial lecture. The micro-lab, designed as a series of short interpersonal experiences, is especially effective as an introductory session to get people directly involved yet simultaneously working on the issues to be raised in the longer workshop. Micro-labs are frequently designed around getting to know others in a group of strangers, interpersonal communication, an examination of stereotyped roles as males and females, or increased sensory awareness. The possibilities are limitless.

Micro-lecture. At times the facilitator may want to speak on the theoretical or research findings related to a particular subject. The problem is that lectures reduce participant response and involvement to passive listening. The micro-lecture uses time pressure for both involvement and integration of material for participants. The facilitator prepares a lecture so that it can be presented in five-minute segments. The main thesis may be presented in the first segment and the substantiating points one by one in subsequent segments. The participants are divided into small groups so that after each five-minute lecture, a ten-minute discussion on that point follows. The pattern continues three or four times—a five-minute lecture on one point, followed by a ten-minute discussion on it. The result is a continued involvement, discussion, and integration of the material in a limited time. Obviously, presentation and discussion time blocks are flexible, depending on the particular situation and the need that arises.

Micro-discussion. On a given topic, frequently only a few of the more verbal individuals participate. Others never get a chance to express their views, or they feel they are peripheral members and not really meant to participate. Sometimes talk is bogged down to a discussion of a tangential point, and returning to the main subject becomes difficult. Once more, time is used actively to promote the facilitator's objectives of enlarged participation. The group is divided in half (and with a larger group, even in thirds). One-half the group comes into the center of a circle and discusses the topic for ten minutes. At the end of that time, the other group comes into the center, and the first group recedes. The discussion continues on the same topic for another ten minutes. Every ten minutes there is a reversal of inner-outer groups. What happens is that with half the number in the circle, there are more opportunities to speak for the more reticent or less involved members. The ten-minute limit on discussion allows the new group to build on previous discussion and not to be stymied by a personality conflict or a peripheral view of the discussion. Once more the limiting of time produces greater involvement, a leap-frogging of ideas as one group builds on the discussion of the previous group, and members build on the resources of members in both groups.

Just as time should not be taken for granted but viewed as a tool to implement the goals of the facilitator, so are other aspects a means to help the facilitator accomplish additional objectives. Grouping especially influences both the process and the outcome.

The Many Ways to Group

In the exercises of this book we have frequently given directions to "divide the participants into groups of 6 to 8." That sounds simple enough, but a consideration of the methods of grouping can produce not only units small enough for conversation but also may be critically important for ensuring implementation of the training goals. By failing to have effective procedures ready for such a simple part of the design, the facilitator may make the group uncomfortable and reduce the rapport so essential for a successful intervention.

Random Grouping. This is the simplest method of grouping. First, the facilitator must decide how many groups are desirable—let us say five; thus participants are asked to count off (1, 2, 3, 4, 5, 1, 2, etc.). Then the facilitator specifies a location for each of the groups (the ones go to one corner, the twos to another, and so on until all of the groups form). Sometimes names are pulled from a hat, with the first five names being group 1, the second five being group 2, and continuing until the desired number of groups is attained. Yet another method is to group people by their birthday month—all January and February birthdays would be group 1, etc. The advantages of random grouping are that whatever diversity exists in the population is likely to be spread among the groups, friendship groups are split, and participants view each group as having equal resources. There are no higher and lower status groups. Random groups are especially effective in a new group in which some people enter with friends and others are alone and feel like outcasts. The random group requires that each individual build a relationship in the group alone and anew. Sometimes, an especially hostile group will perceive even a random grouping as being manipulative. It is the wise (and experienced) facilitator who accepts their suspicions and is sensitive and responsive to their fears. The facilitator may simply ask that participants get together in groups of five with others they do not know and form groups in this manner. Of course, it is unlikely that such a suspicious group will move into "stranger" subgroups. The key is to get them moving and caught up in the plan of the day, which should reduce their doubts or anxieties.

Homogeneous Grouping. For some purposes a homogeneous grouping may be more suitable for the design. There can be one table for elementary school teachers, another for secondary school teachers, a third for higher education, another for administrative staffs. Or there can be women at one table and men at another, or parents at one table and students at another. Homogeneous groupings may be utilized to permit groups with common concerns to work on joint problems, they may be used in an initial grouping to be followed by a pairing of members from each group, or they may be the basis for discussion with a representative from each group.

Stratified-Random Grouping. In some designs it is desirable to have a planned mix in each group—that is, a given number in proportion to diverse populations. Here each group may be composed of a representative from each school, or representatives of different occupations may form a group. This grouping is frequently used to attain diverse populations within a group whose members might not ordinarily distribute themselves in such a manner: blacks and whites, adults and students, inner-city residents and suburbanites, Christians and Jews. There is the predicted tendency for like to sit with like; this form, by design, places representatives of the diverse segments within each group. It is important to let these groups understand how they have been selected so the feelings of manipulation are minimized.

Ad Hoc Grouping. Often involvement itself is the goal, and the type of grouping matters little. In an auditorium, the facilitator might ask those in the front row to turn their chairs so they can speak to those in the next row, and those in the third row to turn so they can speak to those in the fourth row. Sometimes, the facilitator begins by having the room arranged with round tables and chairs. As people enter and as they seat themselves, they are self-grouping. The facilitator then proceeds on the basis that those at a table become a group. These are some of the types of grouping facilitators use. However, at other times there is a very different rationale for grouping.

Dyads and Triads. In a new situation, a large group looks frightening. Talking to one other person, who may be equally apprehensive, becomes a way to enter the group and feel less alone. Dyads, or groups of two, are frequently used in initial micro-labs, in pairing for observations, in sharing of perceptions and reactions. Dyads, used in the micro-concept for a stated short time, increase involvement as well as personal reactions to the subject under discussion.

Triads, or groups of three, are frequently effective in discussing an issue. Triads permit a flexibility of relationships: two may side against one on one issue but align differently on another; in three-person groups there is high involvement, a possibility of utilization of multiple reactions and resources, and a variety of relationships. Groups of four are infrequently used because they permit a formation of sides that could remain deadlocked. Groups of five are used in decision-making or problem-solving groups, but they are used less frequently in situations in which the goal is personal reaction and involvement. In a group of six or more, there is a likelihood that two people will take over; therefore, many facilitators will give two groups of three 15 minutes to discuss a problem rather than assigning a group of six half an hour.

Sometimes the training design might require that participants be in working groups of eight. A common method of creating a group of eight is to begin with a dyad; thus at the simplest level two people are in contact and there is a direct feeling of involvement and a relationship. That pair may then be asked to join another pair and discuss another question. Then that group of four may be asked to join another group of four; the eight then become a team. The rationale is to build to a group of eight gradually so that the participants get to know each other along the way. Starting with eight right at the beginning usually produces a complication of relationships. This same form is used in building groups of sixes or tens or any larger group based on multiples of smaller groups.

Support Groups. Sometimes an anchor group is helpful to achieve the goals of the program; these are called "support groups." In a program in which there are representatives of many schools, the team from a particular school becomes a support group and meets at specified times to discuss the reactions or applicability of the program to their school, or any other questions based on implications of the current program. Support groups may be triads or larger groups that share an interest and discuss it together; they cluster out of the large participatory body.

Fishbowls. Fishbowls are like the micro-discussions described earlier. The group is divided in half, or an even number of units. One-half comes into the center and discusses a question while the other half listens. After eight to ten minutes (or a predetermined length of time), the other group comes into the center and discusses either the same question or another issue. In either event, the group builds as each unit in the center assimilates and responds as if continuing the previous discussion. Thus, by listening to the previous group and then participating, there is a tendency to move over roadblocks encountered in the last period.

A fishbowl is also used in decision making. A representative group may be the inner circle, as in a fishbowl, with the other participants listening to the negotiations, as in the outer circle of the fishbowl. Sometimes the "tap in" is used to allow those on the outside to express their views directly. If someone has something to say that is pertinent and thus far unsaid, the outer member taps the inner member with whom he or she disagrees, or another person who has been silent or uninvolved, and takes the place of the person tapped. The outer member then presents the pertinent view and, depending on the rules, continues to stay until he or she is tapped out or leaves voluntarily, thereby permitting the displaced member to return. Instead of tapping out, another variation is to place two empty chairs in the inner circle. Someone from the outer group who has a comment sits in the empty chair, speaks, and then returns to his or her former place. A fishbowl has the advantage of allowing all to participate in the decision-making process either directly or at least by hearing the negotiations firsthand. Since decision making and discussion of recommendations are often conducted in secrecy and privacy, the fishbowl frequently has great impact on persons who are witness to this procedure for the first time.

The type of grouping used depends on the basic understandings described earlier in the chapter. The method of grouping will be governed by the goals of the facilitator and the kind of problem being examined.

Using Techniques Effectively

A number of techniques are described in training exercises throughout the book, and they are usually self-explanatory to experienced facilitators. To the newcomer, however, a brief review of what is involved in using a technique effectively may be appropriate.

Posting on Newsprint. Using newsprint—large sheets of cheap paper typically purchased in tablets—is one sure way of increasing participant involvement. The newsprint, which is written on with broad felt-tipped marking pens and mounted on the walls with masking tape, is an effective device for having data available and readily evident to participants. It is used to record the reports presented by various groups, to list recommendations, to describe aspects of a situation, and to provide feedback to a group. The newsprint on the wall even serves to remind participants of how much they have accomplished as they see the layers of newsprint surrounding them by the end of a three-day workshop. Like anything else, newsprint can be overused, and it will never save the poorly prepared or unskilled facilitator. But it can help increase idea visibility, reduce credibility gaps, and focus attention of groups composed of from two to several hundred members.

Role Playing. Role playing is an especially effective method for having participants experience a situation in its concrete reality; generally, it is more effective than a discussion in abstraction. It permits analysis of behaviors as well as a possibility for a replay with certain roles enacted in another way. The benefits of role play are inadequately stated here, but there are two good books that will provide the reader with additional information.[1] For our purposes the emphasis will be on frequently ignored steps in a role play that undermine the

---

[1] M. Chester and R. Fox, *Role-Playing Methods in the Classroom*, Chicago, Ill.: Science Research Associates, Inc., 1966; A. F. Klein, *How to Use Role Playing Effectively*, New York: Association Press, 1959.

effectiveness of the technique. Prior to the role play there might be some warm-up activities to help people feel less self-conscious; for example, practicing how people coming to a protest meeting walk in, or where they sit. Such activities create an atmosphere and environment for a realistic role play.

After some warm-up activities, a role play situation is identified, the players are selected, and the role play takes place. First, it is important that the role players have an opportunity to read their roles, become familiar with them, and feel able to perform the behaviors indicated. The players might try imaginary monologues to get them in the mood of the character, or stand outside the room and practice how the role player might act in a given situation. There might even be one or two coaches to help the role player become more aware of nuances and styles. The facilitator checks that all are familiar and comfortable with their roles; if not, the facilitator further clarifies the role or attempts to be helpful to the insecure role player. If there are to be observers gathering data during the role play, the facilitator instructs them in detail, or distributes and reviews an observer's guide, which provides the information needed.

Having ascertained that the players are ready and the observers know their instructions, the facilitator asks that the role players enter and seat themselves according to the role-play situation. Once more the facilitator establishes the situation, and the role play begins. Too often role playing becomes boring because the facilitator does not cut soon enough. The action should be terminated as soon as a decision is made or when it becomes evident there will be no decision. The role play is the focal incident. After it ends, the discussion begins with individual reactions and then enlarges to implications or alternatives for that situation. The facilitator might ask the role players to respond to how they each felt in that role: "Were you comfortable, was it familiar, how did it feel?" Then the debriefing continues as the facilitator asks each to respond to the character out of role: "How different was this from your usual role?" Only then are there reports called for from the observers and other participants. Finally, there is a discussion of generalizations or implications of the role play, in which all enter. As is evident, the role play is only a small portion of what is involved in a training design. The preparation and debriefing are important but often overlooked aspects, and, of course, enough time must be allowed for reporting and for generalizations.

Role Reversal. The objective of role reversal is to understand to what extent one person perceives and can enact the role of another. Usually it is very difficult, or done at a level of superficial mannerisms. It becomes evident that we often see others through the narrow view of our own limited experience. Prior to the role reversal, the participants are given name tags. In the midst of a discussion, the facilitator abruptly cuts the activity and explains that people frequently are concerned only with what they are thinking or trying to say—not with what others are feeling. The facilitator then asks those across from each other to exchange seats and name tags. The participants are to continue the discussion as if they were the person in the seat opposite; they are to attempt to be faithful in their body movements and emotional tone as well as continue the discussion from their point of view. After a few minutes the discussion is again terminated and participants share their experiences. Sometimes, this procedure is done a second time; by then members will have become more aware of each other's verbal and nonverbal behaviors and will be better able to attempt the role reversal. Obviously, the activity can be extended to a variety of situations in which individuals are concerned with how they are being perceived. It is ideal for opening communication between two individuals who are no longer capable of listening to each other.

Alter-Ego. An alter-ego is basically the other persons within us—the "voices" that might urge us to speak when we are silent or express feelings we dare not openly express. The alter-ego as a technique may be used in a modification of a role play, or it may be used to illustrate the conflicts within a person. In a role play, two (or more) participants stand behind a given character and enact hidden parts of the person's personalities. For example, John, the football captain who is a member of a committee to decide on a new dress code, may have his alter-egos behind him. One may remind him that he should vote for short hair; if he votes that way, his regulation short hair will seem less conspicuous. Another alter-ego will remind him to vote for long hair because that is what the students want, and if he is planning to run for class president a vote in that direction will enhance his popularity. The role player continues, but every time the alter-ego (inner voice) wants to speak, he or she puts an arm on the shoulder of the role player, who stops talking. The alter-ego speaks and then releases the role player's arm, signaling the continuation of the role play. It is especially important that the alter-ego and the role players thoroughly understand and are comfortable in their roles. There should be adequate time to warm up and explain the alter-ego concept. Following the role play, the debriefing includes the alter-egos as well as the role players. The prime understanding that develops in an alter-ego role play is empathy for the person who is trapped and who is placed in the position of not being able to express true feelings. At times we have all experienced this pain and frustration.

An alter-ego role play is also a primary example of all the things that can go wrong; those viewing the exercise may be confused about who those people are in the back; alter-egos may not be sure when or how to come in; and role players may be confused about how to respond to the alter-egos. It takes preparation for an alter-ego role play to be successful. However, it can demonstrate in physical terms that sometimes we intend to side with one group and act with another, sometimes we seem to vacillate so that others have difficulty understanding our behavior, and sometimes we are quiet when we have much to say.

Sociodrama, Psychodrama. Both are "acting out" techniques without written formal roles as is usually the case in a role play. In a sociodrama, members will act out a social situation—for example, a mother, a father, and a child discussing an anticipated move to a new city or a job applicant being interviewed. In a psychodrama individuals volunteer problems they would like to work on. One problem is selected. The person whose problem was selected can "play" to another person in the group or to an imagined person. The participants, in each kind of drama, may change roles as a means of further implementing understanding. The sociodrama is used to increase understanding and skill in certain situations; the psychodrama is frequently used to examine and work on unresolved relations with other people or personal issues.[2]

To be effective, there should be a warm-up, or a series of practice activities, so that members feel less self-conscious. Most important, the situation must be clearly presented. After the drama, both participants as well as those observing are asked to respond. It may be in terms of feelings toward this situation, a sharing of similar experiences in their lives, or suggestions for an alternative method of enacting the role or viewing the situation.

Replay Drama. Situations occur in which the members are caught off guard, where an incident occurs that is typical, and the response is anxious and defensive. For example, two Black Panthers were invited to present their platform to a mostly white college graduate class in psychology. In the question-and-answer period the discussion became personal and heated. At the next session of class there was a replay drama; the situation of the previous week was replayed with class members enacting all of the roles. The scene was rekindled, but now the group started where the previous week's discussion ended. Replay drama is a powerful technique that permits people close to a situation to reexamine their behaviors less defensively and more objectively. The replay is different from the original, and some of the most important lessons come from a discussion of what is different and why. Although a relatively new technique, the replay holds promise for allowing persons to reexamine their behaviors in highly emotional areas. This attempt to help the participants to know, to replay, and to understand is fundamental in the facilitator's efforts to help a group.

Gathering Data on Groups

Gathering data is the scientific basis for understanding what is happening. There are a number of methods for observing aspects of groups, but only a few will be described here. Which method is used depends on the training objectives and the readiness of the group to diagnose its situation. It is less threatening to observe a role play than an ongoing group, and comparable resistances are to be anticipated when an ongoing group is to be observed. Groups frequently are fearful of observations because of the assumed implications that the leader might be a poor one or that the group might be viewed as a failure. It is very difficult to ask a group to consider examining its own behavior. The fears are enormous. It is easier in a laboratory group or classroom, where the learning

---

[2] For more information on psychodrama, read J. L. Moreno, *Psychodrama*, New York: Beacon Press, 1946.

aspect can be heightened and the evaluative aspects muted. Sometimes beginning with a simple observation form, like a post-meeting reaction, and allowing the members to discuss the results among themselves and draw conclusions or consider modifications allows the group to begin the observation process without fear of expectations from the facilitator.

Post-Meeting Reactions. A series of questions are developed dealing with the degree of involvement of each member, the amount of participation, the amount of perceived conflict, and the amount of movement toward goals. Each question is followed by a rating scale going from 1 (not involved) to 5 (highly involved). (See Figure A.1.) The sheets are prepared by the facilitator, who explains that they may be a useful instrument to help the group diagnose its present situation. If the groups are agreeable, one sheet is distributed to each member; after all the responses are recorded, the results are determined and read back either by a volunteer or the group itself analyzes the results.

Another form of post-meeting reaction is developed from the concept of bipolar scales. A feeling or attribute is on the left and its polar opposite on the right. Persons are asked to place an X on the scale at the point that best describes their feelings. (See Figure A.2.) Post-meeting reactions are useful for helping a group diagnose its present state; they possibly may lead to more effectiveness as members become aware of the responses of others and find mutual areas of agreement or disagreement.

Post-Meeting Reaction

1. How effectively was the goal of the group accomplished today?

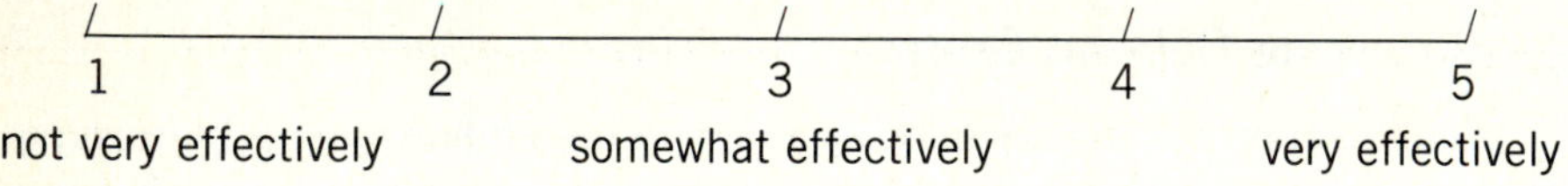

Comments:

2. How thorough was the group in exploring all the possibilities needed to accomplish this goal?

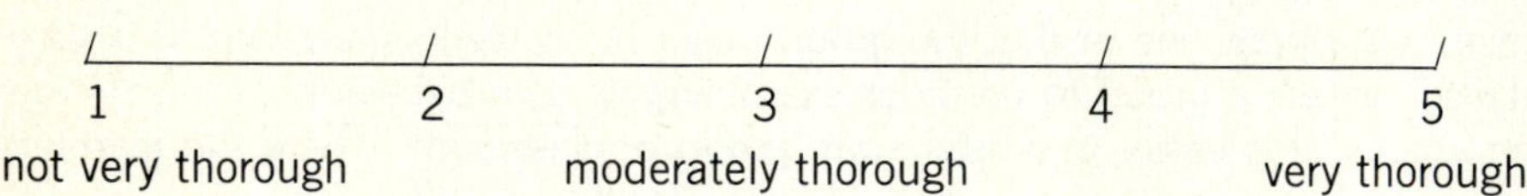

Comments:

3. How well did the members communicate with one another?

/ / / / /
1 2 3 4 5
poorly fairly well very well

Comments:

4. How much consideration did the group give to individual ideas and feelings of each member in making final decisions?

/ / / / /
1 2 3 4 5
very inconsiderate somewhat inconsiderate very considerate

Comments:

5. How satisfied are you with today's session?

/ / / / /
1 2 3 4 5
very dissatisfied dissatisfied, but will accept very satisfied

Comments:

FIGURE A.1. A Post-Meeting Reaction Sheet

Group I.D. ______________________

Individual I.D. ______________________

Group Evaluation Form

Use the following form to evaluate your group by placing an 'X' on the line at the place that best describes how you feel.

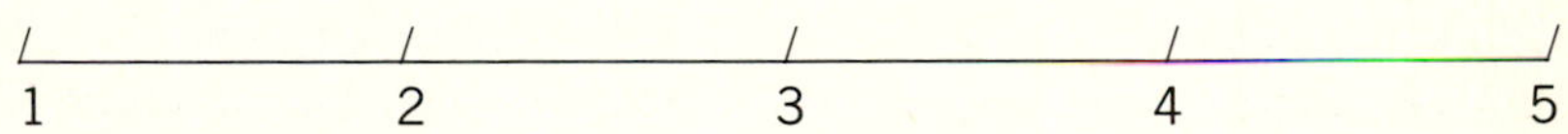

1 2 3 4 5

Unproductive **Productive**

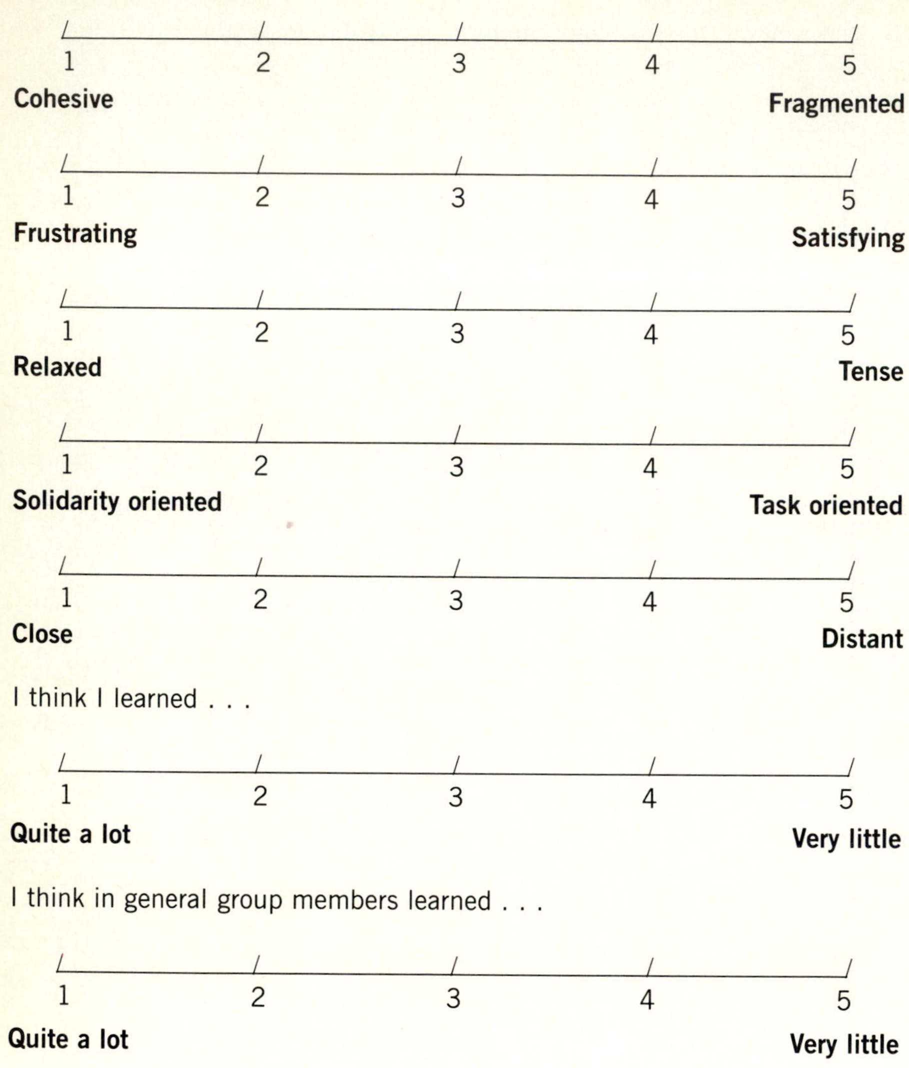
1 2 3 4 5
Cohesive — Fragmented

1 2 3 4 5
Frustrating — Satisfying

1 2 3 4 5
Relaxed — Tense

1 2 3 4 5
Solidarity oriented — Task oriented

1 2 3 4 5
Close — Distant

I think I learned . . .

1 2 3 4 5
Quite a lot — Very little

I think in general group members learned . . .

1 2 3 4 5
Quite a lot — Very little

FIGURE A.2. Group Evaluation Form

Task-Maintenance Observation. Frequently groups understand their work in the problem-solving areas, but they rarely know of the socioemotional areas of equal importance—the harmonizer, the gatekeeper, etc., the roles that influence how members feel about one another. One kind of observation focuses on task-maintenance behaviors. It may begin by dividing the group into thirds. One group performs some experimental task assigned by the facilitator.

One group has sheets listing task behaviors, and one group has sheets listing maintenance behaviors. Following the exercise, the observers report their findings. (See Fig A.3.) The reporting of this data helps participants become aware of the variety of roles in a group and the limited number used by each member. As a result, some members may endeavor to attempt new behaviors. Frequently, the ensuing discussion prompts members to talk about groups they find effective and in which they are comfortable, and it leads to a discussion of implications for that group.

Member Functions Observation Sheet

Use a (√) to indicate each time the group needed a particular function or when it performed one.

Group Needed	Task Functions or Behaviors	Group Performed
	Initiation: proposing tasks or goals; defining a group problem; suggesting a procedure or ideas for solving a problem.	
	Information or opinion seeking: requesting facts; seeking relevant information about a group concern; asking for suggestions and ideas.	
	Information or opinion giving: offering facts; providing relevant information about group concern; stating a belief; giving suggestions or ideas.	
	Clarifying: interpreting or reflecting ideas and suggestions; clearing up confusions; indicating alternatives and issues before the group; giving examples.	
	Summarizing: pulling together related ideas; restating suggestions after group has discussed them; offering a decision or conclusion for the group to accept or reject.	
	Testing for consensus: sending up "trial balloons" to see if group is nearing a conclusion; checking with group to see how much agreement has been reached.	

Group Needed	Maintenance Functions or Behavior	Group Performed
	Encouraging: being friendly, warm and responsive to others; accepting others and their contributions; regarding others by giving them an opportunity or recognition.	
	Expressing group feelings: sensing feeling, mood, relationships within the group; sharing own feelings or effect with other members.	
	Harmonizing: attempting to reconcile disagreements; reducing tension through "pouring oil on troubled waters"; getting people to explore their differences.	
	Compromising: when own ideas or status is involved in a conflict, offering to compromise own position; admitting error; disciplining to maintain group cohesion.	
	Gate-keeping: attempting to keep communication channels open; facilitating the participation of others; suggesting procedures for sharing opportunity to discuss group problems.	
	Setting standards: expressing standards for group achievement; applying standards in evaluating group functioning and production.	

FIGURE A.3. Task-Maintenance Observations

Nonfunctional, Self-Oriented Behavior Observations. When a group is especially conflicted or polarized, yet another observation form can be used. This form focuses not on task or maintenance functions, but behavior that is nonfunctional and individually oriented. A group can be divided into quadrants with one section observing for nonfunctional self-oriented behaviors as others observe for task and maintenance behaviors.

Another way to help the members understand behaviors in the group is to observe only for task and maintenance functions, and then introduce the idea of nonfunctional, self-oriented behaviors by distributing the sheets (Fig A.4) and discussing these behaviors—when they occurred, and the effect on the group.

Nonfunctional, Self-Oriented Behaviors

In addition to task behaviors and group building and maintenance behaviors, a third category should be indicated—actions that tend to be oriented to the needs of the individual member rather than to the needs of the group. They are "nonfunctional" in the sense that they do not *per se* contribute to the achievement of the group's purposes. Illustrative of these nonfunctional behaviors are the following:

1. *Being aggressive:* working for status by criticizing or blaming others; showing hostility against the group or some individual; deflating the ego or status of others.
2. *Blocking:* interfering with the progress of the group by going off on a tangent, citing personal experiences unrelated to the problem, arguing too much on a point, or rejecting ideas without consideration.
3. *Self-confusing:* using the group as a sounding board; expressing personal, nongroup-oriented feelings or points of view.
4. *Competing:* vying with others to produce the best idea, talk the most, play the most roles, gain favor with the leader.
5. *Seeking sympathy:* trying to induce other group members to be sympathetic to one's problems or misfortunes, deploring one's own situations, or disparaging one's own ideas to gain support.
6. *Special pleading:* introducing or supporting suggestions related to one's own pet concerns or philosophies; lobbying.
7. *Seeking recognition:* attempting to call attention to one's self by loud or excessive talking, extreme ideas, or unusual behavior.
8. *Withdrawing:* acting indifferently or passively; resorting to excessive formality; daydreaming, doodling, whispering to others, or wandering from the subject.

Note: in using a classification like the one above, people need to guard against the tendency to blame any person (whether themselves or another) who falls into "nonfunctional behavior." It is more useful to regard such behavior as a symptom that all is not well with the group's ability to satisfy individual needs through group-centered activity. Further, people need to be alert to the fact that each person is likely to interpret such behaviors differently. For example, what appears as "blocking" to one person may appear to another as a needed effort to "test feasibility."

FIGURE A.4. Nonfunctional, Self-Oriented Behaviors

Process-Content Observation. The facilitator who asks, "What are they talking about?" is asking a content question. The facilitator who asks, "What is happening; what do they seem to be doing?" is asking a process question. Who is listened to and who is ignored can be determined by process observations: who has high status and who has low, who is friends with whom—all of these are process questions that, once we obtain answers, permit us to understand the dynamics of a particular group.

A *sociogram* is an instrument that measures interpersonal relations. It may measure productivity; it may ask a member to rate the three hardest workers in the group. It may measure a friendship dimension, and ask, "Who are the three people you like best in the group?" Questions can be designed to obtain information in the area desired. The replies to the questions are tallied and, based on the number of times mentioned, people are rated. The most often rated is the "star"; the least rated may be the "unchosen." The results yield information on members' perceptions of individuals on the dimensions studied, i.e., who is viewed as an isolate, who is the most popular, which are the subgroups. The facilitator might encourage members to design their own sociograms for data they feel are pertinent. Afterward, members discuss the findings as well as their feelings about them. The sociogram is easy to design, administer, and interpret. It is a form of data a group readily understands. It can also be misused or used too lightly in situations that may prove threatening.

A *who-to-whom* is an instrument for collecting information recorded by an observer that completely disregards content. The recorder (this could be the facilitator or a selected observer) tallies each time a person speaks (one tally per sentence) and notes to whom the statement is addressed. The observations are recorded in a matrix, which indicates who spoke to whom. The matrix is illustrated in Fig A.5.

To Whom Spoken (the recipient)

Who Speaks (the speaker)

	Name (1)	Name (2)	Name (3)	Name (4)	Name (5)	Group	Total
Name (1)							
Name (2)							
Name (3)							
Name (4)							
Name (5)							
Total							

FIGURE A.5. A Who-to-Whom Matrix

On the left side are listed the names of the members of the group. (The recorder who is unfamiliar with names lists people by number.) This left-hand column represents the list of possible speakers. Across the top are listed the members, or numbers representing them, in the same order. These top numbers indicate to whom the speaker talks. If person 2 speaks to person 5, a tally is recorded on the row with 2 at the left and in the column under 5, or in the cell 2-5. If the person continues to talk, tallies are continued, one for each sentence. Tallies are recorded in this fashion for a given time unit, usually ten minutes at the beginning, and ten minutes at the end of an observation period. There is a cell for a member addressing the entire group (in Figure A.5, the Group column). Note that there is a diagonal line in the cell in which person 1 might be speaking to himself, or person 2 to herself—it may be possible, but it is unrecorded. Following the observation period, the tallies are totaled, and frequently percentages are computed. The totals at the right represent the number of units (or the percentage) of the total amount of verbal interaction that one person spoke. The totals at the bottom represent the number of times a person was spoken to.

Although content is disregarded, the who-to-whom yields a great deal of information on the relationships within a group. The high-status person is typically the one who is spoken to much more than he or she speaks; the low-status person is typically the one who speaks a disproportionate amount in comparison with the low proportion of times he or she is spoken to. Subgroupings are seen as two members who speak almost exclusively to each other, or speak to each other much more than others. Someone not sure of his or her membership role may rarely speak.

A who-to-whom is an especially valuable instrument for collecting data on a variety of aspects of a group and in analysis allows members to develop new understandings of the dynamics of their group. It should be mentioned that one observation may be atypical, as is a single measure unreliable in many instances; several observations over time are required for a more reliable description of the dynamics of that group.

Feedback

Another method for obtaining data on individuals and groups is through feedback; the individual asks for certain information, and the others answer, based on their perceptions of the person. For example, if Tom notices people looking at him during all of the discussion and thinks he has been informally designated the leader of the group, he may ask the group whether they see him as the leader. Their reply is feedback to him. The whole concept of feedback may be viewed as threatening since it is so alien to the norms of our society. People are really secretive in their feelings toward others and do not tell others how they see them. They not only feel threatened by the prospect, but may view it as harmful. Yet feedback is the means by which we can be more honest in groups and deal more effectively with one another as our behavior is consonant with our thoughts. Of course, feedback can be harmful to individuals or to the development of an entire group. The facilitator should make the rules of feedback clear. The feedback should be requested, be descriptive rather than evaluative, be specific rather than general, be behavioral rather than total, and preferably should be constructive. For example, if Mary asks why no one wants her in the group, a person responding might answer that the last time they were in a project together she never came to meetings and did almost none of the work.

Where appropriate, the facilitator can encourage feedback among members. Among the many kinds of feedback are the results of observation instruments and the reports of observers. The following kinds of observations provide members with data about themselves and their roles in a group:

1. *Feedback on descriptive behavior.* Two people are paired. One, P (Participant), works with others in the performance of an experimental task; the other, O (Observer), observes P's behavior. The observer then describes the behavior he or she saw—how often P spoke, on what subjects, body motions, etc. The two then reverse.

2. *Feedback on nonverbal behavior.* A pairing similar to the situation above is made, except the person doing the observing watches only for nonverbal behaviors. Frequently, nonverbal behaviors give us greater clues to what the person is feeling than verbal responses. The observer shares the findings with the participant. The partners then reverse.

3. *Feedback on coming closer, being more distant.* Yet another version of the observation feedback techniques described above is one in which the observers focus on their partners in terms of behaviors that help people come closer to them (looking at them, listening) or those that make people more distant from them. In each of these observational schemes, the facilitator instructs the observers as to what to look for and preferably develops a list of descriptive behaviors to be checked.

Groups are encouraged to make up their own observational systems. The limitation to be emphasized by the facilitator is that the observations must be descriptive or based on behaviors that can be described.

Ongoing Feedback and Readjustment by the Facilitator. It is so obvious it sounds trite, but the facilitator's effectiveness is directly related to his or her receptivity and sensitivity to feedback. In planning a session the facilitator may meet with other members of the group to get feedback and to ascertain more realistically how the group sees the facilitator role, and where the participants are as a group. The facilitator may test tentative ideas by submitting them to the planning group and carefully watching for the members' reactions. If they say,

"That sounds too much like sensitivity training to be in a teacher's workshop," the facilitator might propose other means for achieving that objective. Even after a preliminary training design has been developed, the facilitator may still be considering others. Upon meeting a hostile "show me" group, the facilitator may decide to alter the opening because the first part of the design does not meet with the anticipated reactions; the design may be revised to get more group discussion in the second phase. The facilitator may also find, as is typical, that there is not enough time to develop the design as planned and that certain sections will have to be eliminated. In a break in the session, the facilitator might ask some of the participants how they feel about what is happening. Finally, following the program, the facilitator might "hang around" so that he or she is available to hear comments. Of course, the facilitator is routinely "reading faces" even though he or she is not always doing so consciously.

Summary

Being a facilitator sometimes looks easy; however, it never is. Facilitators must constantly be aware of themselves, their expectations, and their role in a group; they must be sensitive to that group and its current goals and objectives. Facilitators must have certain basic skills, which, with experience, can be enhanced through observation, gathering data, giving feedback, and developing training experiences. Most important, facilitators have to be sensitive to the feedback they receive. Facilitators plan for a group but do not arrive with "the plan." They have other resources at their disposal so that if they note a change in a group, they can activate an alternative plan as appropriate. With experience and ever-increasing sensitivity to what is going on, facilitators learn how they can be effective.

Appendix B: Illustration of a Student Design and Intervention

The following paper is an example of graduate students learning to design and write up their intervention. It is appropriate for trainers also to write up their experience, for their own knowledge as well as for the purpose of future discussions with colleagues. The paper was written by James Quill and Mary Rounds, students in a Department of Psychoeducational Processes graduate class at Temple University.

Background

Throughout this semester we were involved in a reading course for which students were required to relate information through presentations. The majority of these presentations were of the lecture type and very theory oriented. Subject matter consisted of various psychophysiological factors related to reading such as neurology, psychology, remedial methods, etc. The general approach to the presentation involved individual class members sitting and reading their information from notes or textbook materials.

The listening audience displayed very passive behavior even though they had been requested to read articles pertaining to the topic beforehand. They showed little reaction to the presentations. Very few members of the class generated any questions or comments dealing with the subject matter. It appeared that the classroom group's interest gravitated to the usual pattern of inconsequential note taking. This behavior seemed to indicate a need to withdraw from interaction, which can be interpreted as the common mode of action characterized by the typical college or graduate student group. Overall, the atmosphere could be described as stifling interaction among class members, promoting stagnation, and therefore defeating the learning process. At another level it also seemed to represent what happens in a classroom with teachers teaching reading to their passive, not involved, "remedial" students.

Introduction

Our observation and involvement in this type of "learning experience," combined with our participation in a group processes course, provided us with the opportunity to transform our classroom knowledge into practical experience. We thought it would be interesting to experiment by varying the standard presentation. We thought we would use our group skills to enhance learning here.

Our topic for presentation was based on the use of newspapers and television as an approach to remedial reading instruction. The outline in Exhibit B.1 illustrates the sequence of our presentation:

A. Introduction to Topic and Distribution of Materials
B. Arrangement into Groups
C. Presentation
   1. Interaction 1 — Feedback 1
   2. Interaction 2 — Feedback 2
D. PMR Feedback

Exhibit B.1. Outline of the Presentation

I. Introduction

A. Arrange the class members into groups.
B. Explain how the presentation was organized.
C. State the objectives of the presentation.
D. Define a remedial reading program as one that
   1. Accepts the limitations of the individual.
   2. Sets reasonable expectations.
   3. Desires to meet the needs and interests of the child.

II. Setting Up a Remedial Program

A. Test for strengths and weaknesses.
B. Select materials that are based on the child's needs and interests.
C. Introduce the interest inventory.

III. The Interest Inventory

A. May be administered orally or written depending on the child's ability.
B. Should consist of a predetermined set of questions based on what you want to find out.
C. Have class refer to interest inventory handout (Exhibit B.2) (discuss this).

IV. Group Task—(approx. 10–15 mins.)

A. The groups are to try to develop some sample questions for an interest inventory.
B. The groups are to report their results.
C. Feedback: ask for some feedback from the groups and discuss.

V. Introduce the Newspaper

A. State reasons why the newspaper is a useful tool for remedial instruction. For example, newspapers are
   1. Relatively inexpensive.
   2. Easily accessible.
   3. Have something of interest for everyone—refer to handout (Exhibit B.3).

4. Can be adapted to cover a wide range of reading skills—refer to handout (Exhibit B.4).

B. Give examples of how the newspaper can be implemented in a remedial program (discuss charts).

VI. Group Task—(approx. 10–15 mins.)

A. Using the materials distributed, the groups are to try to develop some sample activities that could be implemented through the use of the newspaper in a remedial program.

B. After the group interactions, ask for feedback on what was developed in the groups.

C. Have a class discussion on the feedback given.

VII. Implications

A. Procedure of newspapers can be adapted for magazines and comic books.

B. The newspaper may stimulate the child with no developed interests.

VIII. Introduce the Use of the TV as a Remedial Tool

A. Discuss the role of the TV in the average child's life.

1. Refer to illustration of the time spent watching TV as compared to the time spent in school.

B. Discuss how poor reading ability may affect attitudes toward books.

IX. Discussion of Various Studies Done on the TV

A. Witte's survey

1. In 1960, TV viewing was approx. 20 hrs./wk.
2. Presently, 20–28 hrs./wk.

B. McLuhan

1. TV is multidirectional.
2. Print is static.
3. TV is attitude-shaping.
4. Consciousness is raised by TV.

C. Marjorie Farmer

1. Phila. Program

D. Mount Vernon study

E. Morriset

1. Interactive TV.

F. Roser

1. Increase productivity and quality of reading instruction, thus possibly decreasing the need for expensive remedial programs.

X. General Discussion

A. Refer to handout on the TV.

B. Have class members suggest other ideas that can be used with the TV.

Group Observation

Group Attractiveness. Once the topic had been introduced, class members were asked to arrange themselves into groups of five. Since class members were already seated next to friends, members formed into groups quite readily. For the most part groups appeared to be attractive to individual members.

Group Atmosphere. The general atmosphere of the groups could be described as being rather apprehensive and guarded. The members were being asked to participate in a different type of classroom experience. They were unsure of their role in the group activity, and their tasks and goals had not been assigned. Nervous laughter and bad jokes were further indicators of a tense atmosphere.

Group Goals. The information given in the presentation included how to devise an interest inventory (see Exhibit B.2). The first explicitly stated group goal was for each group to develop a sample interest inventory based on its own needs in a remedial reading instructional setting.

Exhibit B.2. Developing an Interest Inventory

I. **The Open Ended Inventory**
Example: My favorite TV show is ______________________.

II. **The Question Inventory**
Example: What is your favorite TV show? ______________________.

III. **Multiple-Choice Inventory**
Example: Which of these TV shows is your favorite?
a. The Brady Bunch   b. Happy Days   c. Laverne & Shirley

Directions: Based on the examples above, develop some sample questions for an Interest Inventory (use the space below for questions).

Our observation was that group interaction was not effective. The following problems appeared to hinder group progress:

1. The groups had not experienced this type of learning process in this particular class before.
2. There was insufficient time allowed for interaction—only ten minutes.
3. The instructor displayed a passive attitude toward the process we were implementing.

After the first group interaction, members were requested to share information gathered in their groups. Initial response to our requests was not well received since members seemed unable or reluctant to give any feedback. The one comment that was made did not generate any further discussion.

The second part of the presentation consisted of discussion combined with visual aides on how to use the newspaper in a remedial program (Exhibits B.3 and B.4) or, as an alternative mode, television (Exhibit B.5). The goal was for each group to develop materials related to the use of the newspaper. At this point, group interaction was more task oriented than it had been previously, and group members displayed more overall interest in the group activity. Our observations indicated members were more comfortable and relaxed in this

---

Exhibit B.3. Variety of Subject Matter Found in the Newspaper

News (local, state, national, international)
News index
Weather reports and forecasts
Advertisements
Science
Sports
Theater
Books
Editorials
Letters to the editor
Deaths
Bridge
Legal notices
Human interest stories
Business and finance
Real estate
Career training
Business opportunities
Help wanted
Television
Movies
Music
Obituaries
Society
Transportation
Radio
Crossword puzzles
Art
Women's news
Maps, graphs, illustrations

Exhibit B.4. Reading Skill Areas That Can Be Taught Through the Use of the Newspaper

Word Identification Skills
- Context clues
- Phonic analysis
- Structural analysis
- Syllabication
- Dictionary word pronunciation skills

Comprehension
- Main ideas
- Details
- Sequence
- Following directions
- Drawing conclusions

Vocabulary	**Flexibility**
Sight words	Adjusting style to purpose
Context clues for meaning	Skimming
Dictionary word meaning skills	Rapid reading

Exhibit B.5. How to Use the Television in a Remedial Program*

Reading Skill Area	Materials	Activity	Number of Students
Consonant clusters	Any TV show, paper, pencil	Copy ten words you read from the TV. Circle all the consonant clusters.	Entire class Small group or individual
Recalling information	Any TV advertisement	Student writes ad. info. on a paper but not the name or product. Classmates try to guess ad from given clues.	Small group Partner activity
Alphabetical order	Any TV show paper	Copy 10-20 words that you read on the TV screen; put them into alphabetical order	Entire class Remedial group
Association, picture to word	Any TV ad or show	Write all words that you read in 60 min. that are also "pictured"	Group, class, individual

*Anne M. Adams and Cathy B. Harrison, "Using Television to Teach Specific Reading Skills," *The Reading Teacher* 29 (October 1975), pp. 49–51. Reprinted with permission of Anne M. Adams and Cathy B. Harrison and the International Reading Association.

Programs Offering Response to Viewer Mail Requests*

For best response, photo or letter requests should be addressed to the TV personality by name or the name of the character portrayed in care of the programs listed below. (For other programs, write to stars, using the name and address of the production company listed in the on-air credits for best results.)

Happy Days, ABC TV Audience Information, 1330 Avenue of the Americas, New York, N.Y. 10009.

Good Times, **Sanford and Son**, **All in the Family**, **The Jeffersons**, Tandem Productions, 1901 Avenue of the Stars, Suite #666, Los Angeles, Calif. 90067.

The Waltons, Lorimar Productions, 4000 Warner Blvd., Burbank, Calif. 91522.

Sesame Street and **Electric Company**, Children's Television Workshop, One Lincoln Plaza, New York, N.Y. 10023.

---

*Judith Stecher, "TV As a Two-Way Street in Learning," *Teacher* (November 1976), p. 52. Reprinted from *Teacher,* November 1976.

Exhibit B.6. Bibliography

Adams, Anne M., Harrison, Cathy B. "Using Television to Teach Specific Reading Skills." *The Reading Teacher* (October 1975), pp. 45–51.

Catterson, Jane H. "Print and TV–The Twain Have Met." *Instructor* (May–June 1976), p. 12.

Cheyney, Arnold B. *Teaching Reading Skills Through The Newspaper.* Newark, Del.: International Reading Assoc. Inc., 1971.

Feeley, Joan T. "Reading with TV: British and American Approaches." *The Reading Teacher* (December 1976), pp. 271–274.

———. "Televison and Reading in the Seventies." *Language Arts* (September 1975), pp. 797–801.

Fowles, Barbara R. "Teaching Children to Read: An Argument for Television." *The Urban Review* (Summer 1976), pp. 114–120.

Harris, Albert J., and Sipay, Edward R. *How to Increase Reading Ability.* New York: David McKay, 1975.

Stecher, Judith. "TV As a Two-Way Street in Learning." *Teacher* (November 1976), pp. 46–52.

---

group situation. Feedback on this group interaction was given more readily with more participation from a variety of group members.

A bibliography was distributed and explained (Exhibit B.6).

Post-Meeting Reaction

Following the presentation and group interaction, the class members were administered a post-meeting reaction sheet. Members were surveyed on aspects pertaining to group attractiveness and on opinions of the presentation's clarity, usefulness, and format. Generally, reactions were very favorable since all categories received ratings above three on a scale of one to five. The averages for individual categories were as follows:

1. Overall reaction to the presentation: 4.3;
2. Usefulness of the information: 4.1;
3. Clarity of the information presented: 4.4;
4. Format of the presentation (lecture vs. group centered): 3.9;
5. Attractiveness of the group activity: 4.1.

Although all individual categories computed averages above three, it was interesting to note, however, that the rating for the format of our presentation was lower than the rating for other categories. To understand this score (3.9), we might make several hypotheses. One is that group members were uncomfortable with this question since the presentations they had previously experienced were of the lecture type and this one was different. For members to have given a high rating to this question would have perhaps reflected a negative evaluation of their own presentations. Another hypothesis is that they were unfamiliar with design and working with groups; unfamiliarity may have led to discomfort and a lesser rating.

The overall survey seemed to indicate that the presentation was well received.

Summary

This paper has attempted to present a practical application of the theories related to group processes. We derived the following conclusions from this experience:

1. A realization that groups need to be developed over time with a specific set purpose to enhance productivity; in other words, we believe the ability to work in a group is not innate. Members must be able to adapt themselves to various group environments, roles, and tasks. (The second time the members were asked to share group ideas they appeared to be more comfortable in the process and hence, more productive. This may be indicative of learning from the first group experience.)
2. A successful working group requires common interests, purposes, or goals among group members.
3. The atmosphere plays an integral part in the group process. It was noted in our experimental design that guarded and apprehensive feelings among members hampered even the teacher's progress toward the goal.
4. Generally, from our observations, the group-directed activities provided a better learning experience, especially in an academic

> setting. The sharing of ideas apparently helped to broaden the individuals' scope of knowledge.

This experiment provided us with the opportunity to investigate further group processes and interaction. It convinced us that the use of group processes beyond the limits of the PEP program (psychoeducational processes) would be applicable and beneficial to other types of courses. Of course, implementing this program would require knowledge of the training design, an established purpose for using group process, and cooperation in actual group participation. We believe that if these characteristics of group processes can be maintained, meaningful learning can be attained, and that learning is enhanced beyond the usual lecture/notetaking modes.

Appendix C: Advice to Group Facilitators

In writing this book, we have asked questions to get information beyond our own. For the past year, as part of a training staff, while conducting a training-for-trainers program, or during our work with group leaders, we have asked the same question: *If you had one piece of advice to give group leaders, what would it be?*

What follows are their answers—one per person. They make the same points we make over and over in the book, and their answers serve as a reminder that we need to continuously be aware of the traps and move beyond them.

- Be sure of yourself; act that way and you'll believe it—it's a necessary stance to take.
- Assess group needs if at all possible before planning a design for the group; then design.
- Prepare a group so that the participants know why they are there and what will be accomplished.
- Spend time getting to know the group and having the group get to know you; develop a relaxed atmosphere. You will be able to get a better idea of the group's needs and problem areas when the participants are less threatened by your role.
- Make the group feel comfortable.
- Give everyone a chance to feel safe to share.
- Start out easy.
- Give clear directions.
- Never allow only one right experience.
- Build flexibility into your design.
- Establish acceptance norms and individual difference norms.
- Incorporate a variety of experiences in design. Process them so that the participants understand the full meaning of what they are doing.
- Allow opportunities for each individual to participate in discussions and experiences.
- Listen for body clues in response to group exchange.
- Remember to check regularly with the group, as well as yourself, for group perceptions of events.
- Treat all members in the group as equally important.
- Have constant awareness that you are in *service* to members.
- Stay in control—don't let the group wander all over the place.
- Establish and maintain control by having a design for meeting your objectives.
- Do not hold or show a totally authoritarian position.
- Take time to process the group at regular intervals.
- Have everyone "own" goals of the group.
- Show enthusiasm; you must believe in what you are doing!

- Have lots of energy; your use of yourself is an essential part of the group's development.
- Show you are interested in participants.
- Don't let one person dominate so that it turns others off; seek the opinions of the quiet folks.
- Relax and be yourself—not a copy of someone else.
- Listen with everything you've got, and if you still can't hear what's going on, ask.

Appendix D: A Memorandum

Group facilitators have a world of their own. For example, this memorandum was received, tongue in cheek. It is all very funny, but . . . it is something to think about.

As you know, most problem-solving discussions in education become, sooner or later, a desperate attempt to escape from the problem. This is often clumsily done, causing embarrassment and leaving the group without the comfortable feeling of having disposed of the problem. This is unnecessary; educational leaders long ago worked out adequate techniques for dodging the issue.

One of the most important contributions to the development of such techniques was made by Dr. Paul B. Diedrich over a quarter of a century ago and first published as an important research paper in the March 1942 issue of *Progressive Education*. In his paper, Dr. Diedrich presented 27 different ways in which it is possible to escape from or evade an educational problem. His list, of course, is only tentative, partial, incomplete, a mere beginning, etc., but it at least gives group leaders a command of alternative modes of retreat and enables them to withdraw their forces gracefully, leaving the problem baffled and helpless. The Diedrich list, which I have amended slightly here and there, follows:

1. Find a scapegoat and ride him. Students can blame adults, professors can blame administrators, administrators can blame professors, and everyone can blame the system.
2. Profess not to have *the* answer. That lets you out of having *any* answer.
3. Say that we must not move too rapidly. That avoids the necessity of getting started.
4. For every proposal, set up an opposite and conclude that the "middle ground" (no motion whatever) represents the wisest course of action.
5. Point out that an attempt to reach a conclusion is only a futile "quest for certainty." Doubt and indecision promote growth.
6. When in a tight place, say something that the group cannot understand.
7. Look slightly embarrassed when the problem is brought up. Hint that it is in bad taste, or too elementary for mature consideration, or that any discussion of it is likely to be misinterpreted by outsiders.
8. Say that the problem cannot be separated from other problems. Therefore, no problem can be solved until all other problems have been solved.
9. Rationalize the status quo; there is much to be said for it.

10. Point out that those who see the problem do so because they are unhappy—rather than vice versa.
11. Ask what is meant by the question. When it is sufficiently clarified, there will be no time left for the answer.
12. Discover that there are all sorts of dangers in any specific formulation of conclusions: of exceeding authority or seeming to, of asserting more than is definitely known, of misinterpretation by outsiders—and of revealing the fact that no one has a conclusion to offer.
13. Look for some philosophical basis for approaching the problem, then a basis for that, then a basis for that, and so on back to first cause.
14. Move away from the problem into discussion of various ways to study it.
15. Put off recommendations until every related problem has been definitely settled by scientific research.
16. Retreat into general objectives on which everyone can agree. From this higher ground you will either see that the problem has solved itself, or you will forget it.
17. Find us a face-saving verbal formula like "in a Pickwickian sense."
18. Carry the problem into other fields; show that it exists everywhere; hence everyone will just have to live with it.
19. Introduce analogies and discuss *them* rather than the problem.
20. Explain and clarify ad infinitum what you have already said.
21. As soon as any proposal is made, say that you have been doing it for ten years.
22. Appoint a committee to weigh the pros and cons (these must *always* be weighed) and to reach tentative conclusions that can subsequently be used as bases for further discussions of an exploratory nature preliminary to arriving at initial postulates on which methods of approach to the pros and cons may be predicated.
23. Wait until some expert can be consulted.
24. Say, "that is not on the agenda; we'll take it up later." This may be extended ad infinitum.
25. Conclude that we have all clarified our thinking on the problem, even though no one has thought of any way to solve it.
26. Point out that some of the greatest minds have struggled with this problem, implying that it does us credit to have even thought of it.
27. Be thankful for the problem. It has stimulated our thinking and has thereby contributed to our growth. It should get a medal.

Index

ABCDEFGHIJ-BP-89876543

Student Response Form

We would like to find out what your reactions are to MAKING GROUPS WORK. Your evaluation of the book will help us respond to the interests and needs of the readers of future editions. Please complete the form and mail it to College Marketing, Houghton Mifflin Company, One Beacon Street, Boston, MA 02108.

1. We would like to know how you rate our textbook in each of the following areas:

	Excellent	Good	Adequate	Poor
a. Selection of topics	____	____	____	____
b. Detail of coverage	____	____	____	____
c. Order of topics	____	____	____	____
d. Writing style/readability	____	____	____	____
e. Explanation of concepts	____	____	____	____
f. Use of case studies	____	____	____	____
g. Appendices	____	____	____	____

2. Please cite specific examples that illustrate any of the above ratings.

____

____

____

3. Describe the strongest feature(s) of the book.

____

____

____

4. Describe the weakest feature(s) of the book.

____

____

____

5. What other topics should be included in this text?

____

____

____

6. What recommendations can you make for improving this book?

____

____

____